Hackney:

portrait of a community

1967-2017

Edited by Laurie Elks

THE HACKNEY SOCIETY

The Hackney Society promotes the highest standards in design and protects Hackney's unique heritage. The Society has encouraged positive development of the borough's built and natural environments, through engagement with a broad cross-section of local people and experts. We encourage exemplary new design, regeneration and conservation of our rich heritage through our newsletter, *Spaces*, our publications (see p.238), walks, talks, meetings, website and social media.

info@hackneysociety.org
www.hackneysociety.org

Published in 2017 by
The Hackney Society
The Round Chapel
1d Glenarm Road
London E5 0LY

Editorial team: Laurie Elks, Annie Edge, Monica Blake, Jon Fortgang, Margaret Willes

Designed by design@gloryhall.com

ISBN: 978-0-9536734-3-8

Contents

Ridley Road market stall, 1980. (Photo Neil Martinson)

In the 1960s and '70s, the *Hackney Gazette* every week carried up to 12 pages of advertisements for employment in the clothing trade.

Introduction

Ten years ago, to mark its 40th birthday, the Hackney Society published *Modern, Restored, Forgotten, Ignored* – a commemoration and a celebration by 40 authors of 40 of the borough's most important buildings. This was the most ambitious publishing project undertaken by the Society which has been publishing excellent books about Hackney and its historic environment since the 1970s. One of our members, Steve Szypko, suggested that on our 50th anniversary we could go one better by bringing out a book commemorating the 50 extraordinary years of Hackney's history since we set up shop in 1967; 50 stories, 50 authors, one framing event for each year. It has been a great privilege to have been asked to commission these stories.

I never doubted that I could persuade 50 excellent writers to bring this project to fruition. The borough is rich in people committed to social and environmental causes: intelligent, indomitable, energetic, contrary, idealistic. To turn the epigram of W.B. Yeats on its head, it might be said of Hackney that the worst lack all conviction whilst the best are full of passionate intensity. This book is full of the testimonies of people who have lived in Hackney, stayed in Hackney, fought to make it a better place. Whatever the rights and wrongs of gentrification (of which there is much, possibly too much, in this book), I hope that this fighting spirit will not die. I was very sorry that three doughty characters died as this book was being planned: Joe Lobenstein, whom I would have asked to write about the Conservative interlude in power; Brian Sedgemore, who spoke so eloquently about the conditions on Trowbridge Estate; and Roger Lansdown, who made the improvement of Hackney's public transport his lifetime ambition. They would have made magnificent contributions. But I was delighted to have first-hand testimonies from Chris Sills, Ken Worpole, Stuart Weir, Brian Belton, Geoff Taylor, Alan Rossiter and Julian Harrap of events forty or more years ago. This book is rich in personal memory.

The project has been logistically daunting and I was faced with a jigsaw of events and years, working out how to place each story in a different framing year. I did not, to be frank, scan the pages of the *Hackney Gazette* to find the most important events. We, my editorial colleagues and I, selected the events which we thought of greatest interest, and then worked out a year to assign to them. This seemed perfectly legitimate as the most significant events have run and run, weaving into the history of our place over the years. To give just one example, the stirring story of the restoration of the Hackney Empire started when the irrepressible, bloody-minded Socialist Roland Muldoon walked into the place in 1986, determined to rescue Frank Matcham's great theatre which had sunk to ignominious depths as a bingo hall. It ended, in a way, in 2004, when the restored Empire re-opened its doors having overcome the scepticism of the Arts 'fundariat' and obtained lottery funding. I asked Simon Thomsett, general manager of the Empire over many of those turbulent years, to frame this story around the appearance of Ralph Fiennes as Hamlet in 1995. He has responded magnificently, wrapping the longer story around that one framing event. And of course, the story of the Empire in all its magnificence remains very much alive to this day.

I beg readers' indulgence for the fact that, in a few cases, the connection between the story and the framing event is slightly tenuous but I hope that the logistical difficulties will be understood.

I met a woman recently who had returned to live in Hackney after spending 20 years away. I asked her for her thoughts and she replied "It's exactly the same but totally different". I demurred and said that in my opinion it was totally different but exactly the same! I will return to that thought in a moment but focus first on that 'totally different' question. How has Hackney changed? Or to put that matter emphatically: How Hackney has changed!

It is hard to know quite where to start with that question, but let us recall for a moment 1967, the year of the birth of the Hackney Society. The predominant change in the air at that time was the progressive elimination of the ageing Victorian housing stock – poorly maintained, rent-controlled, and overcrowded. In its stead, Hackney Council, aided and abetted by the GLC, provided housing: modern, spacious, and built to Parker Morris standards which far surpassed the space standards of most of today's 'luxury apartments'. Aspiring families put themselves on the waiting list and waited patiently till they reached the top of the queue. For those who could not wait, or looked further afield for their ambitions, there were new and expanding towns outside London and factories and offices were relocating. The population of Hackney fell by over 100,000 between 1931 and 1961 and by a further 18,000 between the censuses of 1961 and 1971. The tide of falling population was only to turn, unexpectedly, in the late 1980s.

The progressive municipalisation of the borough, its housing stock certainly, but also its life blood, was presided over by successive Labour councils; confident of their higher purpose, unassailed by doubt and seemingly in power for ever. There was an unexpected interlude when the Conservatives took power in 1968 as a result of a national backlash against the government of Harold Wilson. But three years later, Labour was back and it was business as usual. John Kotz, who was later to become leader of the council, wrote an unapologetic political memoir, *Vintage Red*. It captures the spirit of the council leadership at the time, as well as being unintentionally revealing of the poverty of its imagination. He proudly recounts how his first act, on returning to power in 1971, was to unearth the Red Flag which the Tories had stowed away during their term in office.

During the research for this book, I read the report of the inspector who had to rule in 1972 on the council's plans to demolish and redevelop a large area of Mapledene, close to London Fields, now containing some of the borough's most desirable real estate. What comes through is the council's conviction that the waiting list would be cleared, everyone who wanted a council house would get one, and that the Victorian housing stock was doomed. The tenants would be working class and Labour-voting, and the political leadership would be drawn from their number. Indeed, Hackney's political leaders up to the 1970s were predominantly council tenants.

The vision was paternalistic and, to be fair, Hackney was run as a tight ship with experienced councillors, effective management, low rents and rates. Services were mostly of a decent standard and included provisions, such as tea dances and holidays for the elderly, which have long since disappeared. But if the council was benevolent, it was also autocratic. Schemes for the decoration of its flats were dictated by the council, and tenants who fell into rent arrears were dealt with peremptorily without any enquiry into circumstances. No one was expected to argue and very few did.

I remember an inspiring Anglican vicar, John Pearce, telling me, not long after I arrived in Hackney in 1972, how dreadful it would be if the borough were to become one vast council estate. The thought came as a revelation to me – young, naïve and left wing. The tide was to turn sooner than he or I imagined as the ground hollowed out under the council's leadership in the 1970s. Government funds became tight after the oil crisis of 1973-4; national political sentiment was moving against the building of council housing even before Mrs Thatcher killed it off; housing priorities changed after the exposé of homelessness in *Cathy Come Home*, and estates were increasingly the home of the disadvantaged rather than the aspiring. The traditional economic base was also disappearing. Back in the 1960s and '70s, the *Hackney Gazette* regularly carried up to twelve pages advertising work in clothing factories as well as other kinds of manufacturing industry. All of this was to end as factories closed and skilled workers left the borough. Sean Gubbins' article on the Simpson's factory depicts a lost world of skilled, well-paid and secure manual work. All of this is clearer now than it was to the political leaders of the time, as John Kotz's memoir vividly shows.

Then, too, there were the questions being posed by the awkward squad who were beginning to make their voices felt. Stuart Weir settled in Balls Pond Road in 1967 and he was to be a moving spirit in the fight to save De Beauvoir from the bulldozer. He was no friend of the Tories, but as his article on De Beauvoir – and Christopher Sills' article on the Conservative interlude in power – reveal, the three-year intermission from Labour rule applied just sufficient brakes to the momentum of municipalisation to change the outcome. The saving of De Beauvoir proved to be a pivotal moment and, as John Finn's article describes, the infant Hackney Society was to play its part in saving the borough's most valuable physical fabric from destruction.

Things began to move also in the intellectual sphere. Ken Worpole, who moved to Hackney in 1969, describes the impulses which led to the establishment and flowering of Centerprise – bookshop, coffee shop, headquarters for a myriad of community organisations, a place to give voice to the creative spirit of people who had previously been silent. As Anna Harding's article records, this was also the moment when artists started to arrive to take up space in redundant industrial buildings, creating Hackney's status as London's most beloved borough within the artist community. The pioneering community arts organisation, Free Form, set up shop close by in Dalston Lane, later helping to establish Chats Place in deepest Homerton, a celebrated home for community pantos, agitprop, cabaret, jazz and music hall.

Environmentalists started to make their presence felt in Hackney from the 1970s. In 1974, Stoke Newington residents formed the Save Abney Park Cemetery Committee which helped to persuade Hackney Council to buy the cemetery after its future was threatened by the bankruptcy of its owners. Five years later, Save the Marshes was launched by Hackney campaigners to rescue Walthamstow Marshes from gravel extraction. The determination and campaigning nous of this group led to total capitulation by the Lee Valley Regional Park Authority and the preservation in perpetuity of the Marshes. A few years later, Save the Reservoirs launched a campaign to prevent the development of the reservoirs in Stoke Newington. Monica Blake, one of the members of this campaign, records how the battle continued over almost 20 years. The West Reservoir is now a sailing centre, whilst the East Reservoir has been restored as Woodberry Wetlands Nature Reserve. As Margaret Willes' article on horticultural Hackney describes, the movement to make things grow in Hackney has often been counter-cultural, and it still is.

Political protest became more articulate. Hackney has for centuries enjoyed a reputation as a centre of radicalism. Back in the 1960s and '70s there was a small radical fringe, including a strong claimants' union movement. The so-called Angry Brigade, who sent letter bombs to loathed Tory politicians, was based at 359 Amhurst Road in Stoke Newington. But the radical fringe was small and political discourse was mostly relatively docile. Later, as Daniel Rachel observes, Hackney was to play a central role in the Rock Against Racism movement at a time when far-right politicians were targeting support from the white community of Hoxton and the East End, and the British National Party established its headquarters in Shoreditch. As Duncan Campbell describes, there was also forceful opposition on the part of the black community – supported by the political left – against the police, stirred by unexplained events at Stoke Newington police station. The infamous Sandringham Road 'front line', where distrusted police confronted rampant drug dealing, was a tangible expression of a tense and divided community. Political protest was to continue in the 1980s and '90s and beyond, both against the actions and policies of a dysfunctional and near-bankrupt Hackney Council, and against national policies such as Mrs Thatcher's detested poll tax.

Experimentation and innovation spilled out into the mainstream education sector, supported by staff of the permanently Socialist Inner London Education Authority. Geoff Taylor, who taught in the borough in those years, later becoming a Hackney Labour councillor, questions whether that was necessarily to the benefit of young people growing up here. That argument will run and run!

Politically, things were moving too. Stuart Weir, his communitarian instincts sharpened by the successful fight to save De Beauvoir, joined Hackney Council as a Labour member in 1974. He found the inflexibility and complacency of the leadership suffocating and gave up the struggle four years later. But the elections of 1978 and 1982 brought in more young radical councillors at a time when national politics were becoming increasingly polarised and Mrs Thatcher faced up to the so-called 'Loony Left'. The 'Left', though that term is disputed by John Kotz, took control of Hackney Council in 1982 when Anthony Kendall, who, significantly, had been a community worker at Centerprise, defeated John Kotz in the vote for the council leadership. The scope to improve the borough's destinies was certainly curtailed by the malevolence of Mrs Thatcher's government, but it cannot be denied that the inexperienced new leadership, or, to be precise, the dizzy succession of political leaders, substantially messed up, causing Hackney's financial and administrative affairs to fall into a precipitous decline from which it has taken many years to recover. Jim Cannon and Jessica Webb, past and present members of Hackney Council, tell that story.

The population of Hackney has been fast-changing. The Caribbean community was well established in Hackney by the time of our opening chapter in 1967, and there was already a sprinkling of other minorities including Turkish Cypriots, as described in Muttalip Unluer's article. The other large minority in the 1960s was Jewish; not the ultra-orthodox Chasidim, but a more secular and integrated community, most of whom later moved on to further-out suburbs. Instead, into Hackney moved several new minority groups. Vietnamese and Kurds have come to Hackney as a result of political disturbances at home. Linh Vu has told the story of the journey of Hackney's Vietnamese community. Rachel Kolsky's article describes how Chasidic Jews have gathered in Stamford Hill and

Upper Clapton. A fuller and more comprehensive history of Hackney would describe the different experiences and different opportunities of the many communities who make up Hackney today.

In editing this book, my notional reader has been not the Man on the Clapham Omnibus but the Man (or Woman) on Homerton Station. During the rush hour, eight trains pass each way and the platform rapidly fills up with the new generation of Homertonians, mostly on their way to work in Central London. My friend and neighbour Roger Lansdown fought with a tiny band of confederates to bring back trains to Hackney, an objective which included the restoration of a station at Homerton of which no trace, and little memory, then existed. When the trains finally returned to Homerton in 1985 they were ancient, carrying few passengers, with stations en route mostly unmanned and threatening. Before the days of Oyster cards, when I asked for a ticket to Homerton at London Transport offices, the response was always one of puzzlement followed by a search for the correct station code. A ticket-seller helped me – he said "Look, it's 6979. You know what 69 is and just add 10 to that." After that, I always asked for 6979 and it speeded things up considerably! Now most people know where Homerton is and the passenger movements are close on five million each year. I hope that if some of the men and women thronging the platform at Homerton read this book, they will understand better how things have changed in Hackney and how the enthusiasm and energy of campaigners have helped to change it.

But I will return to the theme of change and continuity. Perhaps now is the moment to mention the dreaded 'H' word. The word 'hipster', or one of its variants, appears at various places in this book. It is interesting (at any rate to me) that the word 'yuppie' appears not at all, though that was the term of choice for well-heeled incomers in the 1980s, a period recalled in Suzanne Waters' article on the first post-war wave of private housebuilding. It is a moot point whether the change is mostly one of terminology and facial stubble, or whether it reflects a significant change in the identity of people choosing to make their home in Hackney.

Be that as it may, many of the articles touch in various ways on the impact of gentrification on Hackney: on its markets, its streets and its pubs among other things. Whilst I make no apology for the selection of the themes of these fifty chapters, I do feel that read alone, this book might give a slightly exaggerated sense of the changes that have taken place and, possibly, an over-optimistic view of the future. Just at a physical level on the streets, the greasy spoon cafés and old-fashioned boozers are still there alongside the gastronomic restaurants and hipster pubs. The estates are there amongst the renovated million-pound houses, mostly built to an enclosed design so that it is easy to pass them by without registering them. Your local Tesco, if you pause awhile, is full of people moving round slowly, filling up their day. As Ian Rathbone's article makes clear, the too numerous betting shops are taking money from the community, whilst the money shops are lending it back at extortionate rates of interest.

I sometimes feel, and I am not the only one, that Hackney Council has an agenda to speed the process of gentrification on its way. This narrative lauds the new and the fashionable – the Fashion Hub, Broadway Market, Hip Hoxton, Victoria Park Village, the Olympic 'Host Borough', Shoreditch tech and so forth. Within this narrative there is a view that older institutions and facilities – Ridley Road Market, artists' studios, 'underneath the arches' car repair shops and the like – must make way if they cannot match the rent that the incomers are able to pay. There is an element of economic reality in this. James Watson, who has written about Hackney's new wave of pubs and breweries, pointed out to me that the craft beer pubs attract a clientèle willing to pay £6 or more for their pint whilst the old-fashioned pubs are selling lager and keg bitter for £3 50. If your old-fashioned boozer gets a makeover, stripped floorboards and a bearded clientèle appearing seemingly from nowhere, there is probably not much that can be done to halt the juggernaut of progress. Nevertheless, whilst Hackney has a very mixed population, and that is not likely to change, the council must serve the needs of all the community. Ridley Road Market represents the past of Hackney but also, I very much hope, its future.

Hackney not only remains one of the most under-privileged boroughs in the country but also one full of unfulfilled human potential. Muttalip Unluer remarks how few in the Turkish communities go on to university, or find employment in the financial services industry on our doorstep. And Kirsty Styles, in a very penetrating article on Shoreditch's hi-tech boom, points out how little progress has been made towards enrolling the borough's young people in tech businesses.

That life is improving for many in Hackney is not in doubt. In 2010, Hackney was reckoned to be the second most deprived borough in the country. A range of measures summarising deprivation in local authorities indicates that Hackney was 'only' the eleventh most deprived five years later. As Annie Edge has described, the performance of our schools and colleges has dramatically improved over the space of a few years. A resilient economy and a well-performing education system offer greatly improved life-chances to our young people. But conversely, it is well to be wary of brute statistics. Indices of poverty and deprivation can be skewed by the arrival of wealthier young people who pull up the average without necessarily raising the position of those at the bottom of the pile. It is, or should be, common ground that a great deal has been achieved since Jules Pipe became mayor of Hackney in 2002 and initiated the turnaround in the borough's affairs, but a very great deal remains to be done.

And then there is the question of gangs. Julia Lafferty's article on Clapton's famed 'Murder Mile' emphasises that much of the mayhem was caused by imported internecine strife and turf wars between Yardie gangs hailing originally from Jamaica. Emma Bartholomew, in her article on the senseless death of Shaquille Smith, underlines the fact that gang conflict has become more pervasive and more juvenile. It is a fact that too many young people growing up in Hackney are enmeshed in drug dealing; knife-toting, admiring of false and empty rap idols. Many more, raised alongside the kids in gangs, live in a culture of fear which can be damaging to ambitions and educational attainment.

Where to place the riots of 2011 within this kaleidoscope is a moot question. The riots in Hackney received great attention, not because they were more intense than elsewhere, but because more journalists live in Hackney – or know the way there – than less well-known suburbs further out of central London. As Hackney South MP, Meg Hillier, emphasises, the riots were swiftly over and the process of repair of communities has been prompt and enthusiastic. It is probably true to say that the riots reflect the very different experiences of life in the buzzing world-city that is London more than any specifically Hackney malaise.

To add a personal note, I am the custodian of Hackney's oldest building, St Augustine's Tower, which opens its doors on the last Sunday of the month. On the preceding Monday, I put up banners saying that the Tower will open and that entry is free. I have often asked myself why it is that of the many people who visit us, only a tiny proportion live on nearby council estates. Lynsey Hanley, in her excellent book *Estates: An Intimate History*, suggests that there is a wall in the head of many people growing up on estates, corralling their belief in themselves and their potential. I suspect that that is the explanation why so many of our neighbours pass by our beautiful tower – but perhaps I am wrong.

So the epigram 'totally different but exactly the same' – up to a point, sums it up for me. This book is mostly about the changes that have taken place in Hackney. I celebrate those changes and I played a part in some of them. But I also believe that the borough's vitality depends on the new, younger generation arriving in Hackney having the same commitment to make it a better place as my generation which arrived in the 1970s.

This book has been made possible by the generosity of my co-authors. I would like to thank them for contributing their time and answering my endless questions. The authors of this book have not only shared their knowledge of Hackney, but have helped in different ways to shape its history. Hackney's history owes so much to people who have worked for their community in many imaginative ways to make a difference.

I would also like to thank the professional photographers who have generously donated their work: Simon Mooney, Alan Denney, Neil Martinson, Berris Connolly, Chris Dorley-Brown and Dudy Braun. In addition I thank warmly the other members of Hackney Society's editorial team: Margaret Willes, Annie Edge, Monica Blake, and Glory Hall who has designed the book.

Laurie Elks

The Peace Mural in Dalston Lane, 1985. (Photo Alan Denney)

1967: The Birth of the Hackney Society – John Finn

Shepherdess Walk, Shoreditch. One of the early campaigns of the Hackney Society was to oppose Hackney Council's proposal to demolish the Georgian terrace. (Photo Simon Mooney)

"We shouldn't like people to think we are in favour of propping up old ruins," was what worried Michael Thomas as he first let the world know of his and others' intention to form a society to campaign for the protection of historic Hackney, first announced in the *Hackney Gazette*, 11 January 1967.

The new London Borough of Hackney, the amalgamation of the former Metropolitan Boroughs of Hackney, Stoke Newington and Shoreditch, and only two years old, was facing a massive housing crisis. Hackney had apparently the third biggest housing waiting list in London (*Hackney Gazette*, 20 February 1967), with large numbers of working-class families living in over-crowded, multi-occupied, privately-rented housing – desperate to move into a clean, dry and warm council house. That, I remember, was the great hope of many of my father's family, living in Hackney's Victorian terraces, sharing outside WCs, and some in gas-lit rooms. This problem had been the biggest task of local government in London since the 1930s. Now the 1960s and '70s saw plans to solve the problem that threatened to make a lasting impact upon the built environment.

All three of the former constituent boroughs published, from time to time, official guides. Thumbing through the editions prior to the 1965 amalgamation, the first impression is of a huge amount of advertising by local industries. There was still a big industrial sector, especially in Shoreditch and Hackney Wick: furniture, chemicals and paint, ironfounders, glassworks, timber, clothing, food, laundries – and some famous names amongst them, including Simpson's tailoring, Bronco toilet tissue, Carless Petrol ('100 years in Hackney') and Platignum Pens. There is, states the *Hackney Guide*, "no clearly defined line separating commerce and industry from the residential areas". But even then that industrial profile appeared to be in decline.

While proud of their histories, the boroughs were keen to promote themselves as builders of new housing, and to demonstrate the zeal with which they intended to stride into the golden future inspired by the Greater London Plan, more popularly known as the Abercrombie Plan after its principal author. Shoreditch Council boasted that they had completed their five-year slum clearance and house building programme ahead of schedule, and proudly pointed to the "huge blocks of flats" they had built, with more promised. They predicted that the "majority of Shoreditch will be housed in conditions undreamt of a generation ago".

Meanwhile Stoke Newington took inspiration from the Woodberry Down redevelopment "so vast and complete in itself as to be almost a borough within a borough". While for Hackney, in 1961 "throughout the whole area, building activity continues as the new and finer Hackney continues to rise". Labour's vision in Hackney was for an almost total redevelopment programme. However, the *Hackney Guide* notes that "reluctantly there was no alternative to demolition" of sites like the bomb-damaged sixteenth-century Brooke House.

It was the era of Abercrombie-inspired 'comprehensive redevelopment', where whole areas of sub-standard and bomb-damaged accommodation would be replaced, along with any other viable buildings, shops and factories as necessary, to plan for self-contained estates that would include health centres, community halls, laundries, open spaces with industry segregated away. Constituency Labour parties in London sent resolutions to the Annual Conference calling for total 'municipalisation' of housing. In neighbouring Tottenham for example, which I knew well in the 1960s, it was a regular demand.

Meanwhile, at the level of national politics, Labour and Conservatives competed by announcing ever more ambitious housing targets. Harold Macmillan's government raised the target to 300,000 per annum. His housing minister, Keith Joseph, later admitted that he was a "more" man: "I used to go to bed at night counting the number of houses I had destroyed and the number of planning approvals I had given. . . just more." Harold Wilson's Labour Party promised to raise numbers to 400,000 and to "obliterate London's slums", including Hackney's estimated 2,225 sub-standard dwellings, as part of a London-wide housing programme.

To cap it all, the *Gazette* headlined the news (14 February), that the newly-created Greater London Council (GLC) was planning to create the notorious Ringway 1 or London Motorway Box around central London. Two of the routes, the North Cross Route and Eastern Avenue extension were mapped to push through Dalston and Victoria Park respectively to Hackney Wick, displacing an estimated 3,200 people from their homes.

Mr Thomas and friends couldn't have timed their initiative to protect Hackney's historic environment with greater precision. The previous year, Albion Square residents formed an Action Group "to preserve the pleasant Victorian charm of the square" against compulsory purchase. Michael Thomas commented that "it is encouraging that this has been formed and perhaps there could be a more centralised kind of society ... open to all those who are genuinely interested in the history and character of the borough". He was anxious to point out that such a group would not be what he called a "homeowner's society". The *Gazette* article stated that the idea had gained the support of John Betjeman, co-founder of the Victorian Society, and later to become Poet Laureate and National Treasure. Betjeman had written affectionately in the *Spectator* of trips to Hackney and Stoke Newington by way of the North London Line and the Great Eastern to Clapton. "Hackney", he said then, "is full of the real London". His poem 'The Cockney Amorist' conjures a memory of the Hackney Empire as the "soft electric lamplight/Reveals the gilded walls". He agreed to become the fledgling Society's first president.

And so the *Gazette* was to report that the Hackney Society had held its first meeting on 6 February. A steering committee discussed a draft constitution which included the following objectives:

a. To encourage the preservation, development and improvement of buildings, streets and areas within the London Borough of Hackney which are of historic interest, architectural merit or distinctive character and charm.

b. To encourage high standards of architectural and town planning within the borough.

c. To study critically all plans for the development of the borough and to put forward constructive criticism.

d. To encourage the preservation and improvement of parks, squares and other open spaces within the borough.

e. To stimulate public interest in and care for the beauty, history and character of the area of the borough and its surroundings.

The first public meeting followed in May. Leaflets were printed which opened with words that still seem redolent today:

- I love Hackney. But what will it be like in 10 years' time?
- If you are interested in the place you live in come along to the first meeting of The Hackney Society.

The Agapemonite Church at Stamford Hill, one of Sir John Betjeman's favourite Hackney buildings. He described in the *Spectator* in 1956 how the interior was "a blaze of glory". (Photo Simon Mooney)

John Betjeman was the star speaker along with Patrick Stirling from the Civic Trust, and Paul Kirby from the GLC Planning Department.

A busy programme followed during that first year including a walk along the Regent's Canal, a visit to the Geffrye Museum and garden party ("well attended in spite of the rain") and a walk to visit churches in the Shoreditch area.

These events helped to bind Society members in friendship but there was also serious campaigning work to be done. The new Civic Amenities Act 1967 had introduced Conservation Areas and improved the scheme for statutory listing of buildings of architectural and historic interest. The first committee spent "a considerable amount of time" looking at the likely areas of Hackney that could benefit from the protection offered by this new legislation. They focused on two decaying mansions at 187 and 191 Stoke Newington High Street and Sanford Terrace, a Georgian terrace overlooking Stoke Newington Common. Sanford Terrace was neglected and blighted by a scheme for comprehensive development (now Smalley Estate) and had just come under a compulsory purchase order. The saving of Sanford Terrace was to become one of the first achievements of the Society.

The new Society was eminently respectable. Its first vice-presidents were Ellis Hillman, former LCC member and subsequently of the GLC, Nicholas Taylor, the Sunday Times architectural correspondent, and the Venerable M.M. Hodgins, Archdeacon of Hackney. Initially the Society baulked at confronting the big redevelopment schemes head on – like the De Beauvoir project, which it left to the locals to fight. But by the time of the Mapledene compulsory purchase proposals, the Society had realised that in order to preserve and protect, it would sometimes need to take on planning authorities, locally and regionally. The arduous and sometimes wearisome task of preparing submissions, proofs of evidence, appearing at public enquiries including the 1972 and 1977 Mapledene enquiries, fell on the Society and its hard-working committee members. The Society also weighed into the campaign to resist the ruinously destructive Motorway Box and signed up to the North London Line Committee to save the Richmond-Broad Street Line from closure. Another early campaign helped to save the magnificent Georgian terrace at Shepherdess Walk, Shoreditch, from destruction.

The Society was up and running. Fifty years later, it still has work to do.

1968: The Conservatives take Power
– Chris Sills

In 1964, Labour was elected with a clean sweep in the newly formed London Borough of Hackney. This was no surprise; the old boroughs of Hackney and Shoreditch had been Labour for decades and, although the smaller borough of Stoke Newington had elected Conservative councils in the past, it seemed a fair bet that the new borough would be permanently Labour. And that's what the leaders of the new Labour council confidently believed.

Although we Conservatives had no seats we began to hone our skills in opposition. One example occurred in 1964 when the District Auditor published a highly critical report after the council had been taken to the cleaners by a dodgy builder. We demanded an enquiry and the *Hackney Gazette* gave us full and helpful coverage. Needless to say, there was no enquiry and the Labour leadership's self-certainty continued.

But things began to stir after Harold Wilson's Labour government suffered a dramatic loss of popularity. Labour lost by-elections in unexpected places like Ashton in Nottinghamshire and we Conservatives started to believe that the unthinkable could happen. Secret training sessions were led by Horace Cutler, the Conservative deputy leader of the GLC, supported by experienced councillors in Conservative London boroughs, so we would be as ready as we could be to take the reins if the miracle occurred.

And so it was that in 1968, the unthinkable did happen and, just after 4.30am on 8 May, Conservative Central Office issued an astonishing press release announcing that we had taken control of Hackney Council. Our effective majority was one, and the closest result came in Wick ward where we won the second seat by just four votes. I was 29, the newly elected councillor for Leabridge Ward, and later became deputy chairman of the Policy and Resources Committee. This unexpected victory occurred in the same month that revolutionary students were storming the barricades in Paris.

The outraged Labour leadership were confident that they could wear us into exhaustion. They kept council meetings going by forcing a vote on every possible issue and meetings typically finished around three in the morning. We were politically toughened by the experience. Most of us were under 30, which helped us keep going, whilst the old members perfected the art of taking a short nap in the afternoons before the marathon meetings commenced. Fortunately the personal relationships were mostly civil, even though the politics were intense. I recall that at one meeting, Councillor Mary Watts, a popular retired teacher, turned 80 at midnight. We all stood and sang her happy birthday and then battle recommenced.

There was also an intense mini-cab war going on in the borough at the time. One of our members managed a mini-cab business, whilst several Labour members were taxi drivers. We were nervous that this economic rivalry might spill into our political arguments but, fortunately, it never did.

Some council officers took the view that we were merely keeping the seats warm until Labour was inevitably returned in 1971 (as indeed it was). We had a set-to within the first three months, when the Borough Architect was required to resign after he refused to accept instructions to reduce the size of the Shellgrove Road compulsory purchase for slum clearance. We considered that sound houses in Barretts Grove were being unnecessarily included in the slum clearance order and we lifted the compulsory purchase orders from those houses. The Labour council later tried to reinstate them in the 1970s but they were turned down by the government and the houses are still standing today.

The consequence of this incident was that council officers understood the seriousness of our intent and knew they had to toe the line or they would suffer the same fate.

Housing policy

Housing was the big political issue of the day and the Shellgrove compulsory purchase order typified the main issue between us and Labour. We did not dispute that there was a good deal of unfit housing and did not try to obstruct the slum clearance programme, but we considered that Labour was seeking to turn Hackney into one vast housing estate and believed that sound houses should be restored. We called a special council meeting in June 1969 to reset housing policy when we put forward a resolution proposing the following:

- A target of 2,000 satisfactory homes per year to be achieved "partly by Council building, but mainly by rehabilitation and resuscitation". Six hundred dwellings would be provided by municipal building; the balance by private developers, housing associations and conversions.
- Priority for removal of slums and improvement of substandard property.
- More objective criteria for the choice of sites for municipal development "paying particular regard to the need to preserve and improve all existing housing which can be brought to a reasonable standard".
- Sites not intended to be developed within 10 years to be released.
- Future sites identified for development to take account of the quality of existing housing. We proposed to "overcome the difficulty of owner occupiers arising from planning blight".
- "We will use our full powers to sell to our tenants the houses they are living in".
- Void properties "will as far as possible be offered to housing associations".
- Management agreements with tenants' associations on the running of estates.
- Seven-year tenancies in place of weekly tenancies.

A Labour counter-resolution proposed to reaffirm that the first priority was to make provision for building so as to re-house all families on the waiting list.

We were not able to achieve all of our aims, and some of them, like seven-year tenancies, were not realistic. However, we were able to slow down the juggernaut of redevelopment, particularly in De Beauvoir and Mapledene, where we declared General Improvement Areas. Our 'interlude' in power therefore had an effect in Hackney which lasts up to the present day.

We were also concerned that the existing practice of putting families into bed and breakfast accommodation did not make financial or social sense. We refused to provide any money for bed and breakfast accommodation in the 1970/71 budget so that officers had to find better solutions for families needing temporary accommodation. By the final year of Conservative control there were no families in bed and breakfast accommodation.

Social Services

The Seebohm Report, which was published in 1968, recommended that the fragmentation of social care should be overcome by merging the different social services into a unified social services department. We were keen to implement this change and set up the department. Establishing a social services committee was more awkward because the law still required us to have a children's committee, even though the children's department had been subsumed within the new department. We got round this by keeping the children's committee and doubling up the membership to serve as the social services committee. I believe we were the first authority to do this.

Other policy initiatives

As I look back on the policy disputes of those days there are some which still seem modern and relevant, others which are distant and remote. As Conservatives, we were always keen to see that public money was well spent and we managed to keep rate increases in the last two years to some of the lowest in London. I recall that we uncovered one spectacular case of double counting. A children's home was late opening but the budget assumed the cost of running the home for several months before it was opened, as well as the cost of placing children with other agencies.

There was a difficult issue concerning Shoreditch Town Hall. Health services had mostly been centralised in the town hall and there were central government moves to remove health powers from local councils to new health authorities. We were afraid of losing the town hall along with the health services, so we moved them out to prevent that happening. Now, in the cycle of politics and government, health services are being moved back under the control of local councils.

We were very keen to see Hackney connected to the Tube and in 1970 we formally proposed a new Hackney to Chelsea Line and started measures to safeguard the route. After many twists and turns it now looks as if we will get Crossrail 2, following more or less the same route, some 60 years after we proposed it.

Some issues now seem much more remote. For example, we were very active in promoting child cycling training programmes (then a local authority responsibility) at a time when cycling was much more a minority activity than today. I also remember many lively arguments about town twinning. Labour were keen to build on twinning links with communist councils in the suburbs of Moscow and East Berlin. We were not! It is probably fair to say that both sides quite enjoyed ideological arguments of this kind.

It had to end

As the 1971 election approached, we knew, and Labour knew, that they would take power back. Labour was keen to treat us as lame ducks and we were keen to keep governing. One of the most important decisions we took, right at the end, was to create the General Improvement Area in De Beauvoir South with lasting consequences as described in Stuart Weir's article.

And so in 1971 the end came. We had a much higher share of the vote than in 1964 but – the first past the post system being what it is – no seats at all. Subsequently, our late great leader, Joe Lobenstein, won a seat with a massive personal vote in Springfield Ward, and held it through election after election. 'Tory Joe' bravely held the council to account even when he was the lone Conservative voice in the town hall.

I am now well past 70 and I continue to contest seats at council elections and at by-elections when they come up. Perhaps the wheel of politics will turn again one day, either in my time or afterwards.

1969: The Completion of Trowbridge Estate: council housing in Hackney – Michael Passmore

New and old: Trowbridge Estate rises above the condemned streets of Hackney Wick. (Hackney Archives)

This is an account of the brief life of the Trowbridge Estate which once stood in Hackney Wick. Its centrepiece consisted of seven 21-storey tower blocks; one of Hackney's large system-built estates erected at the end of the 1960s. Those Trowbridge tall blocks have all been demolished and the area has been redeveloped as Wick Village. During their short life the Trowbridge flats became infamous for their persistent structural faults. Finally the botched demolition of one of the towers, Northaird Point in 1985, compounded their association with failure in the public mind.

For a decade from the mid-1950s, the construction of tall blocks was encouraged by a special building subsidy introduced by Harold Macmillan's government to reflect the extra cost of building high and in an endeavour to restrict urban sprawl. A generation of architects and town planners, who were inspired by the Modern Movement, were keen to respond. Yet whereas innovators such as Le Corbusier set their slabs and towers in generous landscaping, many architects and engineers in London were prepared to site them on restricted plots. With little more than scanty grass and hard surfaces surrounding the raw concrete buildings, these 'units of accommodation' often displayed an unrelieved bleakness.

Although the ownership of Trowbridge Estate was later to pass to Hackney Council, its development was initiated by London County Council (LCC) which assembled the site from slum clearance and other land in its ownership. This widespread practice of urban redevelopment, involving the replacement of nineteenth-century terraces and backyard industry with council housing, led to the obliteration of much of the original street pattern. Hence, at Hackney Wick, the redevelopment meant the loss of the quaintly-named Homfray Street, Plover Street and Percy Terrace. LCC architects, who had a worldwide reputation for housing design, sketched out a scheme for flats using a conventional form of construction. These initial ideas were discarded as there was pressure from government ministers to adopt industrialised, or system building, in the fruitless expectation of reducing building costs. For many architects prefabrication conformed to the ideals of early Modernism which envisioned a building consisting of standard parts, or modules, like a machine. Having experimented with system building using large panels in Woolwich, to wide professional acclaim, the architects who took over the project at the newly-formed GLC switched to a similar system at Hackney Wick. They adopted the Cebus system, which had been widely employed in Mediterranean countries, but they failed to notice that the concrete mix was unsuitable for London's damp climate. Cracking occurred in the external walls of the new tower blocks soon after they were built; within a year or two tenants were complaining about rainwater penetration. It was some 15 years later that the first of the towers was demolished.

The close of the 1960s is significant for more fundamental reasons: it signalled a change in the physical form of council housing and a shift in the political culture. The completion of the Trowbridge Estate occurred at a turning point in the story of Hackney's social housing. In 1968, construction of five of Trowbridge's high-rise blocks was nearing completion, with work on the last two under way, when sensational reports appeared about the partial collapse of Ronan Point in neighbouring Newham. Few council tenants, town hall politicians or officials were unaffected by the dramatic photographs that accompanied reports of the disaster which killed three people and injured others. The accident was triggered by an explosion in a gas cooker on the eighteenth floor of the 22-storey building and the pictures showed the flats beneath collapsing on top of each other.

It was too late to pull the developments of system blocks already underway. The GLC was using a similar system of construction at the New Kingshold Estate and at Nightingale Estate beside Hackney Downs. Similarly, Hackney Council was committed at Clapton Park and Kings Crescent, and had just launched the development of Holly Street. Leading borough and GLC councillors were quick to assure tenants that their tall blocks were safe, but there was a widespread public reaction against building more high-rise flats.

There had always been isolated opposition to tall flats, but the Ronan Point incident reinforced professional opinion which had been moving in that direction since the mid-1960s. This was attributable to the high cost of construction and social concern over the undesirability of creating 'streets in the sky' for families with young children. A leading GLC architect, Kenneth Campbell, was one of those extolling the virtues of new methods of construction in the early 1960s. By the end of the decade he was posing the question, "What went wrong with tall blocks?"

Some of Campbell's colleagues had already moved on to designing low-rise forms of housing, which in the 1970s became the preferred option. In Stoke Newington the GLC experimented with small blocks of flats as an extension to the Kennaway Estate. Meanwhile, in 1971 Hackney Council adopted new guidelines for its housing projects resolving to erect no more high-rise flats, except in unusual circumstances. It shifted to building short terraces of houses with brick walls and tiled roofs, and a few low-rise flats. Typical of the style of the early 1970s are the Linzell Estate, Lower Clapton, and the Mountford Estate, off Sandringham Road. By the mid-1990s, when the building of council houses was drastically reduced, Hackney had completed several low-rise schemes, including the huge Jack Dunning Estate in Clapton. Unconsciously, it would seem, Hackney councillors adopted a similar policy to their predecessors who in the 1940s restricted their new estates to three storeys. By chance, the Mountford housing is a stone's throw from Frederick Gibberd's cottagey Somerford Estate, which in 1951 won a Festival of Britain architectural award.

As for those system-built blocks, the GLC and Hackney had financed them using loans predicated on a minimum life of 60 years. All but a handful were demolished in less than half that period and Northaird Point lasted only 17 years – what a waste! Trowbridge was one of the estates most hated by its tenants and it was the first to go. The unhappiness engendered by the blocks was compounded by the catastrophic town planning which permitted the East Cross Motorway that cut off Trowbridge from the rest of Hackney and – it seemed – the world. Brian Sedgemore, the local MP, commented on the Estate in a House of Commons debate in 1983: "Trowbridge Estate was built amid the naivety and optimism of the 1960s. Today it embodies the pessimism of the 1980s. It is a monument to misery and insensitivity, which demonstrates only too clearly how that which can be fashionable but which is not rooted in the needs of the people can quickly become a disaster."

As to the shift in the politics of council housing, in retrospect it can be seen that the completion of the Trowbridge Estate coincided with a waning in the growth of council housing in Britain. During the immediate post-war years both major political parties were committed to building large numbers of council homes, although there were differences of emphasis. For most of the 1950s and 1960s, the success of housing policy in boroughs such as Hackney was measured by the number of new homes completed each year. The housing drive led to the public sector expanding to one-third of all housing in the country by 1969, a proportion which was never exceeded. In Hackney the combined ownership of the local council and GLC was almost half of all housing in the borough. Hackney's Labour leadership of the time envisaged the redevelopment of virtually the whole of Hackney to provide modern homes for the working-class citizens of the borough.

From the late 1960s, government ministers began giving a higher priority to home modernisation with the encouragement of improvement grants. Financial issues came to the fore, making the divisions in policy between Conservative and Labour politicians much sharper and with battles fought over council rents and sales. Before the Trowbridge flats were completed, the new tenants challenged a substantial increase in rent by a Conservative-controlled GLC. They hung a large banner on the outside of one of the tower blocks, Deverill Point, declaring: "NOT A PENNY ON THE RENT". Meanwhile, the influential Horace Cutler, who at the time was a rare proto-Thatcherite at the GLC, expressed the view that "local authorities ought to get out of housing". Only a decade later, the Conservative government introduced the Right to Buy scheme.

Despite the reaction against tall council blocks at the close of the 1960s, in recent years a new trend among private developers for building high-rise flats can be seen in the borough, most noticeably around Dalston Square. Prefabrication is common, with factory-built, modular construction being employed, such as at Raines Court, Northwold Road. Time will tell whether unforeseen faults occur in any of the new forms of construction, as has occurred in some refurbishment schemes at local authority tower blocks.

As the drafting of this piece approached completion in June 2017, people throughout London and beyond were reeling from the pictures and first-hand accounts of the horrific fire at the 24-storey Grenfell Tower in North Kensington. The public grief and anger expressed by relations, friends, and neighbours of those killed, seriously injured or reported missing on the night of the blaze reached extraordinary levels of intensity. The images of the blackened hulk looming large over the urban landscape close to the West Cross Motorway will surely remain in the national memory for a very long time. Checks were being made on the safety of other recently refurbished blocks, and a significant impact is expected on the overdue updating of the building regulations.

Further Information

Brian Finnimore, *Houses from the Factory: System Building and the Welfare State 1942–74*, Rivers Oram, 1989

Miles Glendinning and Stefan Muthesius, *Tower Block: Modern Public Housing in England, Scotland, Wales and Northern Ireland*, Yale University Press, 1994

Michael Passmore, 'From High Hopes to Tall Flats: The Changing Shape of Hackney's Housing, 1945–60', *Hackney History*, vol. 15 (2009)

1970: It started with a Bookshop: the founding of Centerprise
– Ken Worpole

Panel from a cartoon history of Centerprise by Tom Wilson and Brook Walford.

In early 1970 Glenn Thompson, a black American draft-resister turned youth worker, along with his partner, Margaret Gosley, rented a small shop in Matthias Road, Stoke Newington. It was to be the temporary address for a project they had been dreaming about for some time: a shop-front which combined a bookshop, coffee bar and meeting place for young people in Hackney where both now worked. They had solicited help from a number of enthusiastic and well-connected supporters in the arts and education, and had put out feelers to potential co-workers. But it was their original enthusiasm and vision that made Centerprise happen, a model for a new kind of cultural centre which over time was admired and emulated in other inner-city settings, not just in Britain but elsewhere in the world.

Glenn had been influenced by the work of Paolo Freire, a literacy worker and liberation theologist in Brazil, whose pedagogical methods were receiving international interest and acclaim, as well as by the ideas of deschooling guru, Ivan Illich. In Hoxton Glenn had been recruited as an unattached youth worker, while Margaret worked as a librarian at Hackney Downs School. Both were convinced of the power of reading and forms of participatory education to help bring about radical political and social change. Having established an address and opened a bank account at Coutts (Glenn had chutzpah), the search was on for more permanent premises. This was when I first met Glenn, when he and Margaret arranged with my wife Larraine – herself a youth worker – and myself to join them looking for such premises. After a few unsuccessful forays, they found what they were looking for in a parade of run-down shops in Dalston Lane, due for demolition, but temporarily available on short-term leases.

The precise timing of all this activity was outlined in a Centerprise report published several years after, detailing the original funding programme. "An application for financial support was made in March 1970 to the ILEA Experimental Youth Working Party and certain costs for salaries and rent and rates were agreed by that committee in July of the same year." The idealism of the times, not just on the street but even in the corridors of power, can be seen by the fact that even a large bureaucracy such as the Inner London Education Authority had an *Experimental* Youth Working Party. Radical times required radical solutions – or so it seemed then.

Dusty, hard-bitten Dalston Lane has since been much mythologised, and with some justification, by writers such as Patrick Wright and Iain Sinclair, and by performance artist Aaron Williamson, as the forcing ground – or 'incubator' in the current jargon – for many radical and ambitious arts and cultural projects which emerged in Hackney at this time. These included Free Form Arts, The Four Aces Club, Hackney Task Force, Hackney Pensioners' Association, as well as the erstwhile birthplace of punk music in the Music Junction studio in the basement of number 21. There were others too. Elsewhere in the borough community arts projects emerging during this decade included Chats Palace, The Factory, The Fire Station: complementing the long-established Hoxton Hall.

Centerprise proper finally opened at 34 Dalston Lane in May 1971, shortly followed by the opening of the Centerprise Children's Bookshop at 66a Dalston Lane. Glenn persuaded Penguin Books to donate a large amount of shelving, and also secured a (rare at this time) franchise to stock Open University course books. As hoped for, very soon the project was encouraging all kinds of spin-offs, including citizens' rights campaigns, play and under-fives projects, writers' groups and literacy programmes, community publishing and adult education classes. Within three years Centerprise had expanded into the double-fronted building at 136-138 Kingsland High Street where – despite many ups and downs –it flourished for almost 40 years.

Glenn's philosophy, and that of Margaret also, was based on the belief that people's creativity flourished when they became active participants in the fashioning of their lives and identities, especially those who had been, in a phrase then much employed, 'hidden from history', or rendered invisible in mainstream culture.Young teachers in Hackney were aware that while there were many Afro-Caribbeans living and working in the borough, there were no black people in the school reading books they were required to use. Nor was there any reference in history lessons or social studies to Hackney's rich industrial history (and the lives and struggles of its workers) whether in shoe-making, furniture-making and bespoke joinery, tailoring and dress-making, or river-work on the Thames and the River Lea (still then a major working river) – in a borough often demonised for the 'poverty' of its aspirations. New technologies such as cassette tape-

Vivian Usherwood: Poems, by a 12-year-old Hackney Downs schoolboy, published by Centerprise. (Photo Neil Martinson)

recorders, electric typewriters, offset-litho printing, Cowgum and Letraset, put the recording, editing and publishing process within the reach of community groups, and thus a 'do-it-yourself' culture quickly emerged.

The democratisation of culture became part of the zeitgeist. Just down the road, Stepney teacher Chris Searle had been sacked for publishing *Stepney Words*, a collection of school-children's poems, so what became known as 'the politics of literacy' was not uncontested. The first publications from Centerprise included a pack of local history materials, *If It Wasn't For the Houses In Between*, a collection of poems by a young black pupil from Hackney Downs, *Vivian Usherwood: Poems*, and the autobiography of Hackney shoemaker Arthur Newton, *Years of Change*. Over time a tentative stream of small publications became a significant publishing programme acquiring national influence, particularly in education.

The truly radical principle behind Centerprise was that it crossed all the conventional boundaries in public policy and social action, whether between adult literacy and citizens' rights, creative writing and child-care activism, literature and the politics of anti-racism, along with the making and understanding of local history, and the reconfiguring of where and how people lived and made sense of a place like Hackney. It wasn't all peace and love and understanding, especially as the political atmosphere hardened on the streets in the later 1970s, but Centerprise opened doors for many, including those who worked there, and it raised questions about living and learning that are still deliberated today.

In recent years there has been a revival of interest in the radical arts movement of the 1960s and 1970s. The economic case for the arts – that the sector pioneers the refurbishment of run-down buildings, generates new areas of trading activity and community self-confidence, attracts related businesses, and, most importantly, brings young people to the fore of urban regeneration – is now accepted. But the promise that artists and other cultural activists might form a vanguard in creating new forms of community solidarity and identity seems to have stalled. Piggy-backing on the low-rent, high-impact culture of community-minded artists, came the high-rent, short-term culture of the new-build, faux-bohemian apartment blocks and 'place-making' landscapes of private developers, keen to exploit the borough's radical buzz.

Fortunately young people have a habit of 'making it new' all over again, and Hackney's stubborn, renegade heart means that it remains a place of opportunity for those with a creative spark and an independent spirit, particularly at the moment in music, dance, theatre, film-making, publishing and book-selling. The result is that the borough's rich diversity and contrarian culture continues to innovate, dazzle and surprise.

Further Information

Rosa Schling, *The Lime Green Mystery: An Oral History of the Centerprise co-operative*, 2017, available from info@on-the-record.org.uk

Iain Sinclair, *Hackney, That Rose-Red Empire*, Hamish Hamilton, 2009

Aaron Williamson, *Splitting the Atom on Dalston Lane*, Eel, 2009

Patrick Wright, *A Journey Through Ruins: The Last Days of London*, OUP, 2009

1971: The Art Factory at Martello Street: the artist community in Hackney – Anna Harding

Bruce Lacey's studio at Martello Street, London Fields, in the 1970s. (Photo Ingeborg Sedgley)

The creative and artistic scene in Hackney today can be traced back to the 'spirit of 68': Hornsey College of Art, sit-ins, socially conscious artists and revolt against the Ivory Tower.

It is very much to the credit of the defunct GLC that they sought to facilitate and encourage this explosion of artistic activity by their visionary support for SPACE studios' proposal to re-use redundant buildings left by London's industrial decline.

The studios grew out of this twin impetus – creative innovation abetted by political support. SPACE was a new self-help venture set up by artists including Bridget Riley and Peter Sedgley. Its first building opened in November 1968 at St Katharine Docks to provide low rental workspace to artists who previously had nothing. At the forefront of late 1960s art developments, SPACE was home to experimental art forms, such as the Resin Unit, Kinetic, O, inflatables and in the early 1970s the London Film-Makers' Co-op. Artists were becoming conscious of their social role. This was a time of heady excitement, weekend talk-ins, peace and love, psychedelic drugs and anti-war demonstrations, in which artists, writers and musicians played a key part.

Perhaps London's first example of artist-led gentrification, the St Katharine Docks site was redeveloped by Taylor Woodrow two years later. A meeting with the artists about their relocation was featured in a 1970 BBC documentary on SPACE. In 1971 SPACE opened its first Hackney artists' studio building at 10 Martello Street close by London Fields, a former clothing factory offered by the GLC at a peppercorn rent. The area was extremely run down and conditions in the building were basic. The artists had to install lights and plumbing and repair the windows, learning a wide range of skills. They converted the open plan factory floors into individual studios, working collectively for many months without pay. Robin Klassnik, one of the first artists to arrive, remarked to me that nobody seemed to have any money, but you could live for very little in those days.

Martello Street had plenty of dark space and a basement so it was offered to film-makers, installation and op artists. At this time, many artists were mistrustful of conventional commercial galleries. Happenings and installations were part of the artists' ways of working, and a natural development was that artists began to exhibit their work in self-organised studio exhibitions. In 1975 a vast exhibition, 'SPACE Open Studios', was held on 14 different sites throughout London with one-person exhibitions of 138 artists, reaching excited audiences with national and international press coverage.

Martello Street tenants included anarchic performer Bruce Lacey and family, musician, poet and occultist Genesis P. Orridge who with Cosey Fani Tutti ran experimental art group COUM Transmissions, bands Throbbing Gristle and Psychic TV, and P-Orridge's Thee Temple ov Psychick Youth, an informal occult order influenced by chaos magic and experimental music. The experimental artist Robin Klassnik moved to St Katharine Docks in 1968 from art school in Leicester, and then on to Martello Street. He told me that SPACE was his formative education, leading him to abandon painting and begin sculpture, 8mm film, photography and performance. In 1979 he opened his studio at Martello Street as Matt's Gallery, inviting artists to make site-specific work including Rose Finn-Kelcey, Jimmie Durham, Willie Doherty and Richard Wilson's famous 20:50 oil slick installation bought by collector Charles Saatchi.

Martello Street has been home to SPACE studios ever since. Benefitting artists include Turner Prize-winning Laure Prouvost, photomontage specialist Peter Kennard and 20 Canadian artists in residence.

Robin Klassnik, OBE, painting the Crittall windows in his Martello Street studio. (Photo Kathryn Klassnik)

The appeal of Martello Street is captured in *All Nations Hackney*, a blog named after the neighbouring All Nations Club, a Caribbean-themed nightclub that would throb with music from midnight to dawn on weekends. Now a block of flats stands in its place, but All Nations seemed a brilliant name to associate with Hackney and the people who live and work here. The special appeal of Hackney for artists is expressed by some of the contributors to the blog:

"Hackney has got such an amazing atmosphere with lots of artists. London is quite amazing being so multi-cultural but Hackney is especially so. You get lots of things happening, lots of galleries, lots of events and it's still quite shabby chic." Martina Spetlova

"When I was looking for a place to work, Hackney was the major place for studios, because of SPACE. The best thing (about Hackney) is the multicultureness, the openness, the tolerance, the vibrancy and liveliness. Especially in this area there are a lot of activities and I feel this energy and of course my studio is here. I always love to come to my studio; it's like a home for me. I really feel good and contemplative and creative. It's like coming back to your children. My favourite place is this building plus I love the park and the Turkish café, the Anatolia. Sometimes I eat there. It's always been there, it's part of the setting of the place and you see all sorts of people there, the whole of Hackney." Walid Siti, Kurdistan, Iraq

"I like the idea that in Hackney you can be whoever you want to be, no-one gives a damn and everybody's kind of supportive about it, and I think that's very important. This comes together with the fact that this isn't the poshest and richest part of the country, yet the people are very rich in mind and ideas, I think that's the neighbourhood for me." Gergely Barsi Szabo

Since 1971 SPACE has opened 10 studio sites in Hackney and many more across London, each developed as a unique model. These include: The Triangle Mare Street, a 41,000-square-foot building with over 100 tenants, converted with the help of grant funding from the London Development Agency and European Regional Development

Fund; Victor House (now surrounded by Barratt flats) and Richmond Road, both rented from private landlords since the 1980s, with Victor House still going strong today. Eastway Studios, Morning Lane (since demolished), Stoke Newington Library and Sara Lane Court Hoxton have all been leased from Hackney Council. At Timber Wharf in Haggerston, SPACE opened studios in 2011 which met the need of housing association landlords for a mixed-use development including an employment use compatible with residential. Other non-SPACE studio buildings in the borough include The Chocolate Factory, Stoke Newington, and Matchmakers Wharf, Homerton. There are many more studios at Hackney Wick including 92 White Post Lane, Mother Studios, Stour Space, Omega Works, Vittoria Wharf, Cell Studios alongside SPACE's Britannia Works, Bridget Riley Studios and The White Building, which opened in 2012 as a partnership with the London Legacy Development Corporation.

How long these will last in the face of redevelopment is uncertain and depends on the circumstances of each lease and the respective landlords. SPACE was always nimble, taking leases on buildings deserted by their previous industrial users but which the owners had no other use for. But among SPACE's former studio sites Richmond Road has now been converted to luxury flats (The Arthaus) and Morning Lane has been demolished and redeveloped. Others may suffer the same fate in the future.

Artists have contributed to making Hackney the place it is today, attracted by affordable empty industrial buildings, which are gradually being replaced or repurposed. They are potent players in gentrification as they are drawn to areas where they can find somewhere cheap to live and work. Their presence attracts people with more money so that places frequented by artists get taken over by second and third wave entrepreneurs. Martello Street is now in the centre of a hotspot of property development and London Fields has become one of the coolest places on earth.

Hackney has laid claim for many years to having the highest density of artists in Europe, but escalating property prices and shortages of affordable housing and workspace put huge pressure on the low-waged of the borough, including many artists. In response to this, in 2011 SPACE managed, with the help of a large mortgage, to buy its first freehold studio building, Deborah House, a former clothing factory in Retreat Place, Homerton, securing a future for around 60 artists. But many artists in the borough are under threat from unaffordable rent increases and redevelopment. Faced with Hackney becoming more expensive, SPACE has looked elsewhere and secured freehold buildings outside the borough, in Peckham and Poplar, and opened its first non-London site in Colchester. With the increasing cost of property, Hackney's future as a hub for artists is threatened. Despite this, SPACE and Martello Street still provide valued studio space for many artists in Hackney today.

Further Information

David Ley, *Artists, Aestheticisation and the Field of Gentrification*, 2007

On the All Nations Club see https://www.tumblr.com/search/Hackney+All+Nations

1972: Stopping the Bulldozers: De Beauvoir is saved – Stuart Weir

De Beauvoir Square in 1972. The council wanted to demolish the houses, but keep the square.
(Hackney Archives)

It didn't look good. It was on the brink of the May 1968 local elections. Robin Young, my friend and neighbour, and I had trawled the streets of De Beauvoir with a megaphone, inviting everyone to the crypt of St Peter's Church to 'Save De Beaver' from redevelopment. But with only a few minutes to go a mere trickle of people had entered the crypt. "People just don't turn out," said the Labour councillor for the ward, shaking his head complacently. He didn't live in or know the ward; rather he was an emissary from the central Hackney Labour high command to this slightly uppity colony on the imperial fringe.

In fact, it was good, way above our expectations. Suddenly a surge of people burst into the crypt, some 250 or more. I'd never spoken to such a large audience, but they carried me along with their fervour, brushing the councillor and the Conservative candidates aside. I was emboldened, inviting everyone to come back in a fortnight's time to set up an association to take on a Labour council that was intent on driving bulldozers through the homes and local industries in the ward. They did come back again, most of them. I resisted the call for elections to an executive committee, as I wanted to have an inclusive and pluralist enterprise, and I feared elections would be divisive. So I ruled that everyone who came would be on the committee.

The spirit was uplifting. At the end residents crowded round me offering to help. Two older women, Mabel Hall and her sister Nancy, volunteered to "do something for the elderly". They were to be key figures among the stalwarts who sustained the association.

It was a propitious moment. The Conservatives swept through London boroughs in the elections. The unthinkable happened in Hackney: they won a majority on a council on which Labour traditionally had near monopoly control. The local De Beauvoir Labour councillors lost their seats. The spirit at our meeting reflected this greater shift nationally in political opinion. But it also signified something deeper. De Beauvoir, historically a middle-class area, was now a largely working- and artisan-class neighbourhood of strong neighbourly instincts. The long leases of the Benyon family's estate preserved a sense of continuity and solidarity. Families had lived in the same houses since before the First World War. It was common to see neighbours chatting in front of their houses in the early evening.

But De Beauvoir was undeniably dilapidated. Many houses on its spacious streets were in poor repair. Two world wars, bombs, multi-occupation, lack of investment and backyard industry had set the area on to a course of decline. Some houses had only gas lighting. The real damage, however, had been done by Hackney Council which viewed spacious De Beauvoir with its long gardens as an ideal site for 'housing gain', adopting a series of wholesale redevelopment plans for the area. In the late 1950s Hackney moved to compulsorily purchase a first tranche on the south adjacent to the Regent's Canal. Much of De Beauvoir rallied to the defence of the area; Mabel Hall, who lived outside the area to be demolished, recalled the shock and disbelief the proposals caused and clubbing together with neighbours to raise funds for the defence. The inspector at the public inquiry was "impressed by the strength of the objection" made by residents and he found for them.

But in August 1961, Henry Brooke, the Conservative housing minister, insisted that the "substantial housing gain" that redevelopment could bring outweighed the inspector's arguments and overturned his verdict. It was a crushing moment for the neighbourhood. Having come so close to defeating the council, residents despaired of ever doing so. Residents even in the north of the area showed me letters from the council stating when it would require their homes.

Suddenly in 1968 we had three years to convince a new Conservative council that De Beauvoir could and should be rehabilitated, with the force of a major shift in policy under the new Labour government at our backs. The climate in Whitehall was changing fast. The Civic Amenities Act the year before had popularised the concept of area conservation as an alternative to wholesale redevelopment. In 1969, a new Housing Act gave councils powers to generate rehabilitation in designated General Improvement Areas (GIAs).

So it was with a sense of opportunity that committee members met in an upstairs room at the Talbot pub. We were a mixed group, long established residents and professional newcomers, home-owners, leaseholders and private tenants, members of all parties and none. There were some 25 to 30 of us. We created rules to ensure that everyone had an opportunity to speak and no-one could dominate the discussions. Most important of all, we took on the responsibility to work collectively for the benefit of all residents and all tenures. I set up a weekly welfare rights office every Saturday morning.

The *Illustrated London News* recorded that "we unearthed and presented the facts, argued and goaded". Senior town hall officials who wanted to sit out the three-year interregnum and return to Labour's flat-earth policies were forced to pay attention, as we lobbied council members and the Historic Buildings Division of the GLC. We wrote up the area's history, won allies in the Victorian Society, filled the pages of the *Hackney Gazette* and polished our skills in spin.

Robin Young and I both worked on *The Times* Diary column, the nearest approximation to a sinecure in the national press. We had time on our hands. We decided to demonstrate that the houses in De Beauvoir could be modernised by establishing a housing trust to buy up and improve local properties. Over time Robin bought 42 houses, usually tenanted, and some as cheaply as £500. He improved and managed them and their tenants (most of whom wanted to stay in the area) for six years before handing the trust over to Circle 33, a professional housing association.

We also worked hard within De Beauvoir to encourage a spirit of solidarity and fun. We organised a working party to fence off a dangerous refuse area, stealing the planks from a local building site. We organised a student survey of the state of local houses and the wishes of the inhabitants, establishing a semi-independent Southern Area Action Group (SAAG) in 1970 to organise resistance to redevelopment of the vulnerable area. We organised a separate leaseholders' association jointly to acquire their freeholds under the Leasehold Reform Act 1967. We had enough volunteers to deliver a free newspaper, *De Beaver*, to every household; Doffy Weir created a vivid design, while Jo Parsey persuaded local business people to pay for it.

I stood down as chair after two years and was succeeded by Graham Parsey. He was an inspiring leader who chaired the association through the testing period of the subsequent public enquiry. He and Doris Kibblewhite, our long-serving secretary who was known throughout De Beauvoir as 'the lady on the bike', formed the spine of the association, along with many others like Frank Fletcher, who led the resistance in the southern area.

What we might have had: the De Beauvoir South Estate. (Hackney Archives)

We were in luck with the new Hackney Council. Our new Tory councillor, Miss Watts, a starchy former teacher, who regarded me with suspicion as the sort of boy who sat at the back of the class making mischief, was nevertheless on-side. The real 'mischief' was done by Donald Bridgehouse, whom the Conservative party imported on to Hackney Council as an alderman when they realised that their new councillors were incapable of running a whelk stall, let alone a local authority. Bridgehouse was a highly intelligent and snazzy City gent, an exotic creature among his stolid colleagues. He moved quickly on behalf of De Beauvoir, infuriating the once powerful Labour rump. We had already persuaded GLC Historic Buildings officials to begin the process of designating De Beauvoir Square and Northchurch Road as a conservation area (the actual designation was made in 1971).

Bridgehouse, inspired by the GLC, had the 'central area', including the square, declared a GIA in 1970. Younger planning officers responded enthusiastically, setting up a local residents' committee to oversee improvement plans, including blocking off roads that had served as rat-runs. Bridgehouse was not done. In April 1971, in the last moments of Conservative control, he pushed the declaration of a GIA in southern De Beauvoir through the council, in the face of furious Labour opposition.

SAAG had already worked on proposals to protect the area, which had been the next in line for redevelopment and was subject to blight and industrial invasion. Four planning students from the Central London Polytechnic had conducted a structural and social survey and drawn up a sensitive provisional plan with a mix of rehabilitation and development. In 1971, the council rejected the plan, but made it the basis for the GIA declaration. It was a procedurally dodgy decision and Labour, on regaining power, immediately applied to the government to rescind the declaration.

No-one was in any doubt that the restored Labour council intended to carry out as much redevelopment as it could. A public inquiry followed in March 1972, at which the council's case rested on the imperative of housing gain. The inspector ruled that the GIA order had not been improperly made. He found for SAAG, the Benyon Estate and local residents who had given evidence that the GIA should be retained, thus assuring, as he put it, the "prospect of continuity". Subsequently the southern area was designated as a Conservation Area in 1977 and north De Beauvoir in 1998.

De Beauvoir has now become a predominantly middle-class jewel of gentrification, with houses being sold for up to and beyond £2 million each. The New York Times has celebrated it as a "boho-chic buzzing village", a gross exaggeration but a sign of where things are going. A very different De Beauvoir Association still survives which retains something of the communal aspirations of the original. The point of our campaign had been to save the community as well as the houses and environment of De Beauvoir. We saved the fabric of De Beauvoir, but have ultimately lost the community we had.

Further Information

Tony Aldous, *The Illustrated London News Book of London's Villages*, Secker & Warburg, 1980

Patrick Wright, *A Journey Through Ruins; The Last Days of London*, OUP, 2009

The entire De Beaver archive from 1971 to 1984 has been put online by the De Beauvoir Association at http://www.debeauvoir.org.uk/debeaver.html

An advertisement for the Duke of Wellington Pub and Theatre, from *De Beaver* magazine.

1973: The Scrapping of the 'Motorway Box' – Wayne Asher

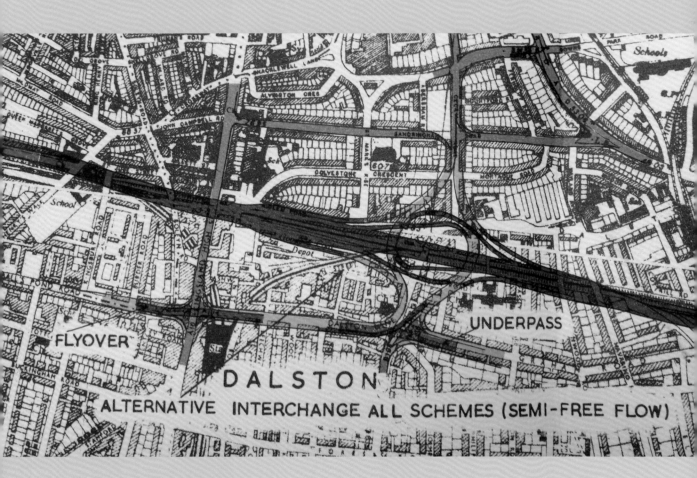

Urban motorways need interchanges. A plan commissioned by the GLC of the proposed Sandringham
Road interchange. Dalston Lane and Graham Road are shown as feeder roads for the new motorway.
(London Metropolitan Archives/English Heritage)

In April 1973 a great shadow was lifted from Hackney – and from vast swathes of the capital as well. Labour had just regained control of the Greater London Council, and its very first act was to kill off the Ringway Project.

What became the Ringways were the brainchild of Professor Patrick Abercrombie, proposed in his *Greater London Plan* published in 1944, a vast set of urban motorways which would have transformed London beyond recognition.

Ringway 1 boxed in inner London and was known as the Motorway Box. It ran from Willesden, via Hampstead, Camden and Dalston to Hackney Wick (the North Cross Route), then following the Lea to the Blackwall Tunnel and Kidbrooke (the East Cross Route), westwards via Brixton to Battersea (the South Cross Route), and back to Willesden Junction (the West Cross Route).

Ringway 2 comprised the North Circular, extended under the river via a new tunnel at Beckton, and then via a new urban motorway across south London to Chiswick.

Ringway 3 was to be built further out and its northern section became part of the M25.

The Ringways would have been Britain's largest civil engineering project since the war. At around £2 billion, (£28 billion in today's money) they would have cost more than Concorde, the Channel Tunnel and a third London airport put together. It was also estimated that from 60,000 to100,000 people living on the route would have to be rehoused

The North Cross Route was originally proposed to follow the south side of the North London Line in a cutting from Hackney Wick to Dalston. From there a viaduct would have taken it over Kingsland Road before following the North London Line again to Highbury. Transport ministry civil servants thought, however, that building the motorway in a cutting through the humble suburb of Hackney was an unnecessary extravagance. They argued that the entire section across Hackney should be built on a viaduct as this would be cheaper.

Hackney would have had two vast interchanges: a spaghetti junction at Hackney Wick where the East Cross Route today meets the M11 Link Road; and another one at Dalston, close to the Cecilia Road/Dalston Lane junction, where the North Cross Route would have intersected with a diverted A10. The Dalston Interchange, shown in the artist's sketch, would have been particularly devastating in terms of wholesale demolition, noise, pollution and a divided community. And the roads around this junction would surely have been filled with traffic trying the join the motorway.

It is easy to grasp what the North Cross Route would have looked like. Just stand on the Wick Lane footbridge in Bow which goes over the East Cross Route, the only part of the Ringway plan to be built in its entirety.

The money needed for the Ringways, which would have burdened public finances for many decades, would have certainly forestalled the current renaissance in public transport. And yet – incredibly – they would not even have worked.

The Ringways were conceived when traffic congestion was expected to grow exponentially and when public transport was out of favour. Building new roads to match the expected demand was seen as the only solution. All over the country, Britain's great cities were attacked by the road builders. In Birmingham, even today, planners are striving to unlock the concrete girdle created by inner urban expressways.

The Ringway project had passed from Abercrombie to the LCC and then to the newly-created Greater London Council. In 1963 engineers started to plan the Motorway Box in detail. Their proposals were unveiled in 1965 on the very first day of the new GLC's existence.

The Ringways were originally a Labour Party project, with the Tories in enthusiastic support and the well-resourced road lobby cheering them on. At first there was little opposition – only wealthy areas in the direct path of Ringway 1 (Hampstead and Blackheath) protested when the proposals were unveiled. But as the impact sunk in, protest generalised. A London Motorway Action Group was set up in 1968 by former Labour minister Douglas Jay, the MP for Battersea but a resident of Hampstead. It eventually represented scores of amenity groups and 13 London MPs of both parties – including Stanley Clinton-Davis, the member for Hackney Central.

However, Hackney was not a centre of road protest. Most residents lived in poorly maintained and often overcrowded rented accommodation and those on the line of the route had the prospect of being rehoused in spanking new council houses. We forget the reality of the swinging sixties – in London in 1966, 600,000 people shared dingy accommodation and half of these shared a bathroom.

Fighting the Ringways needed hard evidence to attack an entrenched 'common-sense' consensus. And so a working party under Professor Michael Thomson of the London School of Economics was tasked to look into the road builders' case. Thomson's report, Motorways in London, published in 1969, showed that road building could never solve traffic congestion as roads generated their own traffic by encouraging more people to buy cars, and existing motorists to make more and longer journeys. This counter-intuitive finding was borne out – to officialdom's utter shock – when the M25 turned out to be full from the day it opened.

The fight against the Ringways was led by the London Motorway Action Group, Although Hackney was not a centre of opposition, the infant Hackney Society enrolled as a corporate member. The Group conducted a genteel campaign respecting the official process by submitting carefully produced evidence to the public inquiry set up to validate the GLC's Greater London Development Plan. There was none of the direct action that would mark road protest in the 1980s. And in that sense the protests failed. Despite all the evidence that road building was doomed to failure according to its own terms, the public inquiry backed Ringway 1, and Ted Heath's Conservative government backed it too.

But the Ringways were ultimately defeated because Jay's group had changed opinion within the London Labour Party. In 1972 the party agreed that if it were to win the GLC elections the following year, it would scrap the Ringways. That promise was delivered when Labour regained control of the GLC in 1973

However, even though the North Cross route was never built, its impact was felt in Hackney for many years. Many properties had been purchased for clearance by the GLC and Hackney Council along the alignment of the proposed route. The traffic engineers continued to dream of a fast route connecting Hackney Wick to Highbury Corner, shifting

The proposed route for the 'Motorway Box' through Dalston. An artist's sketch superimposed upon a contemporary aerial photograph. (London Metropolitan Archives)

their attention to the route via Graham Road and Dalston Junction. The assumption that road widening would eventually take place meant either that new developments were set back (as at Dalston Lane) or that properties were left unoccupied and decaying (as at Morning Lane). The junctions at Mare Street and Dalston (Kingsland Road) in particular were seen as major bottlenecks requiring attention.

The Conservative administration which controlled the GLC from 1977 to 1981 was sympathetic to these objectives and it was not until after the change of political control in 1981 that much of the safeguarding was removed.

Even then, it took many years to reverse the effect of years of planning blight. Dereliction continued in Morning Lane and Dalston Lane until the 1990s and beyond. Indeed, in Dalston Lane, the decay and destruction of Dalston Terrace is in a sense a consequence of transport planning blight – arguably the final legacy in Hackney of the Motorway Box.

Further Information

Wayne Asher, *Rings Around London,* London, 2017

Mick Hamer, *Wheels Within Wheels,* London, 1987

Michael Thomson, *Motorways in London,* London, 1969

1974: Clapton Dog Track is closed
– Brian Belton

Art Deco elegance at Clapton Stadium. (RIBA)

Just before Christmas 1973, I took my last trip to Clapton dog track. This was the place where Joe Coral, who had been a bookmaker at the track, started his empire. I had recently begun work for Coral's as a trainee settler, my job was to calculate the amount due to successful punters.

Taking the tube to Manor House, and then a bus to Clapton Pond, I made the short walk to the stadium, where I made my way past the 'cheap side' (the first turnstile) to the 'dear side', maybe an 80-yard stroll. The track had banked bends, with netting in case a disappointed punter decided to sling whatever might be to hand at a dog that had let him down.

The 400-yard races started in front of the stands, providing a good run up to the initial bend. For longer races the traps were parked at the corner of the back straight, again giving the dogs a fair run to the first bend. I recall that the crowd on that day was quite good, but far short of the thousands Clapton could attract in its heyday.

The arena had been home to a whole range of sports, including boxing and baseball. From 1896 to 1930, as Millfields Road, it was the ground for Clapton Orient football team. Large embankments were built, using slag from the nearby power station, and the first Football League match was played there on 9 September 1905. The home side defeated Hull City 1-0 to send the majority of the 3,000-strong crowd home happy.

In 1922 Clapton hosted the first football match to be attended by a member of the royal family when the Prince of Wales, the future Edward VIII, witnessed Orient's 3-0 walloping of Notts County. Hereafter His Highness was known as 'Teddy the O' in some footballing circles.

Clapton Stadium Syndicate became joint tenants in 1927, when major works were initiated to facilitate greyhound racing. The cost was huge at £80,000: an average house in the area would have cost around £500. Sir Evan Owen Williams, later to be involved in the building of the M1, was put in charge of the design which included an almost circular track encircling the football pitch. It had short straights and easy wide turns, making it one of the fastest raceways in the country. On three sides there was concrete terracing, with a main stand completing the spectator area.

The first race-card was presented on 7 April 1928 and shortly after Major C. Moss, the stadium's racing manager, introduced a new 400-yard sprint. The swift circuit suited this race, which became a classic of the sport: the Scurry Gold Cup. The Scurry, in its glory days, would rival the Derby in status, drawing the most fleet-of-foot dogs: the roster of winners included all the top sprinters of the first era of greyhound racing. However, it wasn't until 1947 that a Clapton dog took the title: Rimmell's Black, trained by the famous Stanley Biss.

The following year another Biss dog, Local Interprize, won the Scurry, and nearly did so again in 1949 before a crowd of 30,000. My grandfather was there that day. For the rest of his life he swore that the race was a dead-heat because, of course, his money was on Local Interprize.

In the final part of its history, Clapton's rural kennels at Claverhambury Farm in Waltham Cross produced a plethora of Classic winners, including half a dozen Derby champions. Claverhambury boasted 200 acres of rolling grassland, with a group of resident trainers and six ranges of kennels, each range encompassing a five-acre exercise area.

Programme covers for speedway at Hackney Wick.

In financial trouble, Clapton Orient left Millfields, but the stadium was the scene of many racing triumphs. Even during the Second World War the racing continued, in between brief periods of closure. In 1951 Clapton won the national *News of the World* title, the start of a golden decade. More than 100 meetings would take place annually, presenting some 850 races on Thursday and Saturday evenings. But in 1963 Clapton Stadiums Ltd ended evening racing, looking to get the jump on the high street bookmakers: this was an ominous sign. Four years later, the shareholders of Clapton sold out to the Greyhound Racing Association, and the stadium was then sold to redevelopers. Although there were no immediate plans for closing the stadium, most punters understood this was the beginning of the end. The end, in fact, came on 1 January 1974. The Scurry Gold Cup was moved to Slough, and by the 1980s Millfields housing estate had been built over the site.

Fortunately, greyhounds continued to run at Hackney Wick until 1997, although the venue went through increasingly hard times in its final years. Built in 1932, the stadium was one of the largest in London, said to have a capacity of 50,000 with six meetings a week before the war. Hackney Wick remained a popular night out into the 1960s. Thursday and Saturday were race nights starting at 7.45 and a proper night out it was, with eight licensed buffets and bars. Hackney kennels were among the best equipped in the country, attracting many of sport's top trainers.

The stadium's popularity, and its financial viability, were supported by the fact that it doubled as a speedway venue. A cinder track was constructed inside the dog track and the stadium was home to the Hackney Wick Wolves up to the outbreak of World War Two. Speedway returned in 1963 when it became home to the phenomenally successful Hackney Hawks with racing every Wednesday and Friday night.

Hackney Wick, alongside Clapton, suffered a major blow when off-course betting was legalised in 1961. In 1970, George Walker (who had shot to fame as the manager of his celebrated brother, the boxer Billy Walker) made a takeover bid through his company Brent Walker for Hackney Wick together with its sister stadium at Hendon.

"It was traditional East London at its best": an afternoon meeting at Hackney Wick Stadium in 1987. (Photo Berris Connolly)

It was clear that property development ran more strongly in George's veins than the dogs, and Hendon Stadium was swiftly pulled down to become the Brent Cross Shopping Centre.

Racing continued, however, at the Wick with afternoon meetings broadcast to a national audience of punters through the Bookmakers' Afternoon Greyhound Service (universally known as BAGS). The stadium itself was starved of investment and looked increasingly forlorn. The kennels, however, remained some of the best in the country and in 1976 local hound Westmead Champ was voted Greyhound of the Year.

Speedway continued at Hackney Wick until 1990, sustained by the success of the Hawks (they became the Kestrels in 1984) who were to win the London Cup four times in the 1980s. But the success of the local team could not compensate for the steep decline in the popularity of the sport and speedway came to an end at Hackney in 1990.

Meanwhile, Brent Walker was succumbing to an unsustainable mountain of debt and in 1991 George Walker was kicked off the board. The bankers took over the company and sold off the stadium in 1994.

The racing journalist, Darrell Williams, described a visit to Hackney Wick in the 1990s:

Hackney was no great looker. It was cheap, cheerful and gave the impression it had probably looked exactly the same back in the 60s. It was a documentary maker's dream, full of characters, old men in caps, many who had probably been coming to the track every Saturday morning since the year dot, and nearly all puffing away, almost as if it was a pre-requisite to attend.

There was certainly nothing flash about the Wick, but it was traditional East London at its best, and I just loved having the chance to be a small part of it. Funnily enough my strongest memory is of the tea bar which was extremely basic and also probably unchanged for donkey's years but an integral part of the operation. And the tea was always very strong, like tar sometimes, having no doubt been standing to brew in the huge urn all morning! But I used to just love the atmosphere, the smells, the sights and the sounds – Hackney was always good for the banter. And while there was always the ensuing battle between punters and the old enemy, given the location, it was always conducted with the deepest of respect for the other side.

The new owners, however, had other ideas for the stadium. Work began on an ambitious £14 million refurbishment project including luxurious dining and state of the art facilities. But their timing was unfortunate. It was too late to revive the jaded image of greyhound racing and too soon to benefit from the rising trendiness of fashionable Hackney. The revamped, re-opened stadium held just two meetings before closing its doors on 4 January 1997.

In the following years, a vast and thriving Sunday flea market established itself in the car park of the derelict stadium, an emblem of the hollowed-out, dilapidated state of the Wick. But then, in 2005, a man in Singapore surprised the world by announcing "London" as the venue of the 2012 Olympic Games and the stadium, market and all were obliterated. The site of the old stadium stretches across the pristine post-Olympic park from The Copper Box to the Here East technology centre. But you would never know it.

1975: Hackney's last Grammar
School goes Comprehensive:
education during the ILEA years
– Geoff Taylor

Until the late 1960s, eleven-year-old children in England were tested to decide which kind of secondary school they should go to. In Hackney, pupils assessed as having academic potential went to one of the local grammar schools – Skinners, John Howard or Dalston County for girls; Hackney Downs, Parmiters or Central Foundation for boys. The rest went to non-selective 'secondary modern' schools. Some grammar schools, notably Hackney Downs, maintained high academic standards and had a good record of sending pupils to university; others had lower aspirations for their pupils, though at least their pupils had not had the bruising experience of having 'failed the Eleven-Plus'. There were plenty of reasons for thinking that this selective system needed reform.

Education in inner London became the responsibility of the Inner London Education Authority (ILEA) on the demise of the London County Council in 1965. In that same year, Labour Education Secretary Anthony Crosland issued Circular 10/65 instructing education authorities to prepare plans to end selective education. Comprehensivisation was enthusiastically supported by Sir Ashley Bramall, the political figure who dominated ILEA from 1965 to 1980. In 1975, the merger was announced of John Howard Grammar School and the secondary modern Clapton Park School to form a comprehensive school for girls that has since become Clapton Girls' Academy. John Howard was the last of the borough's selective grammar schools. Skinners had merged with Mount Pleasant in 1972, while Hackney Downs and Dalston County, along with the other secondary modern schools, simply began to admit pupils of all abilities. Unfortunately the scope of the changes needed to make comprehensivisation a success was seriously underestimated. It was not enough simply to ensure that every secondary school admitted pupils from across the ability range; it was essential to ensure that the provision within each school was capable of enabling all pupils to fulfil their potential. That would have involved wholesale staffing changes as non-selective secondary modern schools began to admit children who would previously have gone to grammar schools.

It would also have required the removal of teachers with persistently low professional standards. Those of us who taught in ILEA in the 1970s will remember the wealth of professional development courses on offer. But it was also true that pupils had to endure teaching by colleagues who were not up to the job yet were practically immune from dismissal. Hackney's militant NUT branch was not solely to blame for this atmosphere; the 1960s had encouraged a widespread hope for human perfectibility – the assumption that teachers, like pupils, would naturally flourish provided they were allowed their freedom. Another outcome of this approach was that detailed records of each pupil's needs and achievements were not kept, which meant that it was all too easy for both to be lost sight of. The result was generally happy, idealistic schools that nevertheless achieved very little for many of their pupils in educational terms.

The decline and closure of Hackney Downs School, where I had briefly taught in the 1980s, became a national cause célèbre. The educational standards of what had been a very successful grammar school, and was for a while a successful comprehensive, declined catastrophically after about 1985. Experienced teachers left. The buildings deteriorated. The school was left only with pupils that other schools did not want. Head teachers came and went. As a new education authority, Hackney Council was unable to get a grip of the situation. In 1995, after a bitter campaign to save the school, the government closed what its detractors called the 'worst school in England'. Hackney

Downs showed that a market approach to education creates sink schools that cannot be made successful simply by repeated inspections. They need skilled leadership, significant investment and long-term professional support. Perhaps the vast improvement in secondary education in Hackney, and in London generally, shows that the lessons of Hackney Downs were learned.

The febrile political climate in the 1970s did not provide a promising background for the new start that successful comprehensivisation needed. On top of that, Hackney schools were struggling with falling rolls. Hard as it now is to believe, Hackney's population steadily fell for most of the twentieth century. Repeated school mergers were needed, and the effort of coping with these reorganisations absorbed much of the available attention of education leaders.

Although distinct in many ways, the four Hackney secondary schools I taught in during the 1970s had common features that now seem a world away. The pupils were largely white British; there were also pupils of Caribbean, Cypriot or West African heritage, but although many of them had been born outside the UK, all spoke English. We suspected that many ethnic minority children were not doing as well as they should. No doubt there was racism in the education system, but a major factor in our failure to redress their underachievement was the absence of systematic record-keeping, sometimes justified in terms of anti-racist rhetoric.

The school-leaving age had been raised to 16 only in 1972, and the lack of emphasis on success in the 16-plus exams (and particularly A Levels) meant that few pupils stayed on into the sixth form. Where they did, their curriculum was said to be à la carte, which was often a euphemism for 'disorganised and inadequate', with far too many 'study periods'. The result was that hardly any students went to university directly from school, though some did eventually go in their twenties. Proposals for a sixth-form college were countered by secondary school teachers' desire to spend a pleasant few hours teaching sixth-formers. Only the church schools held the daily Christian assembly that the law still required. Other secondary schools generally held no daily assembly (although most primary schools still did). School uniforms mostly disappeared, being widely seen as an undesirable curtailment of freedom of expression.

Classroom teaching did not conform to any overall teaching programme. This had the advantage of allowing teachers and pupils to exercise a considerable degree of independence in methods and materials. This certainly gave scope for inspirational teaching by a few gifted teachers, but without a clear programme or written lesson plans, teaching tended to be inchoate and unchallenging. That in turn fed teachers' low expectations of children who already suffered other kinds of deprivation. The lack of a rigorous inspection regime suggested that, despite the high-flown rhetoric of ILEA and its enthusiastic sponsorship of innovative methods, there was insufficient attention to the quality of education in the frontline.

In primary schools, the curriculum was entirely in the hands of individual teachers. Some of them were inspired and inspiring and made good use of their freedom. Harrington Hill, opened in 1970 to serve a tough estate in Upper Clapton, was a case in point. It was led by a progressive head teacher, John Bryce, and was later pulled into more rigorous shape by Barbara McGilchrist who became ILEA's chief inspector. But other primary schools undoubtedly failed their young pupils. And even where individual teachers were inspiring, their efforts did not form part of a well-organised educational system built on sound evidence and proven methods to attain clearly defined objectives. And as a result, while schools like Harrington Hill excelled, their attainment was precarious, easily lost when inspiring teachers moved on.

Maybe I was unlucky in the schools I happened to teach in. Certainly Woodberry Down Comprehensive School, under the leadership of Michael Marland, established good academic results and an enviable reputation, at least until it fell victim to the 'falling rolls' mergers in 1981, when it combined with Clissold School to form Stoke Newington School. Marland left Hackney to become the founding head of North Westminster Community School. What Woodberry Down and Harrington Hill demonstrate is that it was possible to combine progressive methods of teaching with measurable success. But they also demonstrate the indispensability of high quality, committed professional leadership.

In the late 1980s the ILEA was abolished and education became a borough responsibility. This spiteful and costly act of the Thatcher government proved to be the straw that broke the back of Hackney's education service. The ILEA had its faults, but it had been able to provide wonderful education support services co-ordinated not only across all of inner London but across all sectors of education. These included teachers' centres, a music service, rural studies centres, a film library, museum education and much more. Colleagues from that time recall the wealth of development courses which inspired them to persevere in the teaching profession despite the challenges of working in Hackney at a time when its communities were being hollowed out by industrial decline, falling population and rapid demographic change. All this has now became fragmented and often lost altogether.

The government hoped that its top-down managerial regime of imposed curriculum, target-setting and tougher inspection would improve matters. But while this was a necessary corrective to the laissez-faire approach left over from the 1960s, it turned out not to be sufficient for success.

Further Information

Two books offer contrasting views of the Hackney Downs saga and also of the wider debate about educational standards:

Geoffrey Alderman, *A Study in Menace: Hackney Downs 1876-1995*, The Clove Club, 2012

Maureen O'Connor, Elizabeth Hales and Sally Tomlinson, *Hackney Downs: The School That Dared to Fight*, Cassell, 1999

1976: Chats Palace opens in Homerton: a community arts legend is born – Alan Rossiter

"Come on in!": a publicity poster for Chats Palace. (Courtesy of Chats Palace Archive)

1976 was the year of 'East goes West', the third Hackney Marsh Fun Festival and the year that the old Homerton Library became Chats Palace. Chats Palace was soon to become a beacon of innovative, immersive community-based arts programming, a legend which lingers today.

But the story starts earlier with the Hackney Marsh Fun Festival.

I was Senior Playleader of Hackney Marsh Adventure Playground and organiser of the festival. I started at the playground in 1972, the same year that the Free Form Arts Trust moved into their premises in Dalston Lane. Free Form, founded by Martin Goodrich, Barbara Wheeler-Early and Jim Ives, was a pioneering community arts organisation. They had been successful in making the case to the Arts Council for a community arts panel; this was to make funding available to artists working with communities as part of their arts practice. A telling slogan of the time was 'investing in the imagination of the people'.

The first project that we did together was the Hackney Marsh Firework Show, a cabaret with fireworks. This led to the Hackney Marsh Fun Festival and both events were to become part of the Homerton calendar. We were determined from the outset that this should be a celebration with the local community. Homerton was at this time an almost wholly working-class community – with only the thinnest scattering of middle-class newcomers – and sub-committees were formed with local residents and tenants' groups to ensure that our activities reached deep into the community. They all played a part in reaching out to people and making the festival a success.

The Fun Festival and Firework Show took place each year on Daubeney Fields next to the adventure playground, close to Clapton Park Estate and the somewhat notorious Kingsmead Estate, and looking across the Lea Navigation to Hackney Marshes.

The year 1976 was a scorcher and Daubeney Fields looked like a prairie; the playground became Fort Apache. The huge 'East goes West' music stage rivalled Woodstock and there were decorated stalls from local community groups and tenants' associations, arenas both large and small, and decorated marquees including the all-important beer tent, exhibitions, non-stop events and a variety marquee.

The festival began with a carnival around the streets of Homerton with decorated floats and marching groups. Two fine examples were the steam locomotive float from Cardinal Pole School and, on foot, the Clapton Park Hill Billies led by Brian Walker. Brian Walker was working as a delivery driver at the time, but the festival and Chats Palace unlocked his talents as a singer, performer, signwriter and raconteur. One of the highlights was the Johnny Concho Wild West Show when the ranch house being attacked by Red Indians went up in flames. This made it into the *News of the World*. Then there was the famous Free Form's Boston Tea Room where you could sit and have a nice cuppa while listening to a string quartet or order a suprisimo, a custard pie that you might deploy to adorn the face of the head waiter to a chorus from the waitresses.

Leading up to the festival, a whole series of fundraising events was held in local pubs and community halls; this mirrored the spirit of the time with alternative theatre such as Ken Campbell's Roadshow performing shows in similar venues. There were also alternative venues such the Albany Empire, Oval House and Hoxton Hall reaching out to involve local people in artistic creation. The Hackney Empire, the borough's traditional palace of varieties, was closed but the Fun Festival provided a new embodiment of

Cockney Culture, working outside the commercial sector and combining local vitality with the creative guidance of young community artists. It was apparent, however, that a building, a centre, was needed to develop this creative impulse and provide a perennial home for community arts.

Mike Gray, the Chairman of the Hackney Marsh Fun Festival, was approached by Joe Noble, a local community worker, to see if the Fun Festival would be interested in using the vacated Homerton Library as a community centre. Mike was a talented photographer and a Communist Party member – a modernising Eurocommunist for whom co-operation between intellectuals and communities was an article of faith and practical belief. Over a dozen local organisations were involved in Chats Palace's inception – to create a coalition with deep roots in the community. The affiliated groups formed a management committee, agreed a constitution and were successful in gaining the support of Hackney Council with a small grant and a peppercorn rent. Mike was elected chairman and it was he who came up with the name of Chats Palace, based on Joan Littlewood's People's Palace combined with the familiar name for Chatsworth Road. The *Hackney Gazette* announced that, "Plans include arrangements for a nursery and playgroups, an old folks' luncheon club, an art gallery to exhibit the work of local artists and photographers, a theatre for live entertainment, meeting room facilities and a coffee bar." As these plans developed, the coffee bar became a licensed bar and it is fair to say that the moderate consumption of alcohol came to lubricate many of Chats' liveliest events just as it did for Old Time Music Halls.

Free Form was successful in applying to the Arts Council community arts panel for my post as full-time organiser of the Hackney Marsh Fun Festival. At the end of September 1976 I built my office out of the bookshelves at the end of what had been the reference library. Among my first tasks was to build a Chats Palace sign for the front of the building using the font of Broadway lettering from the Chats Palace letterhead. The bookshelves also came into play literally as a medieval backdrop to one of the first projects to take place: the Lady of Spain film with the children of Hackney Marsh Adventure Playground. The basement took little transformation for the dungeon scene, the climax to the film was a battle on the adventure playground edited to the soundtrack from Eisenstein's film Alexander Nevsky.

One of the first events at Chats was Professor Alexander's Old Time Music Hall. Mike had seen the show at the Victoria public house in Queensbridge Road. Music Hall performances, staged 'at enormous expense', became a regular feature of the Chats Palace entertainments programme for years, as did benefit events and live music. Music Halls were enjoyed by white-haired ladies who had lived all their lives around Chats (and knew the words of the old songs) along with middle-class newcomers (who did not).

Free Form began local children's workshops funded by Hackney's Urban Aid Programme in what is now the bar, which in turn encouraged parents to come and join in. It was also responsible for the first Christmas show *'A Hackney'd Show'*, a magical mystery tour down memory lane. It starred Nicky Edmett as good old Dr Jelley, a much loved character in Homerton from pre-war days. "There's nothing as jolly as a good old east end knees up," commented the *Evening News*. "But these days it has reached an art form."

The show was a forerunner of the very popular pantomimes which involved many children and adults from the local community working alongside professional artists, actors and musicians. This fusion of amateur and professional performers within a visually stunning environment was a perfect example of what community arts could achieve. Subsequent productions, such as the *Thief of Ragbag* and *Robbin the Rich* were subversive and immersive affairs. In *Robbin the Rich* the entire auditorium became a glade in the Greenwood with a huge cast of performers, musicians, extras, prop-makers and costume-makers mostly from the local community – innate talent drawn out by artistic direction and enthusiasm. At the end of each Christmas show under the guidance of Brian Walker, Chats' children would stage their version of the show, a humorous aping of the adults that came close to being better than the real thing. The Christmas shows played for lengthy runs to sell-out audiences and were renowned throughout London.

Chats survives to this day and its spirit lives on too – a beacon and forerunner for the explosion of creative activity that is Hackney today.

In the Greenwood: the Chats Arkestra playing the panto, *Robbin the Rich*. (Courtesy of Chats Palace Archive. Photo Mike Gray)

1977: Mapledene, the Final Victory: a Victorian jewel is saved
– Julian Harrap

Saved from the bulldozers: the Victorian villas of Mapledene. (Photos Julian Harrap)

Mapledene and De Beauvoir have much in common. They represent in many ways the ideal of mid-nineteenth-century suburban development. They are amongst the earliest examples in Hackney, close to the City of London and were designed to provide for the burgeoning army of workers employed in the capital of the Empire.

Mapledene extends from Queensbridge Road in the west to Lansdowne Drive in the east. The area was part of the Rhodes family estate and formerly used for market gardening. The advantage of growing vegetables, fruit and flowers close to the City was undermined by the development of the railway, enabling produce to be delivered overnight for central distribution to the metropolis. The estate became more valuable as the site for a Victorian suburb than as a market garden.

Mapledene was built by Thomas and William Rhodes between 1840 and 1860 and largely designed for middle-income households. This was reflected in the spacious accommodation provided by the houses with interconnecting ground-floor rooms within a standard London plan. Some of the houses had (and have) exceptionally generous gardens by London standards and these were to become known as the 'backlands'. Originally the backlands were laid out with extra space to enable rear access by horse-drawn vehicles supplying goods and services to houses facing the main street. This made a particularly interesting arrangement as the safeguarded area was for access only and did not resemble the mews courts of the great estates of inner London. The backlands formed an integral part of the Victorian suburb and have been retained as open space for the residents over a period of 130 years.

By the period following the Second World War Mapledene had lost its social cachet and the population was declining. Houses were predominantly rented, multi-occupied and mostly poorly maintained. Hackney Council, anticipating development in the future, had been buying houses at scandalously low prices and leaving them empty. There was also a scattering of industrial uses, including the renowned Sindall's tassel factory in Middleton Road. A handful of individuals were also buying these houses, including the redoubtable Communist and community campaigner Ernie Greenwood, and Gayne Wells, later to be the Secretary of the London Society. They were to be two key figures in the fight to save Mapledene.

By this time urban clearances and housing redevelopments were moving northwards from Bethnal Green and Hoxton to Mapledene and De Beauvoir. Comprehensive development was originally motivated by the objective of slum clearance, but by the 1960s this had transmuted to the wider aim of providing spacious and modern public housing to replace the deteriorating (and often overcrowded) Victorian housing stock. 'Housing gain' was the mantra of the time and Mapledene, with its large gardens and low density, was an obvious target. However, at the public enquiry which was to follow, it became clear that the council's case exaggerated the housing gain, which was in truth only marginal.

Local authorities used compulsory purchase orders to provide clear flat sites for their system-built high-rise estates. South De Beauvoir was one of the first incursions using this methodology, to be followed by Holly Street to the west of Mapledene. Both brought gale-ridden microclimates to their unfortunate tenants and neighbours.

In 1972 plans for Mapledene were announced in notices which suddenly appeared on lampposts around the area. The council proposed to purchase compulsorily a large area involving 320 houses. The notices warned that anyone moving into the area after the date of the notice would not be eligible for rehousing. Despite the assiduity of the council officers, they forgot to put a date on the notices!

The Mapledene Residents Association was hastily established to combat this threat – as in De Beauvoir, it was a coalition of relatively recent owner-occupiers and longer-standing residents. They argued for restoration – and for the preservation of community. As Ernie Greenwood put it, Mapledene was "one of these areas where bricklayers and doctors, book-keepers and artists, all kinds and any kind of person cannot just co-exist but feel themselves to be part of the community". Some 40 years later this characteristic remains fundamental to the character of Mapledene.

The Residents Association presented the case for retaining Mapledene at the ensuing local public enquiry in the following terms: the council had laid out a series of demolition orders affecting 320 houses providing some 450 households with civilised residential accommodation within a settled community; the orders were served without consultation with the community in a sudden and peremptory manner; the redevelopment was to be piecemeal and would impose severe hardship on local residents, disrupting the lives of many people with close ties to Mapledene and Hackney.

The Association emphasised that many houses were in good condition with an active programme of improvement and repair under way. Houses in council ownership had brought a sense of planning blight to some otherwise pleasant streets by their neglect. The redevelopment proposed by the council was considered a social disaster, implying the dispersal of a long established community enjoying local employment and schooling over many generations.

The public enquiry to consider the compulsory purchase order proposals took place in May 1972. The nub of the council's case was that the large housing gain to be achieved by the scheme would make substantial inroads into its housing waiting list. The presumption was that every eligible family seeking council accommodation should get it and the waiting list would be cleared by the 1980s. To be fair, at a time of falling population, this was a much less unrealistic aspiration than it appears today. The council argued that the Victorian houses were life-expired and, in response to local residents' arguments that they could be improved and repaired, they argued that even if done up, the houses would last no more than a further 20 years!

The inspector found for a scheme of rehabilitation and against a compulsory purchase order, a momentous victory. It is clear from his report that he was antagonised by the council's arrogant attitude and a belief that its higher purpose made its duty of consultation no more than a meaningless formality.

In November 1977, the council returned to the fray, coming forward with proposals to redevelop two backland areas. One was north of Albion Drive and the other north of Mapledene Road where number 73 was to be demolished to gain access to the landlocked ground. Once again, housing gain was the rationale behind the council's proposals.

These two backlands were extremely valuable to those living in the surrounding houses. The Hackney Society worked with the Mapledene Residents Association to research and develop the case objecting to the council's proposals. Both organisations were deeply indebted to Christine Huggins, a professional conservation planner who marshalled an enthusiastic and dedicated band of residents from every sector of the community. The council's proposals would have caused great distress to residents who

Mapledene Road in 1977. After the compulsory purchase order was lifted, Tony and Cherie Blair bought their first house in the terrace in the centre of the picture. (Hackney Archives)

enjoyed their gardens for recreation, cultivation and tranquillity. Moreover, since the 1972 enquiry, scholarship in Victorian town planning had developed considerably and it was argued that redevelopment would obliterate an increasingly rare example.

The Hackney Society also made the case that the whole area was still suffering from the blight arising from the 1972 enquiry. Two dozen houses, mostly owned by the council, were unoccupied or derelict in the streets surrounding the backlands. The Society argued that the council's need for housing could be reasonably met by sponsoring housing associations or private individuals to repair the existing housing stock.

And so the long-suffering residents organised for a second time to defend Mapledene. The final outcome came in a letter from the Department of the Environment to Hackney Council on 11 July 1978, stating that the department was unwilling to confirm the compulsory purchase orders. It was a triumphant victory by a local amenity society working with local people.

Today, the term 'Mapledene' is little used and estate agents are wont to refer to the area as 'London Fields'. It has of course become immensely desirable real estate and it is interesting to note that the first house purchased by an ambitious young couple called Tony and Cherie Blair, 59 Mapledene Road, would have been demolished if the first proposed order had taken effect. But more importantly, the Victorian houses have already survived beyond their predicted short life and are likely to stand for many years to come. The wide streets have been enriched by street trees, the generous front gardens are stocked with shrubs, flowers and specimen trees behind restored railings and paved paths. The conservation movement of the 1970s and 1980s has informed the restoration detailing in a beneficial and harmonious way. Overall the impression is of an immensely successfully rehabilitated early Victorian suburb, one mile north of the City of London.

1978: Rock Against Racism Concert is held in Victoria Park: fighting the Fascists in Hackney – Daniel Rachel

Tom Robinson performing in Rock Against Racism in Victoria Park. (Photo Syd Shelton)

"There were one and a half million on the dole, belts tightened, cuts biting, prices soaring, wages frozen, the government looking for someone to blame," recounts Red Saunders, founder of Rock Against Racism (RAR), "and the loony fascists cashing in by stirring up hate. Three Asians killed in London. Notting Hill Carnival attacked by the police. The right-wing activist Robert Relf doing his house for sale – 'to an English family only' – bit. Enoch Powell ranting about 'alien wedges' in our culture and predicting a racial war in Britain."

It was in this climate, on 30 April 1978, that an estimated 80,000 people marched the seven miles from Trafalgar Square to Hackney to make a stand against racism and to be entertained by an array of bands including X-Ray Spex, The Clash and Steel Pulse. "Victoria Park was a statement," says RAR committee member Kate Webb. "The East End was the place of the forgotten."

A year earlier, in the Greater London elections, the National Front had polled an impressive 119,000 (5.3 per cent of the vote and a tenfold increase on the previous election). It had prompted the formation of the Anti-Nazi League (ANL) backed by the slogan 'The National Front is a Nazi Front'.

"Within their ranks," says ANL co-founder Paul Holborow, "they had people who denied the Holocaust." Deputy Leader of the National Front, Martin Webster, said "We are busy building a well-oiled Nazi machine in this country." Bloody confrontations between anti-fascists and neo-Nazis were regularly enacted across the capital from Brick Lane and Chapel Market to the Battle of Lewisham and the Southall Riots. On The Clash's appropriately named single English Civil War, Joe Strummer sang of a fight "still at the stage of clubs and fists". Rock Against Racism brought the anti-racist fighting into dance halls by attempting to unify a divided youth with the power of music. The simple principle behind an RAR gig was to put on a white punk band, followed by a black reggae band before ending the night with musicians from both groups together on stage in a statement of black and white unity.

"I went to a very early Rock Against Racism gig at Hackney Town Hall in August '77", remembers Neil Spencer, editor of *NME* from 1978 to 1985, "with Generation X snarling their way through Wild Youth and The Cimarons chanting down Babylon. My jaw was on the floor. I thought, 'Wow, I've never seen anything quite like this.' There was this juxtaposition of the municipal surroundings and photographs of these Victorian councillors looking down on us, and the ultra-modern and something that had never been seen before."

Red Saunders, similarly, recalls a "mother-fucker of a gig" and the terrible mistake Hackney Town Hall had made. "The whole place was seething with punks and people pissed and stoned, and they turned the music off. But the jam at the end was fantastic."

Rock Against Racism concert poster, commissioned by the Anti-Nazi League and designed by Dave King.

Rock Against Racism was established in reaction to Eric Clapton, who in August 1976 had made repeated inflammatory racist remarks at a concert in Birmingham, calling for "wogs" and "Pakis" to "leave our country". In response, a letter written by Red Saunders and published in all the major music papers, called for "a rank and file movement against the racist poison in rock music", and signed off with a PO Box address. The response was immediate. More than 200 letters of support were received within a week and Rock Against Racism was born.

The growth of Rock Against Racism across the country was stunning and within eighteen months of its inaugural gig at the Princess Alice in Forest Hill – headlined by the blues artist Carol Grimes – an idea formed to put on a carnival in the lead up to the 1978 local elections. "RAR's unannounced ambition", declared David Widgery, a GP in the East End, RAR committee member and author of the book *Beating Time*, "was to turn the event into the biggest piece of revolutionary street theatre London had ever seen, a tenth-anniversary tribute to the Paris events of May 1968."

The term 'carnival' had been inspired by the annual Notting Hill celebrations of black culture and it was in this spirit that the tone of the rally was set. Since the late summer of 1977, RAR had cut an alliance with the newly formed Anti-Nazi League which proved critical in providing political and national mobilisation, but culturally the Carnival Against the Nazis was pure RAR. Congregating in Trafalgar Square, tens of thousands of protesters, arriving from all corners of the country, held aloft lollipops daubed with anti-racist slogans whilst listening to speeches from Peter Hain MP, and singer Tom Robinson.

As the march set off for the East End there was singing, dancing, 10,000 whistles blowing, flag-waving, badges, street performers, stilt artists, clowns, papier-mâché heads of Adolf Hitler and Martin Webster, and bands playing on the back of mobile trucks. When the demonstration passed the infamous right-wing pub the Blade Bone on Bethnal Green Road, marchers were greeted by shouts of 'Sieg Heil' and 'red scum'. Wave after wave of demonstrators remonstrated with aggressive neo-Fascists who, faced with unrelenting opposition and, increasingly, sheer fatigue, were forced to beat a retreat. Musician Billy Bragg was amongst the protesters. "I saw this little old guy with a pint of beer and a fag on doing a Nazi salute and we were jeering at him. I remember thinking, 'That's him. He's the last of Mosley's Blackshirts.'"

At Victoria Park a representative of Tower Hamlets Council had been paid off with a large bottle of whisky and an invitation to join Steel Pulse's pre-gig ritual involving the delights of 'herbal jazz' cigarettes. Meanwhile, the ever-swelling crowd pogo-ed to Poly Styrene's screams of "Oh Bondage! Up Yours!" and by mid-afternoon "London's Burning" by The Clash.

"It said in our publicity we wanted to see 20,000 people in the park," remembers Syd Shelton of the RAR central committee. "We had no idea it would be as big as it was." The night before, Red Saunders had gathered a group of friends in his Hackney home to make cheese rolls for the anticipated moderate turnout. The reality was beyond his wildest dreams. Shelton remembers Saunders coming backstage saying, "Syd, how many people do you reckon are here? " "I said, 'Maybe 60,000?' He said, 'Let's say 80,000,' and went straight out to the front: 'WE'VE JUST HAD THE OFFICIAL COUNT THAT THERE ARE 80,000 PEOPLE HERE!'" By the afternoon, exhilaration had replaced any lingering doubts. "I went out on the stage," Saunders says, "and shouted, 'THIS AIN'T NO FUCKING WOODSTOCK. THIS IS THE CARNIVAL AGAINST THE FUCKING NAZIS,' and the whole crowd went, 'AARRGGHH'. It just lifted me for the rest of the day."

Likewise, Billy Bragg was having a life-changing experience epitomised by the Tom Robinson Band's rousing anthem '(Sing If You're) Glad To Be Gay'. "I realised this was how my generation were going to define themselves, in opposition to discrimination of all kinds. This was our Vietnam; our Ban the Bomb. It had a very powerful catalytic effect on me." Four days later, the National Front vote at the London Borough Council elections fell by almost 30,000 votes, despite their party headquarters sitting in the heart of Shoreditch, which the Front had recognised as fertile recruiting territory.

The political and cultural success of the Carnival Against the Nazis was replicated two months later in Manchester with Buzzcocks and Steel Pulse, and then in September in Brixton's Brockwell Park, headlined by Aswad and Elvis Costello and The Attractions. By the end of the summer, David Widgery estimated, "more than a quarter of a million people had rocked against racism. The fascists didn't know what had hit them. In London their local elections vote plummeted and in their so-called West Midlands strongholds their vote also fell; in Wolverhampton for example from eleven per cent to three per cent." Significantly, when Peter Hain later sued Martin Webster for libel, the latter admitted in court, "Wherever we were the Anti-Nazi League was. Whatever numbers we had, they had more, and that destroyed us, both in physical opposition and through propaganda."

The anti-racist euphoria amongst young people carried through to the general election of May 1979, when the National Front was crushed at the ballot box. But it came at a price. "Margaret Thatcher getting in was an absolute disaster", says Syd Shelton. "That was the beginning of the end of Rock Against Racism." Red wrote, "Suddenly there was a frightening new set of cherries come up on the great fruit machine of life… now the real gangsters have come… ."

As the newly-elected Conservative government took office, 2 Tone music swept the nation – The Specials, The Selecter, Madness, The Beat. The mix of black and white musicians in the same band was a visual embodiment of Rock Against Racism. "When you saw 2 Tone," asserts Red Saunders, "you went, 'job done'." This is what we dreamt of in 1976. 2 Tone music and their spirit and their story and everything Jerry Dammers went on to do for Nelson Mandela. It trumped the whole fucking lot of us."

Editor's Note: Until 1994 the boundary of Hackney and Tower Hamlets ran through the middle of Victoria Park. The RAR concert was (just) on the Tower Hamlets side, but I hope readers will agree that it is part of Hackney's story.

Further Information

Robin Denselow, *When the Music's Over*, Faber & Faber, 1989

Roger Huddle and Red Saunders, *Reminiscences of RAR*, 1976-1982, Redwords, 2016

Daniel Rachel, *Walls Come Tumbling Down: the music and politics of Rock Against Racism, 2 Tone and Red Wedge*, Picador, 2016

David Widgery, *Beating Time*, Chatto & Windus, 1989

1979: Shoreditch in the Dumps
– Ray Rogers

Photographs of decaying industrial buildings in Shoreditch taken between 1975 and 1980.
(Hackney Archives)

On 4 September 1979 the following news story appeared in the *Hackney Gazette*. "Fire ripped through the premises of a Shoreditch furniture firm on Sunday afternoon and caused hundreds of pounds worth of damage to stock. The blaze began at around 3pm in a furniture store at 103 Shoreditch High Street, belonging to Haywain Warehouses Ltd. A spokesman for Haywain said that the fire had damaged furniture and stock in an annexe building used as a storeroom. The spokesman for the firm added that the fire had not affected their trading position."

The warehouse at 103 Shoreditch High Street no longer exists, gone along with the rest of the furniture trade. The fire may not have affected the trading position of Haywain Ltd but a bonfire had been lit under the Shoreditch furniture trade well before this incident.

For over one hundred years Shoreditch had been a thriving industrial quarter, the hub of the London furniture trade and a significant centre of the printing industry. But by 1979 it had hit rock bottom and politicians and planners were beginning to think seriously about how the relentless tide of decline in the inner cities could be turned around.

But first, let us go back to the beginning. By the end of the eighteenth century South Shoreditch was a busy residential and manufacturing suburb, home to a wide variety of artisanal trades supplying the needs of the nearby City. Its character started to change from the early nineteenth century as industrial and commercial uses intensified. With a growing mass market for lower priced, ready-made goods of all kinds, certain trades began to dominate in different areas and Shoreditch, Bethnal Green and Hoxton became the centre of the London furniture trade. It was a classic example of what economists now call a 'cluster', in which manufacturers, sub-contractors, ancillary trades and suppliers gathered in a mutually beneficial way. There were also smaller but significant clusters in other trades including printing and shoemaking.

The furniture trade evolved three main building types. First, there were the workshops and factories for manufacturing. Second, there were showrooms and wholesale warehouses for displaying and storing the goods, selling them on to West End retailers and across the British Empire. Third, there were the buildings of associated firms and suppliers such as ironmongers for hinges and handles, polishers, timber yards and sawmills. With a practised eye it is possible to identify surviving examples of each of these building types in South Shoreditch today, now re-used as clubs, restaurants, hi-tech offices, graphic designers and in some cases chic apartments – all the paraphernalia of a post-industrial economy.

The East End of London had long been a focus for new immigrants and some of these went on to create firms that became household names such as Beautility and Austinsuite. Hille and Co was established in Shoreditch in 1906 by Salamon Hille, a Russian Jewish immigrant. It became known for its post-war association with the designer Robin Day during the Festival of Britain in 1951. Luciano Ercolani came from Tuscany in 1898 and learnt his trade at the Shoreditch Technical Institute before moving to High Wycombe where, in 1920, he founded his own firm, later to become the Ercol furniture company. By the late 1890s Harris Lebus, founded by German Jewish immigrant Lewis Lebus (and succeeded by his son Harris), was the largest furniture manufacturer in the country with over 1,000 workers, with its showrooms in Tabernacle Street, Shoreditch. In addition to these giants, many smaller firms supplied West End shops, such as Maples and Waring & Gillow, with high quality furniture.

The golden age of the furniture and printing industries in Shoreditch lasted from the mid-1870s until the outbreak of the First World War. As the more successful furniture manufacturers grew, they gradually moved out to sites in the Lea Valley where they had the space to set up modern production plants. This process began in the early twentieth century and by the late 1930s many of the larger firms had made this move. Harris Lebus moved to a vast site in Tottenham Hale (now the site of Hale Village) and after the Second World War Hille moved first to Leytonstone and then to Watford.

The continuing loss of industry in Shoreditch in the years following the Second World War was part of the wider flight of industry from the inner cities. By the 1970s the furniture trade was in steep decline and the printing industry had never fully recovered after the war. The large furniture manufacturers had moved out and smaller firms gradually closed down, unable to weather the economic challenges of the time. A rump furniture trade clung on but buildings were emptying and the area, once a seething mass of energy and industry, lapsed into a quiet backwater.

In 1982 I joined an architect's practice based in Leonard Street. It was my first encounter with Shoreditch, which by then had become a byword for dereliction. A few cabinet-makers and veneer dealers still hung on in Curtain Road, along with some printing firms, but it was all very rundown. Empty buildings were occupied by hard-up artists (my brother among them). Photographs of the time bear witness to boarded up, empty buildings with fascia signs still carrying the names of departed companies. A trawl through the street directories for 1979 shows very few surviving furniture makers, but numerous rag trade sweatshops that had set up in the empty properties.

By the late 1970s the Labour government of the day introduced a range of policies to tackle the 'hollowing out' of inner city areas. The Inner Urban Areas Act of 1978 promoted the idea of the 'Industrial Improvement Area' to be controlled by local partnerships set up under the Urban Programme, and the Hackney-Islington Partnership lost no time in creating an Industrial Improvement Area in Shoreditch. This was intended to direct money towards environmental improvements, build advance factories and bring derelict sites back into use.

This policy had hardly got under way when Margaret Thatcher's Conservative government was elected in May 1979 and immediately put more emphasis on encouraging private sector investment. In December 1979 South Shoreditch was on the government's shortlist as one of the first Enterprise Zones but, fortunately for the future of the area, London Docklands was chosen instead.

In a speech on 2 November 1979 Ron Brown, MP for Hackney South and Shoreditch, deplored cuts to the Labour government's scheme. "As a result of the Government's decision to cut this fund, the whole project is now in chaos. No one knows whether he can go ahead, and as a result an initiative has been killed… ." But in reality there was never really sufficient funding for this programme and the resulting contribution to inner city regeneration proved to be marginal.

The tension between Labour's public sector-led policy and the Conservatives' private sector emphasis was reflected in the letters columns of the *Hackney Gazette*. "Private enterprise has failed Hackney," was the by-line over a letter published on 10 April 1979. The writer referred to "a plethora of letters from local Tories" which had condemned "thirty years of socialist domination" in Hackney and called on the council to encourage private enterprise. He went on to point out that "despite having had Labour controlled councils for most of the last 30 years, the local economy in Hackney remains firmly capitalist". The letter concluded, surely correctly, that the growth of unemployment in Hackney was a product of the general post-war decline in manufacturing industry and of the small firm as a viable unit of production.

Housing conditions in Shoreditch, especially in the crowded Victorian tenement blocks, also reflected contemporary problems. Around City Road there were substantial numbers of these, most in shockingly run-down condition as many of the tenants who had worked in the furniture trade followed the move to greener fields. "Sell off these tenements says Shoreditch liberal" was the by-line over another letter published on 6 February 1979 demanding that the council dispose of all vacant tenement blocks in Shoreditch to private developers as "Shoreditch's location on the edge of the City makes it an ideal place for the development of luxury flats for many businessmen". Although many of Shoreditch's tenement blocks disappeared at this time, this was not for luxury flats but mainly in an attempt to make way for new commercial units, although some of the sites remain derelict to this day.

Despite all the brave words nothing much actually happened to improve the area for at least another decade. In hindsight it was the neglect of the area in the 1970s and the failure of regeneration policies from 1979 onwards that helped to preserve the buildings and character of South Shoreditch for a later generation. Over the following decades, new and wholly unexpected uses came to Shoreditch, beginning with artists and galleries, followed by the 'night-time economy' and the world of hi-tech. The reinvention of Shoreditch in a completely unexpected form to become the epitome of gentrification, giving rise to the term 'Shoreditchification', is yet another story.

Further Information

William I.Massil, *Immigrant Furniture Workers in London 1881-1939 and the Jewish contribution to the Furniture Trade*, the Jewish Museum in association with the Geffrye Museum, 1997

Joanna Smith and Ray Rogers, *Behind the Veneer: The South Shoreditch Furniture Trade and its Buildings*, English Heritage, 2006

1980: Hackney Central Station Re-opens: the rebirth of the North London Line – Laurie Elks

Broad Street nocturne: a slam door train waits to depart for Richmond in the station's last days.
(Photo Gordon Edgar)

Hackney in the 1970s was a surprisingly remote place. Famous as the borough without a tube station[1], it lacked decent connections with central London in general, and the West End in particular. True, buses trundled forth regularly on long and heroic journeys, such as the No 6 which went from Hackney Wick to Kensal Rise and the 22 which journeyed from Chatsworth Road to Putney but, at a time when there were few bus lanes (and those which existed were unenforced), it was usually an hour's journey, or more, to reach central London.

There were trains to the City via Hackney Downs but these were old and dingy; the stations were more so and in strange remote places such as London Fields(!) and not too many people used them.

And there was the famous problem child – the North London Line joining Broad Street in the City via Dalston Junction to Richmond in distant Surrey – described by the railway enthusiast John Betjeman as a "smooth, beautiful and useless journey".

Poster of the Save the North London Line Committee.

So unappreciated and neglected was this line that it was earmarked for closure by Dr Beeching in the 1960s and came under renewed threat of closure in the 1970s. There was a vicious circle of under-investment and neglect which drove away customers; ancient trains, long service intervals, forbidding stations and cancelled services. I recall persuading a footballing team mate to get the train back to Dalston from Willesden Junction after a match at Wormwood Scrubs. We just missed one train, the next was cancelled and the one after late; forty-five minutes on a freezing platform. My friend swore never to travel that way again, and he never did. Broad Street station itself was cavernous, underused and neglected, already being eyed up by British Rail for property development.

The fact that the North London Line hung on – just – through these dark days owed much to a small group, the North London Line Committee, formed in 1970 to fight closure. The campaigners who fought to save the Line (just like the campaigners who opposed the Motorway Box), were based predominantly in and around Hampstead. Hackney's destiny as a centre of resistance still lay in the future.

But there was a solution to hand – if the powers that be could but see it. Between Dalston and Stratford was a railway line, used for freight traffic but closed to passengers since 1944; linking two transport hubs and passing right through the middle of Hackney. Roger Lansdown, a young economist living in Clapton, was the leading light of Hackney Public Transport Action Committee (HAPTAC), formed to campaign for better public transport for Hackney, in particular the re-opening of this 'missing link' to passenger

1 Manor House tube station is actually just in Hackney but that is a quibble.

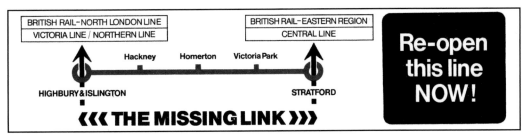

The Missing Link: a guerrilla lamp-post poster issued by HAPTAC.

traffic. He was supported by his next-door neighbour, Richard Gee, who joined the council in 1978 and later became chairman of the planning committee. Roger provided the passionate vision and Richard the political know how.

As a result of HAPTAC's efforts, very soon every other lamp post in Hackney, it seemed, bore a sticker bearing the slogan <<< THE MISSING LINK >>> Re-open this line NOW! Lansdown also worked closely with the North London Line Committee which was still working away to improve the line.

Given the popularity of the line today, it may seem mystifying why this campaign did not achieve instant success. There were two main reasons. First, Hackney was far more economically cut off then than now. It was still a substantially industrial borough with many people employed in local manufacturing industry, so the line was not missed as much as it would be today. Second, British Rail saw their role as moving passengers in and out of central London, not across it; the concept of an orbital railway had not caught on. And so the line was trapped by the low expectations of BR management of the time.

The ground started to shift in the late 1970s as growing appreciation of the potential of Docklands prompted interest in improving the little-used Stratford to North Woolwich Line which ran through Canning Town and Silvertown. A service was launched in 1979 between Camden Road and North Woolwich – passing through Hackney but with no stations as yet to stop at! This was a cut-price job with ancient diesel trains running at 30-minute intervals and 20 minutes at rush hour. The momentum increased after a Labour Greater London Council, led by Ken Livingstone, was elected in 1981 and sought to direct more resources to public transport.

The new route reached the borough when Hackney Central Station was re-opened in May 1980 along with a new station at Hackney Wick. The old Victorian station at Hackney Central was still owned by BR and could have been restored but BR opted for an 'economic station' – as their then boss Peter Parker called it – which we still have today. Dalston Kingsland, a much better job, followed in 1983. Homerton Station opened in 1985 only after the line was electrified. HAPTAC advised, lobbied and pressed at every stage to make the new service as good as it could be.

Passenger numbers rose but the new line was scarcely the vital artery we know today. BR kept investment in the line to a minimum. In 1985, after the GLC had paid for electrification of the route, BR introduced ancient two-car slam door electric units dating from the 1950s – a tangible sign of the low esteem in which they held the line. The old bugbears of low service frequencies, cancellations, and unstaffed stations continued to depress usage. Stations were desolate and threatening at night, particularly Hackney Wick, situated in an area which was no longer industrial but not yet trendy. In December

1985, 19-year-old Alison Day was murdered after she got off at Hackney Wick to meet her boyfriend. Her body was dragged from the nearby Lea Navigation a few days later.

A further drawback was that no agreement was reached to incorporate the line into London's transport zonal system. Thus, whilst it was possible to buy a through ticket from my local station, Homerton, to my workplace at Green Park, the cost was the aggregate of two journeys, Homerton to Highbury and Highbury to Green Park, making it by far the most expensive route into town.

But despite the institutional neglect, passenger numbers rose steadily through the 1980s, sustained by demographic changes in Hackney where increases of population and owner-occupation outstripped almost every London borough. Through ticketing was eventually introduced and, in 1989, the 1950s slam door trains were replaced by three-car sliding door Class 313 sets, a mere 12 years old and practically brand new by comparison.

But rising passenger numbers, coupled with lack of investment and lack of vision, spelt misery for passengers. Three-car trains at 20-minute intervals were insufficient for the increasing passenger numbers, resulting in appalling rush hour scrummages with passengers regularly left behind on the platform to try their luck on the next train. Privatisation of the service in 1995 made little difference. The new private operator, Silverlink, managed to increase the service to four trains per hour but this extra capacity trailed far behind increases in demand.

The situation was only transformed when, in 2004, the Labour government committed to transfer the line to Transport for London. TfL took over, rebranding the railway as the Overground in 2007, and they have created a virtuous circle which would have utterly confounded Dr Beeching. New trains were ordered, initially three cars but extended to four cars and then five (requiring major investment to lengthen platforms). Signalling works now permit eight trains per hour at rush hour and six at other times, whilst still allowing freight paths in between. The bonanza of the Olympic Games at Stratford formed part of the business case for the necessary investment. Stations are now manned at all times and evening services, which were once threatening, are now thronging.

My own station, Homerton, had nearly 5 million passenger movements in 2015-16 and a mobile coffee stall to boot. The line has helped to make Homerton an eligible place to live for the first time since it was a country village.

Roger Lansdown, the driving force of HAPTAC, died unexpectedly as this book was being planned – he would otherwise have written this chapter. The crowds who throng the platform each morning – if they but knew this story – would be grateful that his imagination helped these events to come to pass.

Further Information

Wayne Asher, *A Very Political Railway: The Rescue of the North London Line,* Capital Transport Publishing Limited, 2014

John Glover, *London's Overground,* Ian Allan, 2012

Dennis Lovett, *The North London Railway 1846-2012,* Irwell Press, 2012

Vic Mitchell and Keith Smith, *North London Line: Broad Street to Willesden Junction via Hampstead Heath,* Middleton Press, 1987

1981: Simpson's, a Cut above the Rest – Sean Gubbins

The Finishing Room at the Simpson's Stoke Newington factory. (Courtesy of DAKS)

Had you walked along Dalston Lane in 1981, up Ashwin Street, through Ridley Road and on to Shacklewell Lane, you would have passed signboards for Denelight, Mindy, Rimplan, Palenstar, Multimodes – all factories making clothing for British high street stores. Continuing down Somerford Grove, you would come to the House of Simpson on the corner with Stoke Newington Road. A shadow of its former self, it was in 1981 that Simpson Ltd. finally vacated their factory. No longer to be seen was the once-familiar sight of Simpson's vans, advertising 'Comfort in Action', driving out to distribute the world-famous DAKS trousers.

In 1981 the clothing industry still represented 33 per cent of all manufacturing firms in Hackney, employing 12,000 people. Clothes were made via a number of routes: in-house, sub-contracted workshops, smaller outworking units or homeworking. Unlike Simpson's, the average size of a Hackney clothing firm was small.

The area's connection with the clothing industry dates back at least to 1609 when silk weavers were recorded in Hackney. Successive waves of entrepreneurial immigrants – Jewish, Cypriot and Turkish – had dominated the industry through the twentieth century, setting up factories which offered a quick response when it came to serving the British high street. If one high street store brought out the 'must have' dress, the factories of Dalston could produce lookalikes in short order.

But though the clothing industry had been the bread and butter of our borough for many years, Hackney had attracted a variety of other industries. The River Lea powered mills and transported raw materials to chemical works in Hackney Wick. The coming of the Regent's Canal brought gas works to Haggerston; the railway and a growing population provided a transport network and workforce for industry to be established all over Hackney.

By 1938 the metropolitan borough of Hackney had 2,071 factories, including the manufacture of cigarettes in De Beauvoir Town, pipes in Homerton, Turkish delight in Stamford Hill, fountain pens in South Hackney, pencils in Lower Clapton, artists' materials in Dalston and furniture in Upper Clapton. Only three of London's boroughs had a larger industrial workforce than Hackney.

The departure of large firms, such as Simpson's, was part of the decentralisation of London's industry which gathered pace after the Second World War. Industrial decline became more marked from the 1970s. One firm that for some time bucked this trend was pressure die casters, Lesney Products, which began to make Matchbox model vehicles in 1953. Lesney's technical innovativeness kept it ahead of Far Eastern competition for many years and its blue double-decker buses carrying staff to work were a familiar sight around Hackney. With 1,500 workers, it was probably Hackney's largest employer when it went into receivership in 1982, the year after Simpson's finally vacated their factory in Stoke Newington Road.

Aged 16, Simeon Simpson set himself up in 1894 as a bespoke tailor in Middlesex Street, London's 'Petticoat Lane'. He had a vision that one day machine-made, ready-to-wear clothing would surpass men's clothes produced purely by hand. By 1917 he had created one of the UK's most successful clothing companies.

Success meant his business's capacity, including a factory in Shacklewell Lane, was overflowing. A larger factory was needed. By the 1920s the Simpson family, like many other Jewish immigrant families, had moved north-westwards from Whitechapel and

The last days at Lesneys: the company still employed 2,000 workers when the main factory closed in 1982. (Photo Neil Martinson)

were living in Bethune Road. Along with his younger son Alex, Simeon planned to build a new factory close by in Stoke Newington Road, to centralise production. This location appealed because of low rates, proximity to outlets in the West End and the local availability of the skills required.

Almost every clothing factory in America and Britain worthy of consideration was studied by the Simpsons before the new factory was opened in 1929. The architects were instructed to achieve as much light as possible and allow no shadows – essential to produce first-class workmanship. A few years later the factory was extended down Somerford Grove. Now covering almost 200,000 square feet, it was considered to be the most advanced clothing factory of its time.

Menswear was beginning to change in the 1920s. Alex Simpson, like many keen sportsmen, was irritated by the braces holding up his trousers impeding his golf-swing. He patented the DAKS trouser: the world's first self-supporting trouser, freeing men "from the bondage of belts and braces", by sewing rubber pads into the waistband to hold the trouser in place and prevent the shirt riding up. Confident in his new product, Alex Simpson commissioned 100,000 pairs ahead of launch in 1934. DAKS trousers were an instant success. "Purchasing your first pair" of DAKS, noted fashion writer and journalist John Taylor, "was as symbolic as a Masai warrior killing his first Lion." The success of DAKS allowed the company to open their store in Piccadilly in 1936. With all menswear departments under one roof, it supplied "everything a man needs for every possible occasion". Simpson's started making women's clothes in 1937.

It was at the Stoke Newington Road factory that DAKS were made, employing over 2,000 people. The factory was also the company's head office, including the sales and

A cutter at work in Simpson's last days in Stoke Newington. (Courtesy of DAKS. Photo Neil Martinson)

Staff were provided with "wholesome well-cooked meals". (Courtesy of DAKS)

advertising departments. One of the most important areas in the factory was the Cutting Room. By the mid-1930s Simpson's used 15 miles of cloth each week and employed 206 hand cutters working on cloth spread out on cutting tables. Modern electric knife cutters, operated by men with years of experience, were used on bulk work.

Whereas most of Hackney's clothing firms contracted work out, Simpson's made all its clothes and pieces in-house. The Cutting Room's output was distributed hourly to the factory's making-up departments. Two large goods lifts and wide gangways helped keep the half-finished garments moving between departments. It was in these making-up departments that the majority of employees worked: the Coat, Vest, Jacket and Trouser Rooms, the latter producing 6,000 pairs of trousers every week in the mid-1930s. And every finished garment had to be inspected by viewers before being sent to the packing department and dispatched in the company's fleet of vans.

The clothing industry had traditionally provided a large number of jobs for women in Hackney but pictures of the factory at work in the mid-1930s show mostly men. In the company's picture archives, women can be seen – always seated – working as hand-tailoresses in the Coat Room, sewing shirt-controls into the DAKS waistbands or as hand-finishers in the Trouser Room. The men can be seen smartly dressed in three-piece suits or with waistcoats but jacket off, often perched, one leg crossed over the other, whilst sewing on a work-table.

Simpson's prided itself on the care of its staff and the long service of many employees. Mrs Mabel Tapp, a room clerk in the Jacket Department, received her gold watch for long service in December 1968. She also had a sister, sister-in law and brother-in-law working at Simpson's with 94 years' combined service. In some cases two or three generations of the same family were employed and the company would continue to employ staff well over the retirement age provided "the standard of work of their work was sufficiently high to warrant continued employment".

Staff were provided with "wholesome well-cooked meals" and the canteen was provided with a "radiogram concert" every lunchtime. Young workers were thoroughly trained, progressing from the Trimming Room to the Cutting Room where they were taught their trade. There was a staff newsletter entitled The Needle and Thread, teams for football, men's darts, ladies' darts, table tennis and snooker, a swimming club and a drama group. Children were given a party at Christmas and there was the opportunity for boxing instruction on Thursday afternoons. And of course there was an annual dance for staff, held at a top class West End venue such as the Lyceum Ballroom.

At the beginning of the Blitz, bombs dropped on the factory. Canvas walls were erected so that production could continue but, to keep up production, Simpson's acquired additional capacity in Nottingham, and in Larkhall, near Glasgow. It was the beginning of Simpson's slow withdrawal from Hackney. By 1969 Simpsons' manufacturing base was centralised in a modern, custom-built factory in Larkhall and there remained only a small number of staff in the Hackney building after 1976. In 1979, a buyer was found for the Stoke Newington Road factory and, within a couple of years, the few rooms still used by the company were finally cleared and left.

Most of the large-scale clothing manufacturers had deserted Hackney by the 1980s. In addition to Simpson's, this included Moss Bros, Swears & Wells and Horne Brothers, whose art deco factory remains a fine landmark in King Edward's Road. Burberry in Chatham Place were the last of the large manufacturers to go, but their connection continues with their outlet shop, patronised especially by the Japanese. And just the other side of Morning Lane is rising up Hackney's new Fashion Hub, so starting a new chapter in the borough's association with the clothing industry.

1982: The Left takes Control
– Jim Cannon

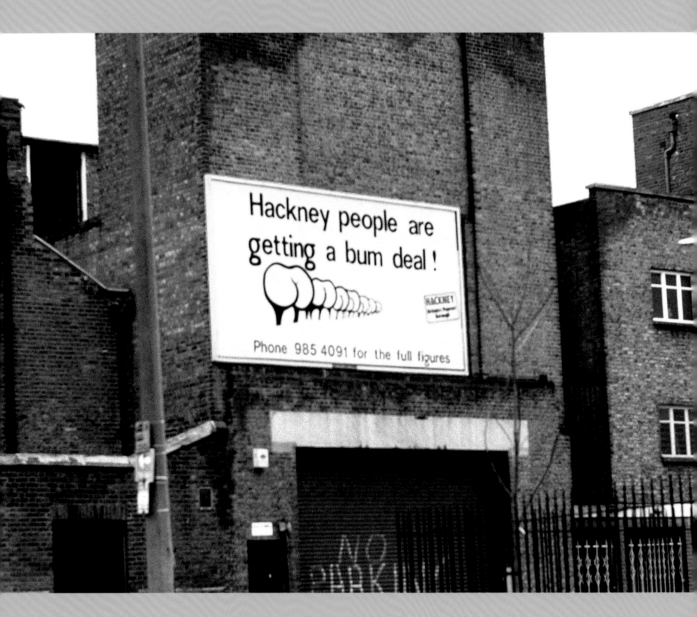

Bum Deal: Hackney Council takes to the hoardings to ventilate its disagreements with Mrs Thatcher's government. (Photo Alan Denney)

After Labour resumed power in 1971, it was business as usual in Hackney. Labour had crushing majorities in the following elections. In 1978, for instance, 59 Labour councillors were elected alongside lone Tory Joe Lobenstein. Successive leaders, Lou Sherman, Martin Ottolangui and John Kotz came from a close-knit ruling group. All three had served as councillors in the old Hackney borough predating the merger with Stoke Newington and Shoreditch. All were proudly working class, council tenants and with a fierce belief in municipalisation of the housing stock, facilitated by compulsory purchase where required. Social services, libraries and parks were also seen as priorities. The council ran a tight ship financially and the leadership had no time for the more abstract Socialist notions of some younger members. John Kotz's memoir, *Vintage Red*, is a magnificently unreconstructed apologia for the old guard including the plausible, but controversial, argument that they were more left-wing than the new wave of Labour councillors who succeeded them in power.

After the election of Mrs Thatcher in 1979, there was a lot of infighting on the left and the Social Democratic Party was formed in 1981. In Hackney, the local elections of 1974 and 1978 brought in younger members of the council amid a time of major turmoil nationally. During the late 1970s and early 1980s, the National Front had been very active in the Shoreditch area and some of their policies, including preference for housing to be given to sons and daughters of existing tenants, led to considerable tensions. In the general election of 1979, the leader of the National Front stood for election in Hackney South and Shoreditch and polled one of the highest percentages of votes ever received by a racist organisation in the UK. In Shoreditch, the Liberal Party were seen as espousing some of the National Front's policies

This led to local elections in May 1982 where there were candidates from the Liberal Focus Team Alliance (LIBFTA), and the SDP as well as the National Front and the Labour and Conservative parties. The outcome was 50 Labour, seven LIBFTA (all in the South) and three Tories in the North.

The elections brought in a different mix of councillors with a big drop in the average age and an increase of middle-class, university-educated Labour councillors, working as lecturers, teachers, social workers, or in charities or NGOs. Many of the newer members had grown up outside the borough and had bought their own homes.

After the election, the Group of Labour Councillors met to elect new officers and committee chairs. Anthony Kendall, a former community worker at Centerprise, won the election to be leader and defeated John Kotz. The new policy committee was made up of the chairs of the committees and was tasked with implementing the manifesto. This had focussed on decentralisation of services as a means of combating the cuts in funding imposed by the Thatcher government and bringing the council closer to local communities. There was considerable effort put into involving groups with a community development committee as well as extra attention to such issues as equal opportunities and a women's committee.

Other policies also received considerable attention – far more than was merited by the council's ability to influence national policy on the topics. As an example, Hackney became a 'nuclear free borough' which was impossible to implement since the trains which carry nuclear waste went along the North London Line (and as far as I know they still do!). The new council also adopted a more strident rhetoric about the problems faced in Hackney, including the much-publicised (and unhelpful) strapline of Hackney as 'Britain's poorest borough'. The decentralisation policies were debated at length but in reality weren't implemented since the resources weren't available.

Anthony Kendall was keen to involve members of the Labour Party more in the direction of the council and introduced the Annual Borough Conference which was intended to give the opportunity to hold the council to account. As part of this process, the leader, deputy leader and chairs of committees were selected in open forum. Previously chairs were chosen by the Labour group of councillors but now it was thrown open to the delegates who attended from local branches. This change, which was against

Storming the Bastille: occupation of the council chamber (Photo Neil Martinson)

Labour Party rules, led to the election of the ultra-left leadership of Hilda Kean in 1984. Interestingly only 14 of the 44 Labour councillors voted for Hilda Kean – her main support was from the organised left wing among the general membership: a not dissimilar situation to the election of Jeremy Corbyn as leader of the Labour Party in 2015.

The major issue at this time was the continuing squeeze by the Tory government on local authorities and the introduction of rate capping. Prior to the introduction of the Poll Tax, local authorities raised their money by levying a rate against residential and commercial properties. Most authorities relied heavily on central government grants to cover their expenditure. In 1978, Hackney Council had one of the lowest rate levels in the UK. As a result of the central cutbacks, Hackney met some of the shortfall by increasing the rate level. The Tory government was not happy with this approach, which was also being followed by several other authorities, and introduced the rate capping legislation which limited the rate that councils were permitted to charge.

The financial year 1984/85 became a major breaking point with much acrimony within both constituency Labour parties and conflict with trade unions and others. During that year, as an example, the Woodberry Down housing offices were occupied by tenants for four weeks in October with more occupations of housing offices in March 1985 and the occupation of the Town Hall, as a means of preventing a rate from being set, in May 1985. The key working relationships between the senior officers of the council and the political leadership became untenable with a loss of experienced officers. An expensive review was commissioned from Andrew Arden QC to investigate the impact of Freemasonry on the council.

The policy of the left became known as the 'three noes': no rent increases, no rate increases and no cuts to the budget. The argument was that it wasn't enough to oppose the capping as such, but it was a means to face down the Tory government and compel

Occupation of the town hall. (Photo Neil Martinson)

them to provide more resources. Sadly, nothing was further from the truth. Refusing to set a budget was illegal and the campaign singularly failed to move Mrs Thatcher's government. The Labour Party nationally did not support this approach and the first break in the solidarity was when the GLC (led by Ken Livingstone and John McDonnell) set a precept. Eventually, after legal challenges in court and occupation of the Town Hall on two separate occasions, a rate was set at a council meeting.

The Labour group had voted (on the casting vote of the chair) to set a rate but in the event a number of Labour councillors voted against in the council meeting and the vote went through with support from the Tories and Liberals. This was a most divisive time in Hackney and the leadership of the council was not prepared to work out a realistic way forward. As a result, Hilda Kean and her deputy, Andrew Puddephatt, decided to resign their posts in May 1985. Tony Millwood was elected as leader and many councillors decided not to stand for re-election in May 1986.

After the initial solidarity shown by the 15 Labour-controlled authorities which had been capped, the gradual setting of the rate ended up with only Liverpool and Lambeth failing to do so. This led to 81 councillors from those two authorities being surcharged and disqualified from standing for office.

In the case of Hackney, a public enquiry was held in the Town Hall. This eventually allowed Hackney to continue without any surcharges being levied.

The disputes in the Labour Party in the 1980s were set to continue into the 1990s. Different leaders generated more division as exemplified by the formation of a dissident group called Hackney New Labour in 1996. The challenges following the disbandment of the GLC and ILEA led to Hackney and other boroughs taking on education and housing from the GLC during a period when central government was continuing to cut the resources available. In 1998, a Tory/ Liberal Democrat Coalition was formed (after elections which were marred by fraud) which led to even more turmoil. It would need a new Labour council in the twenty-first century to sort it all out.

1983: Well Settled: the An Viet Foundation – Linh Vu

Domino players at the An Viet Foundation. (Thanh Vu)

From about 1978, the newspapers in Britain started to be filled with harrowing stories about the 'Vietnamese boat people'. The boat people were refugees from political oppression in Vietnam who risked everything to take long and perilous journeys to seek a better life and freedom, travelling in tiny boats – at the mercy of the seas, the weather and pitiless pirates. Many perished during the voyage, but of those who survived and made their way to the UK, a large proportion settled in Hackney. I was one of those boat people, just seven years old when I left Vietnam with my father Vu Khanh Thanh.

This is the story of our community in Hackney and of the An Viet (meaning 'well-settled') Foundation which my father established to help us settle well into our new host country. It was born out of my father's wish that Vietnamese refugees might integrate, become self-sufficient and independent in their new home.

Unofficially, An Viet Foundation started in 1982, when my father and I moved to London after being in refugee camps on the south coast for three years. My mother, sister and brother were left behind in Vietnam after many failed attempts to escape. We were reunited five years later, after much bureaucracy in Vietnam.

We came originally to Hackney because it was one of the few boroughs that visited the camps to offer accommodation. There was a resettlement policy under the Thatcher government to disperse new arrivals in order to prevent ethnic 'ghettos'. However, some were sent to places not suitable for finding employment and lacking services and support networks. People became very isolated and moved to London to find work, often staying with relatives. Some even resorted to squatting in the many empty properties in Hackney at the time.

When other Vietnamese arrived in London, they found out where we were living, and would turn up at the flat regularly to ask for help. These spontaneous gatherings in our home led to the birth of the Vietnamese community centre, An Viet Foundation, in Hackney. My father had gained experience from the camps, not only as a refugee, but also as a member of staff, initially working as a translator and then senior field worker.

The first public event organised by An Viet was in 1983, at Hackney Town Hall, for a Vietnamese New Year celebration. I often had to help out, wearing my national costume, reading speeches and introducing guest speakers from the local community, mayors and councillors. Going to school in Hackney, I found it much easier to gain a command of English than my father's generation. The New Year Festival became a successful way of bringing people together and raising awareness and carried on annually for the next 20 years.

An Viet Foundation eventually got its proper office away from our flat, in a disused public bathhouse in Englefield Road in De Beauvoir Town. It could now give support and advice on a larger scale. Projects set up included youth schemes, a drop-in centre for the elderly, and language and job training in fields such as nail treatment, catering and food hygiene. Our people wanted to work and get on and An Viet was all about helping them to realise that objective. An Viet also created the first Vietnamese housing association, officially recognised by the Housing Corporation. Most minority housing associations had previously concentrated only on one local region but An Viet Housing grew to offer services not only in London, but around the UK. Unfortunately, in 1999, An Viet Housing was taken over by a larger association. It seemed to be marginalised under the new management systems and bureaucracy. My father no longer wanted to be a part of that and concentrated more on community work. Consequently, important links in housing and community that had been developed were lost.

Many Vietnamese who arrived during the 1980s initially found work in the clothes-making factories in Hackney as little English was required. Links were established between An Viet and local Turkish, Jewish, Cypriot and Greek manufacturers. Over time, some went on to open their own clothing factories. An Viet would help them set up and get started. Some became very successful, employing up to 400 workers by 1989. Unfortunately, in the following years competition from the Far East eventually led to factory closures.

The Vietnamese went on to open nail salons. The phenomenon started in the US, where there is a much larger and more established Vietnamese community. People would visit their relatives, start learning new skills and then pass them on. By opening their own salons, families became more independent, dealing directly with customers rather than the middleman as in the clothing industry. They came to own most of the nail shops in Hackney and the surrounding areas. Now, the Vietnamese have also come to own most of the nail supply companies and it is a major source of employment.

Many people were using the community centre throughout these years and also needed to be fed! This led to the celebrated and much loved Vietnamese Canteen being set up by my family at the An Viet Centre in Englefield Road. People did not know much about Vietnamese food or culture at this time and were very curious. The canteen began to open to members of the public. This was the first Vietnamese restaurant in Hackney and started the food boom that we have today. 'Little Vietnam' can be found mainly along Kingsland Road, with further restaurants on Mare Street. The extra income generated by our restaurant helped to fund projects and training at An Viet. It became a place of service and cultural exchange, with the wider public coming into contact with the community.

The food boom led also to the growth of Vietnamese mini-supermarkets around Hackney. The arrival of regular direct flights from Vietnam to Heathrow in 1995 made trade much easier. Many of these supermarket owners have reinvested back in Vietnam, by opening factories or importing goods directly to supply their shops and restaurants.

Resettling into a new life in the UK was not always easy. Some had mental problems due to their experiences in Vietnam and their traumatic journeys while trying to escape. The open seas were prone to pirates. Some lost relatives or experienced torture at the hands of pirates looking for gold and jewellery.

The community also had to deal with problems of drug addiction. The problems started from camps in Hong Kong, where there were large numbers of unaccompanied minors, without parents or siblings. Many came from rural farming or coastal regions of Vietnam, and grew up in a more open, carefree network of large, extended families, but with little education. It is not surprising that some of these later immigrants faced problems adjusting to life in London. These problems did not occur with the earliest refugees from the late 1970s, including my family. We early refugees came mostly from cities and the South and were often more educated and politically active, and had attracted hostility from the Communist regime as a result.

The community has changed throughout the years. The elders contributed and loved using the community centre, but wanted their children to have a better education than themselves. Children like myself were often over-pushed to achieve good grades. There was endless extra homework after school, weekend classes and private tuition. As I got older, kids of my generation became less involved in the community, as we went on to universities and colleges. We had also got used to the way of life in Britain, together with our new office jobs.

In 2006, my father was awarded an MBE, for his valuable service to the community.

Thanh Vu, founder of the An Viet Foundation. (Thanh Vu)

One of the challenges moving on is how to connect children from the first generation of refugees like myself, who have settled and integrated into a more open, Western way of life, with the generation of later arrivals, who do not often share the same views and do not have as much of a 'chip on their shoulders' about the politics of Vietnam.

Some of the later comers' connections are still with Vietnam. They have grown up as young adults there, their parents and families are still there. Some arrived as students in later years and have stayed on. They have gone on to open new restaurants and businesses funded by their increasingly wealthy parents back home,

Englefield Road bathhouse became the An Viet Centre. (Photo Lisa Shell)

since the US lifted the trade embargo on Vietnam in 1994. Their loyalty is changing. They have begun to enjoy the freedom that London enables them to have, to develop themselves and enterprises without the corruption often experienced in Vietnam.

It has also taken a long time for the earliest refugees to make their peace with Vietnam. This making peace, aiming to create greater cultural links and business connections between those here and in Vietnam, and linking these to a wider extended community, would be positive progress for the whole community.

Further Infomation

My father's autobiography written with Christina Puryear, *Catholic with Confucian Tendencies: The True Story of the Extreme Adventures of a Vietnamese Boat Person*, 2016

'Passing Tides – Story of a Young Girl Escaping Vietnam with her Father': https://childmigrantstories.com/2016/06/09/passing-tides-story-of-a-young-girl-escaping-vietnam-with-her-father

1984: The Inquiry into the Death of Colin Roach: the police and the black community in Stoke Newington – Duncan Campbell

Police face off protestors demanding an enquiry into the death of Colin Roach. (Photo David Hoffman)

Few events cast a greater shadow over Hackney throughout 1984 than the death of Colin Roach. The 21-year-old died the previous year in very puzzling circumstances in the foyer of Stoke Newington police station. An inquest later concluded by an eight to two majority that he had committed suicide, but the angry local reaction that his death provoked was a symptom of the deep distrust between the local police and the black community.

Roach, from Bow, who suffered from depression and had recently been released from a short prison sentence for theft, died from shotgun wounds. His family told the inquest into his death that the police had broken the news to them in a callous fashion and there was immediate suspicion that the official version might not be true. Demonstrations were called. Musicians and poets, including Benjamin Zephaniah and Linton Kwesi Johnson, gave voice to the dismay.

Local politicians became involved. Brynley Heaven, the chairman of Hackney Council's police committee at the time, described how the officers who policed the area were "recruits... from Scotland, Somerset and Suffolk and many are meeting black people for the first time in any serious way. To deny there is a problem is a screamingly dangerous absurdity." There were disagreements on party lines. Joe Lobenstein, who led the Conservative group on the council, denied that there was local distrust : "Mr and Mrs Hackney are not in opposition to the police."

The demonstrations grew in size, frequency and turmoil. After five of them, there had been 96 arrests. There were echoes of the events in Deptford three years earlier when 13 young black party-goers had died in a suspicious fire and the local black community had also been angered by the police and media response. When it was announced in 1984 that there would be no official public inquiry into Colin Roach's death, an alternative was launched, commissioned by the Roach Family Support Committee. Its conclusions were published under the title of *Policing in Hackney 1945-1984* and the report asked why, if Roach had shot himself, his fingerprints were not on the gun and why it was not close to his body.

The late Stuart Hall, who wrote the foreword to the report, suggested that "any unbiased and objective person reading what is written here must conclude that contrary to everything which has been officially put about, nobody has the slightest idea why and how a young Black man lost his life in the foyer of one of the most controversial police stations in London. Further, that steps have been consistently blocked which might have led to these matters being systematically and satisfactorily inquired into. Why this should have been so is not for the Committee to say. But that it is so is clear. And the fact that it is so is a prima facie case for extreme public disquiet, not simply in Hackney or in the Black community but in the society at large."

The anger surrounding Colin Roach's death and the perceived failure of the authorities to investigate it fuelled the distrust between the police and the black community in Hackney. Nor was it by any means the only source of dismay. In January 1987, another young black man, Trevor Monerville, was arrested and detained in Stoke Newington police station and suffered a blood clot on the brain which required surgery. Again the circumstances of his injury were clouded in suspicion; sadly, he was murdered in unrelated circumstances seven years later.

By the end of the 1980s, Sandringham Road had become the main battleground between the two sides. To people living outside the borough, Sandringham Road – the 'front line' – was best known as a place for buying drugs. It was described by the then Metropolitan police commissioner, Kenneth Newman as, along with All Saints Road in Notting Hill and Railton Road in Brixton, a place where "crime is at its worst, where drug dealing is intolerably overt and where the racial ingredient is at its most potent". The local disquiet was reflected in the work of the Hackney Community Defence Association which was located appropriately enough at the Colin Roach Centre in Bradbury Street. They catalogued the many complaints of police behaviour on the front line with accusations ranging from the planting of drugs to the taking of money and drugs from dealers.

In the early 1990s, when I was the *Guardian's* crime correspondent, I was approached by people representing those who claimed they had been framed by the police and I visited a number of them in prison. It transpired that there was a major anti-corruption investigation, code-named Operation Jackpot, into some of their allegations. Such was the continuing

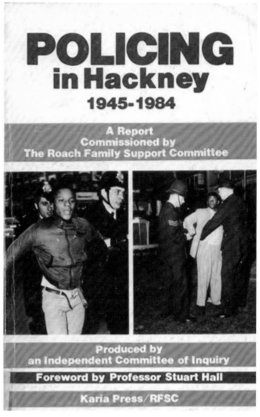

The Independent Enquiry Report.

distrust that we were asked by the anti-corruption team to try and persuade people to cooperate with them as most people were still too distrustful of the police to want to help. In 1992 eight police officers from Stoke Newington police station were moved to eight different stations and the *Guardian* reported this and the background to the investigation without naming the officers who had been moved or suggesting that they were in any way involved. Nearly three years later the eight officers, backed by the Police Federation, sued the *Guardian* for libel, an action which we eventually won in court in 1997 at a cost to the Federation of around £600,000. We were fortunate that it was left to the jury to decide the case as the judge, the late Mr Justice French, made it very clear that he favoured the police and informed the jury that it was open to them to award up to £125,000 to each officer.

In the meantime, in March 1993, the convictions of four of those accused of drugs offences in high profile cases connected to Stoke Newington police station were quashed at the Court of Appeal and they were awarded substantial damages. The prosecution in their cases acknowledged that "there are police officers upon whom suspicion has fallen as to their reliability". Something of an understatement. Then in 1996, Maxine Edwards, who had been convicted on drugs charges in equally controversial circumstances, also won her appeal after her case had been referred back to the Court of Appeal by the

Home Secretary in light of what had emerged about policing in the area. Just how seriously the police took the work of the Colin Roach Centre did not become apparent until 2013 when the *Guardian's* Rob Evans and Paul Lewis reported how Scotland Yard had used an undercover officer posing as a political activist called 'Mark Cassidy' to penetrate the centre in the 1990s.

The death of Colin Roach and the questions it raised would have a parallel on the other side of the Atlantic more than three decades later. The slogan 'Black Lives Matter', which was adopted by the campaigns that followed the deaths of young black men in the United States at the hands of the police in 2013 and 2014, echoed in many ways the campaign formed in the wake of Colin Roach's death so many years earlier. One of the greatest sources of distrust, of course, was the lack of police officers from ethnic minorities across London. This has changed significantly: by 2016 there were more than 4,000 ethnic minority officers, 13 per cent of the Met which, while it still did not mirror the 40 per cent of London's population that it should, was a vast change from 1984 when a black officer was rarely to be seen. The eventual acceptance by many within the police service in Hackney and elsewhere in London, that there were very good reasons why there had been such distrust of them and that those reasons had to be addressed, are part of Colin Roach's bittersweet but abiding legacy.

Further Information

Policing in Hackney 1945-1984 Karia Press/Roach Family Support Committee, 1989

1985: The Fate of Hackney Wick – Chris Dorley-Brown

Hackney's first tower block demolition, Northaird Point in the Trowbridge Estate.
(Photo Chris Dorley-Brown)

The events of 7 November 1985 appear increasingly pivotal to the recent history of this area of north-east London. The botched demolition of Northaird Point, one of seven 22-storey tower blocks on Hackney's largest council estate, resulting in 'the Leaning Tower of Hackney', heralded the beginning of an area of what we now call regeneration. But the anti-climax experienced that day was probably nothing new for an area with a reputation for opportunity and uncertainty.

Northaird Point. (Photo Chris Dorley-Brown)

I was just one of many photographers covering the event, but the images we took show little or no perspective of how the imposition of the tower blocks affected the community. Moreover, there are relatively few archival images that illustrate the significance of the Wick's contribution to Britain's industrial and military powers of the early twentieth century, and even fewer that document the area's decline after the Second World War. However, the recent emergence of archival aerial photos online has provided opportunities for reappraising history from a topographical perspective, and those of Hackney Wick are a good example. Taking three photographs, from 1921, 1971 and 2011, we can illustrate the transformations that have defined the story of the Wick, and in some way serve as a metaphor for modern London and its economic, post-industrial role.

***

1. In June 1921, the Aerofilms Avro aircraft, with the acclaimed cinematographer Claude Friese-Greene aboard, flew sorties over the Lea Valley. The late afternoon sun picked out this densely industrial neighbourhood, focussing on the area around White Post Lane. The scale of the Clarnico sweet factory is evident, occupying both sides of the waterway, emblazoned with their sweet purposes, 'British Standard Chocolates', 'Cream Caramels' and 'Lily Caramels'. Beyond the Atlas Works on the eastern bank of the canal is a vast flooded quarry and an area of 200 allotments, ringed by new avenues with freshly planted trees heading out to Walthamstow.

The Hope Yards of Carless Capel & Leonard were the first place where crude oil was refined into petroleum spirit. It is almost unimaginable to think that this volatile invention was still manufactured in a small London yard with wooden outbuildings and horse-drawn carts, selling to the 70,000 or so motorists in Britain in 1921. Over the railway line to Stratford is the India rubber factory of J&G Ingram making finely vulcanised surgical implements. In Queens Yard, can be seen the skylight windows of Britain's first dry cleaners, Achille Serre. The entire area appears as a huge chemistry set: the Empire at its peak, but also in its dying throes.

By far the most shocking image is the entire square mile occupied by the National Projectile Factory, which around the time of the Battle of the Somme was knocking out 16,000 six-inch shells a week, containing both high explosive and chemical warheads.

Aerial view of Hackney Wick in 1921. (Britain from Above)

The factory was demolished in the mid-1920s and its centre in what is now Mabley Green, is marked by the 80-ton monolith in granite by the artist John Frankland. Half climbing wall, half sculpture, it was hauled by road from a Cornish quarry as an unwitting but pertinent epitaph to the fallen.

In addition to the myriad industries, the picture shows that the Wick was a place where people lived. If the camera zoomed in on Wallis Road, well-dressed women could be seen inspecting the shop windows and strolling with their children in the afternoon sun.

***

2. Another image available on the website of the National Collection of Aerial Photography was taken at 9.06am, 2 May 1971. London is in the middle of an early spring, week-long mini heatwave. In contrast to the entrepreneurial scene of 1921, the picture is less optimistic. The rows of Victorian terraces have mostly been replaced by warehouses, and the landscape is dominated by railway tracks and parked trains. The site that is now Westfield shopping centre is one huge depot of rail and road interchange. The 'island' between the waterways that now hosts the Olympic Stadium is largely abandoned marshland, but over a footbridge, the toxic traditions of the Wick survive in the form of the concrete laboratory of Queen Mary College, containing a nuclear reactor the size of a washing machine.

Printer's Paradise in Queens Yard is knocking out counterfeit £20 and £50 notes by night, hard core porn by day. Adaptability, ducking and diving define this era

The woodyard of Gliksens dominates the island between the river and the cut, with

Aerial view of Hackney Wick in 1971. (National Collection of Aerial Photography)

tons of timber seasoning in the sunshine. On Fish Island the giant distribution depot of Courage's Brewery is keeping London in pale ale. To the north is an area that has been largely flattened – the last glimpse of Hackney Wick before the motorway pushes south towards Bow. Apart from a few warehouses and a church, the whole swathe has been cleared.

Moving across the branch line to Stratford, the new Wick 'village' and phase one of the Trowbridge Estate is ready to be occupied. Looking like the architect's model, the seven blocks cast their long shadows on the newly planted grass. The second phase, yet to be completed, is a building site. Hackney Stadium – speedway on Fridays, greyhounds on Wednesdays, is at its peak.

Remnants of Wick's chemical heyday remain, albeit on a small scale: Zamo bleach, Daro knobs and knockers, Matchbox toy cars, Percy Dalton's peanuts, Algha wire-rim glasses factory – at one time manufacturing annually a million and a half pairs, including John Lennon's. These stalwarts will hang on till the end of the century but most will have left for Essex.

***

3. The third image is taken in 2011, with one year to go before the opening of the 30th Olympiad. The site looks almost finished. We are not allowed in beyond the blue fence, but the photographer is, hovering low over the Wick while his gimbal rig keeps the

Aerial view of Hackney Wick in 2011, featuring the Olympic Park in the making. (Photo Giles Price)

vibrations to a minimum. The result is a precision digital, state of the art study. It's as if every stage of the construction process is an event in itself. We now inhabit diagrams of tarmac, concrete and polyurethane.

***

The Lea Valley of today is a matrix of computer-generated geometric forms looking like intricate microchips or printed circuits, almost abstract, but in fact loaded with information. This is a state of control, security, power and politics. If you zoomed in, the canals are lined with narrowboats. Micro-breweries, pizza ovens, artists' studios, think tanks, skate parks have all appeared in the four years since the Games. The cycle continues, the Wick is Britain's technical showpiece once more, a design for living: a rare vision in a world of uncertainty.

Furrther Information

The Britain from above image (1921) may be seen on line at:
http://www.britainfromabove.org.uk/image/epw006776
http://ncap.org.uk/frame/11-1-4-80-12

1986: The Mothers' Hospital closes, the Homerton opens: maternity services in Hackney – David Sloan

As it used to be: mothers and babies at the Mothers' Hospital in the mid-1950s. (Courtesy of the Salvation Army International Heritage Centre)

I remember reading a letter in a woman's medical records, dated 1968, from a consultant obstetrician thanking the GP for referring her and saying that he could see no particular reason for a hospital delivery. Up to the mid-1960s about one in three women had their babies at home, with midwives as their main and often only attendants. Things had changed dramatically by the time I became a GP in 1978 and by the mid-1980s less than one in 100 babies were born at home.

In 1986 the Mothers' Hospital in Lower Clapton Road closed and the Homerton Hospital opened, symbolising the fast changing times. New technology was bringing great advances but it was also challenging the culture of care. Nowhere was this more evident than in maternity services.

The Salvation Army Mothers' Hospital was built in 1913. Initially set up to provide maternity care for unmarried mothers, it grew as demand increased and expanded to care for married women as well. When it was taken over by the NHS in 1948 it was agreed that a proportion of the staff would continue to be Salvation Army officers and it retained, to some extent, its evangelical atmosphere right up to its closure. In its early years it boasted a spirit of research and innovation. For example, during the Second World War it pioneered getting women out of bed soon after childbirth, primarily to get them to the safety of the air-raid shelter. But it was also observed that this reduced the rate of post-natal venous thrombosis, a major cause of maternal death.

I came to know the Mothers' when I was working as a GP in Lower Clapton. My first impression was of its domestic scale and ambience. The frontage, housing the administrative offices, was made up of adapted Victorian terrace houses. A rather ungainly arch then led into the hospital proper. The single storey, bungalow-like wards were set off from a central covered walkway and separated by patches of lawn planted with trees which had a spectacular show of blossom in the spring. The light and airy wards were divided into one-, two- or four-bedded bays serviced by a kitchen, so there was a sense that the whole had been designed more like a dwelling than a hospital.

There was an operating theatre, a basic nursery and rudimentary lab facilities but it relied heavily on support from outside if anything went wrong. There was no resident anaesthetist or paediatrician; if needed they came across from the Hackney Hospital. Babies requiring special or intensive care or mothers with any serious complications had to be transferred out.

By the early 1980s recruitment to medical posts had become difficult and anxieties grew about safety and the quality of care. So the Barts and Hackney hospital group transferred some consultant obstetricians from St Barts, the other maternity unit serving Hackney residents, to the Mothers' to 'help'. It was an uneasy alliance, fraught with mistrust and cultural difference.

To understand why, despite these problems, the Mothers' was still a much-loved institution in the early 1980s, it is worth looking at what else was happening at the time. The technology of obstetrics was advancing at a great pace. Ultrasound scanning was becoming more sophisticated, electronic foetal monitoring was becoming standard practice, epidurals were increasing in popularity and the caesarean section rate was rising. I had spent a year in Latin America in 1976 and came straight back into an obstetric job and was very struck by the growing focus on safety and risk. It seemed to me that the new technology was being introduced in an uncontrolled way and that some midwives and doctors were spending too much time watching machines and had forgotten how to listen to women.

This increasingly technological and defensive view of pregnancy and childbirth was at odds with what women were saying they wanted and it reinforced their demands. Women wanted choice, a say in how and where they gave birth and for pregnancy to be treated as a natural process, not an illness. The National Childbirth Trust, founded in 1956, was strong in Hackney and campaigned in support of women resisting the appropriation of pregnancy and labour by mostly male obstetricians. Perhaps it is of note that the Mothers' had two female obstetricians at the time. People respected the values the Mothers' espoused; not necessarily the hymns and prayers, but the attempt to humanise the process of childbirth. So they continued to choose it. My first wife, Helen, gave birth to our two children there in 1981 and 1983.

But it was not sustainable. The Mothers' was isolated, some would say unsafe and its registration as a teaching hospital was threatened because of the perceived poor quality of care. At the same time Hackney was due to get a new hospital, the Homerton, as part of the great shake-up of medical schools and hospitals across London during the 1970s. The Homerton was to be the first hospital built in Hackney since the Mothers' in 1913. This was the opportunity to get our own modern hospital with up-to-date facilities and no longer to depend on hospitals outside the borough.

In relation to maternity services, the health authority proposed to close the Mothers' and the maternity unit at St Barts and move all in-patient maternity services for Hackney women to the Homerton. There we were to get a well-equipped labour ward, state of the art operating theatres and a neonatal intensive care unit. There would, however, be a shortage of space for all the antenatal activity. Some of us saw this as a great opportunity to move antenatal care out to where we thought it belonged – in the community, where women lived.

The result, after a lot of talking, was the establishment of seven community antenatal clinics, in general practices, based on a model pioneered by Professor Ken Boddy in Sighthill, Edinburgh. This was important in helping us to get buy-in from our initially sceptical hospital obstetric colleagues. Staffing of the clinics was by midwives and GPs, with consultant obstetricians attending, if necessary, to give advice. The system was backed by a risk-assessment protocol to decide when it was necessary to escalate to hospital care.

After extensive planning and negotiation we got the clinics launched in 1985 prior to the opening of the Homerton. Community antenatal care proved to be popular with women and professionals and to be as safe as hospital care.

On reflection it was only possible to persuade GPs to take on this extra work because there was a small group of us who were very much in sympathy with the demands women were making. We responded to their requests for a less technology-centred approach to pregnancy, including offering care during delivery, either at home or in hospital, sometimes working with independent midwives. Following the opening of the Homerton in 1986 GPs continued to have access to the labour ward and women continued to ask us to look after them in labour.

But during the 1990s midwives, whose authority as independent practitioners had, I believe, been threatened by the new technology, began to regain their voice as advocates for women. This was given traction with the publication in 1993 of *Changing Childbirth*, the report of the enquiry into maternity services led by Dame Julia Cumberlege. This emphasised the importance of care being centred on women's needs and wants and choice of care provider, place of delivery and interventions, based on sound impartial information.

In response the Homerton opened a low risk unit, the Elizabeth Suite. In 2011 this approach was further developed with the opening of the larger, midwife-led Birth Centre. This is for women whose risks are low and who want a natural birth but do not want to deliver at home. It has a relaxed and home-like atmosphere and there are pools for women who want a water birth. Being near the main labour ward, anyone who develops problems can be transferred quickly. Since 2007, the Homerton has also had a dedicated home birth team who support around 120 women a year having their babies at home.

So the Homerton has been responsive to what women want. But not all has been well with maternity services in the past few years. Between 2013 and 2015 five women have died as a direct or indirect complication of pregnancy. This is a reminder that the Homerton serves an area in which many women are at very high risk during pregnancy. Staff recognise that this means that attention to risk and quality of care is even more important than in areas with lesser risk, but it is challenging.

I greatly valued the time I spent as a GP providing maternity care. I think we filled a vacuum at a time when midwives were feeling overwhelmed. GPs now do very little maternity care but that is because the star of midwifery has risen again and that is appropriate and very good to see. It probably would never be appropriate to return to the days when a third of women had home deliveries. Technology has brought many benefits but the balance between reducing risk and being compassionate and empathetic remains as important as ever.

1987: The Bobov Sect takes over Egerton Road Synagogue: the changing Jewish community in Hackney – Rachel Kolsky

The jewel in the crown, Egerton Road Synagogue. (Photo Simon Mooney)

In 1987 the New Synagogue, known as 'Egerton Road' or 'The New' was acquired by the Bobov community, one of the world's largest Chasidic sects of ultra-orthodox Jews. The Chasidim together with other ultra-orthodox groups make up what is today known as the Haredi world. The two terms, Chasidic and Haredi have become synonymous.

'The New' is but one of a large number of synagogues in Hackney today, with estimates suggesting around 120, most linked to Haredi groups. The Chasidic sects are often named after the villages of origin, including Bobover, Belz, Ger, Satmar, Vishnitz and Lubavitch, and they each have their own dynastic rabbinical family. Chasidim are instantly recognisable by their long black silk coats and fur hats, reminiscent of seventeenth- century Polish nobles. To an outsider they all look similar but subtle variations in the clothing differentiate each sect. The *lingua franca* on the streets is Yiddish, albeit nowadays spoken into mobile phones.

The core beliefs within all sects are that every word of the Torah (Five Books of Moses) was dictated by G-d to Moses on Mount Sinai, and they adhere to the strictest interpretations of the laws.

Egerton Road, completed in 1915, had been one of the foremost synagogues of the 'mainstream' orthodox Jewish community with more than 1,000 members in the 1960s. But numbers dwindled rapidly and the handover to the Bobover confirmed a transformation in Hackney's Jewish community.

Most of London's Jewish community arrived through immigration from Russia and Poland during the late nineteenth century and early twentieth century. London's Jewish population rose rapidly with the majority living in close and overcrowded conditions in Whitechapel and Stepney.

The move northwards from the East End to Hackney and Stamford Hill had already begun by the late nineteenth century as earlier settlers migrated to less crowded areas, and this migration gathered pace after the First World War. The new arrivals dispersed widely and established large and small synagogues in Dalston and Hackney. But the jewel in the crown was Egerton Road. Its predecessor had been first established in 1761 as the 'New Synagogue'; it was rebuilt in 1838 in grand cathedral style at Great St Helens in the City of London.

The New Synagogue was encouraged to move north by Marcus Samuel, the founder of Shell, and its relocation to Stamford Hill in 1915 heralded Hackney as the 'new Eden'. A community hall remains in his name and glorious stained glass windows commemorating the Sabbath and Jewish festivals were later added, designed by rabbi and artist David Hillman.

As the growth of the Jewish community gathered pace, Stoke Newington, Stamford Hill, Dalston and Hackney all witnessed an influx of Jewish shops and businesses. There were synagogues for all levels of religious observance but overall it became a largely secular community. Tradition, culture and family ties defined Jewish identity. The great majority sent their children to local state schools – most notably Hackney Downs School, still widely known by its old name of 'Grocers'. By the 1930s Grocers was 50 per cent Jewish. Alumni were to become some of London's best known writers, academics and artists including Nobel Prize-winner Harold Pinter, Alexander Baron, author of the definitive Jewish Hackney novel, *The Lowlife*, and Abram Games who devised the iconic Festival of Britain logo of 1951. Many members of the community threw themselves enthusiastically into politics (mostly on the left) and Hackney Council had several successive Jewish leaders up to the 1970s.

After the Second World War a number of Jewish organisations migrated from the East End to Hackney, including the Jewish Maternity Hospital, the Workers' Circle, London Jewish Bakers' Union and Victoria Youth Club, confirming Hackney as the new Jewish East End. Jewish welfare organisations established in Hackney included the Jewish Deaf Association and Hackney Kosher Meals Service. By the 1950s the Jewish population of Hackney reached its height of some 100,000 people. The Kosher Meals Service, based at Egerton Road, was making 60,000 meals a year by the 1960s, reflecting the aging population. Rapid migration to the suburbs followed, mainly to Southgate and Cockfosters, leafy north London suburbs, and Newbury Park and Gants Hill along the post-war Central Line extension. By the 1980s the old Jewish community had almost completely dispersed.

As the mainstream orthodox and secular communities moved out, their institutions closed down and the Haredim began to predominate, many of them survivors relocating to London following the Holocaust of the Second World War.

Between 2001 and 2011 the Jewish population in Hackney grew by 44 per cent, predominantly Haredim. Their family size averages 6.3 children per family, ahead of the national average of 2.5. Closed pubs, such as the British Oak on Oldhill Street and the Swan off Clapton Common are now community centres for the Belz and Bobov, and Skinners School on Stamford Hill is now owned by the Lubavitch. Notices in shops and community centres are mostly in Hebrew script and Saturdays are tranquil, and free of motor traffic.

At first glance this close-knit community looks steeped in the past but relationships are being forged with other local communities. Rabbi Herschel Gluck, a leader in this work, liaises with other faith groups as a spokesperson for the Haredim, whilst Interlink, founded in 1991 and led by Chaya Spitz, provides support for navigating the bureaucracy of secular modern life. With large families, houses are often extended out and up and in the early 2000s Hackney Council was criticised for allowing unregulated loft conversions to remain. Today, Agudas Israel Housing Association, founded in 1982, works with social housing organisations to meet the needs of large orthodox families. Apprenticeship schemes are encouraging young orthodox men to become electricians and plumbers as they understand the requirements of orthodox homes such as time switches, large sinks and preventing fridge lights automatically activating on the Sabbath.

Haredim have gone some way in constructing parallel social institutions. In Lordship Road the former Bearsted Maternity Hospital has been rebuilt as a health centre catering for orthodox mothers and babies. Next door is Schonfeld Square, founded in 1993 for elderly Holocaust survivors but now a housing complex for orthodox families.

The education of Haredi children has become contentious. Haredi students attend their own schools, several of which were found to operate outside the national curriculum because much of the timetable was concentrated on Talmudic studies (classical Jewish texts). However, other schools, including the Beis Chinuch Lebenos in Woodberry Down and Yesodey Hatorah in Egerton Road, both for girls, are well regarded. The long established Avigdor Primary School survives and plans were approved in June 2016 to increase capacity by 30 per cent.

In the early twenty-first century, Jewish Hackney is also experiencing a renaissance centred on Stoke Newington Church Street and Stoke Newington High Street. Kehillah North London, founded in 2002, worships at the Community Rooms of St Mary's Church, and in 2008 Masorti Judaism arrived with the New Stoke Newington Shul, currently worshipping in members' homes. The Masorti movement, in contrast to Haredi beliefs, maintains that the Torah was not dictated by G-d to Moses on Mount Sinai at one point in time but was a divinely inspired record of Man's search for G-d.

Masorti children typically attend Simon Marks Jewish Primary School, formerly Clapton Jewish Day School, which relocated to Cazenove Road in 1973.

Jewish Hackney is represented in the House of Lords by several Jewish peers with a Hackney background including Alan Sugar and Maurice Glasman. They both honour their childhood home as Lords: Baron Sugar of Clapton and Baron Glasman of Stoke Newington and Stamford Hill. Within the Jewish community, the boundaries of Stamford Hill and Stoke Newington have often been difficult to differentiate but today few would dispute that the former, leading down to Clapton, is Haredi and the latter is more progressive.

Rabbi Herschel Gluck has worked tirelessly to promote inter-faith understanding.
(Photo David Braun)

Further Information

Alexander Baron, *The Lowlife*, Black Spring Press, 2010

Sharman Kadish, *The Synagogues of Britain and Ireland*, Yale University Press, 2011

Rachel Kolsky and Roslyn Rawson, *Jewish London*, New Holland, 2012

1988: The Construction of Watermint Quay: private housing in the 1980s – Suzanne Waters

"A charming cul-de-sac ending at the river": Watermint Quay. (Photo Simon Mooney)

"A modern variation of the old-fashioned London square": Sutton Square with St John at Hackney Church in the background. (Photo Simon Mooney)

In the 1980s, Hackney still had a slightly dubious reputation. Its council was in a mess and revelled in its status as 'Britain's poorest borough'. Unemployment was high at nearly 20 per cent, the schools were poor and, although physically close to the City, Hackney was considered to be remote from the rest of London.

Yet changes were taking place. Stoke Newington was becoming established as a cheaper alternative to Islington, especially for young left-wing professional types. Further east, Docklands was beginning to develop after a 20-year impasse. Aggressive and expanding building societies were ready to lend in areas which they had once blue-lined. People began to notice that a train line now served Hackney. New and assertive estate agents, such as Alan Selby and Shaw's, arrived to give older-established firms such as Bunch & Duke a run for their money. For more or less the first time since the First World War, private house-builders began to take serious interest in Hackney as a place for development.

Their interest was stimulated by some 'low-hanging fruit', brownfield sites (as we now call them) created by departing industrial behemoths. These included: Atlas Works in Hackney Wick (where Bronco toilet paper was made); Metal Box, makers of tin cans in central Hackney; Lathams timber merchants who were contracting their operations by the River Lea; and Shoreditch gasworks. These and other vacant industrial sites were all to go for private housing. Furthermore, by 1980, with the abolition of subsidised public housing, the council was keen to foster relationships with private developers.

The preferred style was Post Modern with its eclectic and sometimes architecturally witty references to past styles (particularly Georgian). The preferred cladding material was brick, often imitative of traditional London stock, although very modern construction methods were used. Densities were low (at a time when London's population was declining). There was also a continuing reaction against the high-rise architecture of the 1960s. That reaction had already begun in the public housing sector with the construction of low-rise housing estates in the 1970s, such as the huge Jack Dunning Estate in Lower Clapton.

Within this overall format, there were significant variations; architecture ranged from the daring and innovative to the dull and derivative. This was matched, as we shall see, in the financial and development models adopted by different builders.

Most interesting and most innovative was the collaboration between the architectural practice Campbell, Zogolovitch, Wilkinson & Gough (CZWG), and the developer Kentish Homes, which had begun in 1981. From 1983 to 1988 they built four schemes in the borough, largely on former industrial sites.

In 1981 Kentish Homes' managing director Keith Preston was impressed by CZWG's conversion scheme for a disused school in Hackney. Although this scheme wasn't carried out, it led Preston to contact the firm a year later to produce designs for a new-build scheme on Harrowgate Road, near Victoria Park. Preston's method was for the architect to produce the plans and apply for planning permission, for a flat fee (£250 per unit), only paid once permission was secured. CZWG designed 14 semi-detached houses with integral garages and arranged in pedimented pairs, with a hint of the Spanish villa owing to the dark pink stucco on the front façades and metal balconies. The houses were very popular and 10 were sold before completion in 1983.

Their next scheme was Sutton Square, close to Sutton Place and St John at Hackney Church, on a site that had been occupied by the Metal Box factory which closed in 1982. Here CZWG came up with a modern variation of the old-fashioned London square. Although Preston liked it, he wanted to be sure it was both economically viable and socially acceptable to the planners, who were not convinced of the apparent jokiness of the architecture. It is a mixture of 49 houses and a block of 16 flats, facing onto Urswick Road. The 'square' is actually a long, narrow cul-de-sac, set back from the road with the entrance flanked by two 'tollbooths'. Again, it was a highly successful scheme: all the properties were sold before completion in 1985.

Orchard Mews, built at the same time, is located off Southgate Grove in De Beauvoir Town on the site of a former factory. The layout is similar to Sutton Square, but much smaller with 15 houses arranged in three blocks around a narrow quadrangle, open on the west side for access. Architecturally quite different from the surrounding late Georgian terraces, here is Edwardian pastiche with the houses topped at each corner by a large dome similar to Edwin Lutyens' New Delhi.

The final scheme was at Watermint Quay, on a former timber yard, completed in 1988. The long narrow site is adjacent to the sports ground beside Springfield Park and the River Lea. CZWG used it to create a charming cul-de-sac ending at the river. It was built as a series of three-storey terraces facing one another, distinguished by pairs of gate piers at the top end, decorated by crossed oars and other nautical features, such as the odd porthole. These are family houses mainly occupied today by Hackney's Chasidic community.

While CZWG with Kentish Homes were producing their highly successful housing schemes, local architects Levitt Bernstein were setting up as house builders for the development of the old Shoreditch gasworks between Whiston Road and the Grand Union Canal. This became Gloucester Square, completed in 1988.

Previously, Levitt Bernstein's work had been predominantly public housing, but now they were adapting to the new commercial world of private house building. They set up a company called Pilot which acted as purchaser and developer. The site was bought without planning permission for residential use (initially refused, but granted after appeal in 1986). Similar in size to Sutton Square, the scheme was a mixture of one-bedroom flats and two-bedroom houses. Included were six one-bedroom flats specially adapted for people with disabilities to be sold at cost price (25 per cent off the market value). Unfortunately very few sold, so some were converted back and sold at full market value. The buildings were arranged around a small courtyard, with some fronting on to the canal, distinguished by pediments and columned porches. The courtyard was landscaped with a circular 'temple' in the centre.

We have seen the impact of architects designing these schemes in conjunction with enlightened developers. But the development on the former Atlas Works site, close by the Lea Navigation in the de-industrialising but interesting environment of Hackney Wick, is much less imaginative. Developed by Land and Urban, a company promoted under the Business Expansion Scheme to exploit tax incentives to build property to rent, Leabank Square is laid out in terraces around a central grassed area. The houses are very plain with the only distinction being the pedimented centrepieces.

Another private development with few architectural pretensions is on the site of the former Lathams timber yard by the River Lea. Riverside Close was built in the late 1980s as a series of three-storey blocks, with pitched roofs, some facing on to the river and the rest around a courtyard. This type of private housing was to become ubiquitous in the 1990s. A particularly dull example is the development on the former filter beds site in Stoke Newington, from 1996, by PRP Architects, a mixture of flats and houses.

These were all purely private schemes and the sales pitch was mostly aimed at people outside the borough. The sales literature described these areas as 'up and coming' and having a named architect was a key selling point. Wages were low locally, so very few of Hackney's longer-standing residents were able to afford these new houses. But this is not to denigrate the architects, or the developers. Cough and Wilkinson were aware of the disparity and admitted that it is "like opening up a cream cake shop in an area where the population can only afford bread". With the impact of the recession in the early 1980s and the collapse of large public projects, architects had to cut their cloth accordingly and team up with developers to survive. Parallels can also be drawn with eighteenth-century methods of urban building where builders and developers were in charge and the architects were there to provide some stylistic features to encourage a sale. But as we have seen, CZWG and Levitt Bernstein, with their careful planning and layouts, were keen to provide good quality, attractive homes.

This significant phase in Hackney's housing development more or less ended when the property market dried up following the collapse of the 'Lawson boom' in the early 1990s. When developers returned to the fray in the present century, it was in the context of more constrained sites and rising population pressures. Verticality increased and traditional building methods and materials were to be eclipsed, heralding a new phase of Hackney's development.

1989: Hip and Hype, Hoxton gets cool – Carolyn Clark

Hoxton hip happening: the 'Fete Worse than Death' poster.

Early years

At a Roman crossroads, and sufficiently distant from the City to be out of sight and earshot, Hoxton was destined to be a socio-economic and cultural cauldron.

Five hundred years ago, a scattering of shanties and a mansion or two were joined, not always amicably, by those heading to Hoxton for archery, the spas or country air. Ribbon development along the highways attracted the wealthy. Inns, pleasure gardens and The Theatre, opened in 1576, attracted gaming houses, cutpurses and ragged queens who earned the area a 'suburb of sin' tag.

But Hoxton had market gardens too, which may have influenced the creation of one of London's oldest garden squares in the 1680s, after plague and fire had turned City eyes beyond the walls. Hoxton Square

Damien Hirst and Angus Fairhurst dressed as clowns at the 'Fete Worse than Death'. (Alamy)

and its twin New (Charles) Square sandwiched Hoxton Market, creating a well-to-do suburb. Hoxton Market was doomed as a market square, but provided the setting for the much-loved Daddy Burtts Mission alleviating poverty, and the Shoreditch Generating Station bringing 'Out of Dust, Light and Power' to local people in Victorian times.

Hoxton Square's development coincided with the persecution of dissenting ministers who moved into its relative safety as the first bricks were barely laid. Hoxton Square became a hotbed for secular and non-secular radicals.

During the period of transition from wealthy suburb to inner city, almshouses and Hoxton's notorious asylums filled the void until the opening of the Regent's Canal superhighway in 1820. This brought timber, stone and lime to build alongside it, as well as industries requiring warehouses, workshops and workers. The local population almost quadrupled between 1800 and 1891.

Hoxton's notable small industries were shoe-making, printing and clothing, but the furniture trade dominated for 100 years. "Hoxton Square is almost entirely given over to cabinet makers" according to social commentator Charles Booth, writing in 1899.

Hoxton had factories, warehouses and housing, often with outworking in homes, cheek by jowl. There was little open space to relieve the intensity of the packed narrow streets. Hard graft and a hand-to-mouth existence made Hoxton's close-knit, working-class community, which created its own ways to support, survive and celebrate, backed by a progressive borough.

The area played a full part in World War Two, not least as a Luftwaffe target. Hoxton Square remained remarkably unscathed but took a hit from post-war strategic planning, slum clearance and industrial decline. By 1980, many industries had disappeared. In Hoxton Square, the last man standing was Fox's Safes, a large local employer until it was forced to relocate in around 2000.

Hoxton has always had the grit, defiance and resilience to get by as it ducked and dived into an uncertain future. As the twentieth century ended, it had turned full circle as a fashionable area to live, work and play. Hoxton Square was at the heart of the change.

Hip Hoxton

Was this turn-of-the-century cool that new? Culture and commerce have long run in Hoxton's arteries: from Shakespeare to the Britannia Music Hall, to May Scott's Community Theatre at Hoxton Hall to Whirl-Y-Gig Dance Trances; from Gainsborough Film Studios to the Silicon Roundabout; from artisans in wood and marble to community art murals and chair design fanatics. And not forgetting the creativity of Hoxton's population over centuries to earn a crust. Little wonder that local eyebrows arched at media claims that "When I first came to Hoxton, there was nothing there," and that artists "discovered" Hoxton – "a place known more for its bomb sites than its culture".

The Vanguard

In 1968, the short-lived Antiuniversity of London set up in Rivington Street. In the late 1970s, the area's industrial charms were seized on by other outsiders: the owner of Flip, selling American vintage clothing in Curtain Road, told me that Hoxton would be the next Covent Garden. In the early 1980s, the London Apprentice lost its rock bands to become a gay bar overnight, and the Bass Clef Jazz Club opened in Hoxton Square. By the mid-1980s, acid house warehouse raves and the Strong Room sound studios had arrived. The Bricklayers Arms, a real ale haunt complete with Morris Men, became the artists' rendezvous, later rivalled by the Foundry Bar. Small publishing firms, fashion designers and wholesalers located around Old Street gave some continuity with the past. A relaxation of live/work and designated 'employment areas' planning rules enabled the inward migration of artists and designers, notably Alexander McQueen, attracted by the space, low rents and edgy feel of Hoxton's warehouses. The Young British Artists had landed and Hoxton Square was to get a Banksy.

Supercool

The height of 'Cool Hoxton' was possibly 1993, when the YBAs own art entrepreneur, the late Joshua Compston, organised the 'Fete Worse than Death' in Hoxton, with the arteratti in active attendance. Tracey Emin read palms, Damien Hirst ran a stall where people could make their own spin paintings for £1 which he signed. The author's favourite stall was 'Jackson's Bollock' where bursting a paint-filled balloon with a dart won a small alloy effigy. Shoreditch has always loved to party and this event had a similar hedonistic anarchy to some home-grown fayres. In 1994, the second and last Fete took place in Hoxton Square.

Cooling down

The early arrival of the artists, often struggling to make ends meet themselves, had an organic quality. Some came from left field: Circus Space parachuted into Hoxton Market in 1994. Standpoint artist-run gallery and studios arrived in Coronet Street in 1997 with a local arts and education programme. Both are success stories. The Lux Cinema at 2-4 Hoxton Square was a public funding disaster. Purpose built in 1997 on a former timber yard as a base and venue for experimental and independent film, its modern design contrasted starkly to the rest of the Square. It closed in 2002 due to serious debt. The White Cube Gallery adapted a 1920s publishing company's building with a similarly modern design showcasing the YBAs from 2000-2012 before relocating to South London. It attracted queues around the Square, as well as Stuckist demonstrations against "the sterility of the white wall system". The Stuckists had their own gallery in Shoreditch and opposed "the pretensions of conceptual art" claiming that "artists who don't paint aren't artists".

While creative industries colonised Hoxton, the night-time economy had stormed in. Hoxton had a touch of the Klondike, with absent or ineffective local controls as the bars and clubs ran roughshod over local concerns. Visitors came from all over the world: Hoxton got slick and a Holiday Inn.

So has Hoxton lost its cool? According to Dr Lida Hujic writing in the *Guardian* in 2006, satirical local fanzine the *Shoreditch Twat* which ran from 1999 to 2004, "distinguished between the genuine creatives who were drawn to the area in search of similarly minded people and the fakes – opportunists who wanted to cash in on this creative hub, or faux artistes pretending to be scruffy and yet having loads of money from their parents". The YBAs moved on. In 2006, Michael Wylie declared in *The Times* that "The Ditch is Dead!". In 2016, an event boasted of its "beautiful and exclusive Hoxton Venue".

What Next For Hoxton?

Number 16 Hoxton Square provides a case study of change over time. It was a typical 'mission to the poor' school for the first 100 years of its life, a Latin American Centre in the 1970s, a nursery in the 1980s, an architect's live/work space and martial arts gym in the 1990s, a social enterprise training restaurant and base in the 2000s, a commercial restaurant and design studios in the 2010s. There will be further changes, but let's hope the listed building stands the test of time.

In 2011, 'Shoreditch Unbound' documented the area's continuing creativity: "Parts of Shoreditch are new and gleaming but most is old, patched up and made over… .It is evidence of a frequently ignored history, one of work and honesty, which is the essence of Shoreditch and it lives and breathes because of the people who create it and live it."

Many long-term residents, proud of their Hoxton heritage, are still here. But the wealthy have returned, squeezing out those with less deep pockets, ironically including the artists. Luxury flat land grabs put even listed buildings at risk. New trades in old buildings provide jobs, albeit specialised. Independent shops and cafés abound – but the chains are circling. The march of development from Bishopsgate threatens to destroy the goose that laid the golden egg as Hoxton's historic streetscape is trampled on.

The plane trees in Hoxton Square may well sigh as they have seen it all before and survived. Whatever the future holds, Hoxton's fighting spirit is needed now as ever. Hoxton is up for it.

Further Information

Carolyn Clark and Linda Wilkinson, *The Shoreditch Tales*, Shoreditch Trust, 2009

David Mander, *More Light More Power: An Illustrated History of Shoreditch*, Sutton Publishing, 1996

1990: Hackney becomes a Local Education Authority: chaos and rebirth in the borough's schooling – Annie Edge

National educational statistics published in October 2016 show the performance of Hackney's schoolchildren to be amongst the best in the country. From the performance of five- to seven- year- olds in reading, writing and maths to achievements at GCSE, the borough took top place. The Department for Education rated Hackney as "outstanding" and above London and national figures on all attainment measures.

These results are even more impressive when one considers the situation just 20 years earlier. In reports published between 1997 and 2000, Ofsted concluded that Hackney Council was providing "unsatisfactory or worse" support to its schools and, of the schools inspected between 2000 and 2002, two thirds were judged less than good – either satisfactory or inadequate. Hackney's Key Stage 2 results, for primary children aged seven to eleven, were the worst in the country.

The journey from worse to best is an extraordinary story. The tale starts in 1990 when the Inner London Education Authority was abolished, almost as an afterthought to the abolition of the GLC by Margaret Thatcher's government four years earlier. The ILEA had inherited the mantle of the LCC Education Committee and survived several earlier abolition proposals, but the 1988 Education Reform Act passed responsibility for education to the thirteen Inner London boroughs. Whilst the transition went smoothly in most boroughs, Hackney started chaotically. Payroll services broke down immediately, causing immense distress to desperate unpaid teachers, until other authorities stepped in.

Unfortunately, this was only an augury of things to come. Education directors came and went, often in a welter of recrimination. In 1996 Education Director Gus John retired early, saying councillors had failed to defend him against attacks by left-wing teachers and gay activists and no new education director was appointed until 1998. In 1997 Ofsted reported that Hackney's education service had collapsed, with Chief Inspector Chris Woodhead stating that Hackney "set new standards in disorganisation and bureaucratic waste". As former Mayor, Jules Pipe, commented, "The whole council was in crisis and the fact that Hackney schools were failing badly was just one symptom of that malaise that affected every part of local services."

In 1997 the new (and New) Labour Prime Minister Tony Blair outlined his three priorities as "Education, education, education," promising to put classrooms at the top of the agenda. Education ministers made no secret of their determination to be tough on Hackney. In March 1999, Hackney became the first LEA to have some of its responsibilities contracted out to a private company, Nord Anglia. But just over a year and a half later in November 2000, a further Ofsted report noted the recent resignation of another director of education, Elizabeth Reid, and commented that this was "only the latest in a series of crises resulting from the continued ineptitude of the corporate management of the council". Apprehension and disquiet among schools in Hackney culminated in head teachers making an unprecedented request to be removed from the control of the LEA. The Ofsted report concluded that "the time has come for radical change".

Nationally, policy changes throughout the 1990s had given increased powers to schools and their governing bodies. The introduction of the national curriculum, key stages with SATs, and league tables designed to encourage parents to make informed choices between schools, reinforced the growing independence of schools. The management of this cultural and organisational change, requiring autonomy for schools on the one hand and a reducing core of administrative and support services on the other, was beyond the capability of the enfeebled council.

The government's naming and shaming of poorly performing schools in a list of what became known immediately as the '18 worst schools in the country' exacerbated the situation. At Morningside School, which was already on an improving trajectory, pupils and staff found themselves in the press spotlight and were seriously demoralised. The problem of attracting good teachers to work and to stay in Hackney became even harder.

Within this framework schools complained of being viewed by Hackney Council as an homogeneous group with very little recognition of their different needs and different capacities. Many, but not all, secondary schools were struggling, though a significant group of primary schools were doing well and were popular with parents. There was a view that the council was predominantly in transmit rather than listening mode. Frequent changes of leadership, poor management, a lack of support and, on occasions, punitive responses to bad Ofsted reports led to mistrust between schools, teachers and their unions, and the council. According to one head, there was no collective optimism. Schools tried hard to co-operate with the council but they were surrounded by things going wrong.

The government's solution was the creation of the Learning Trust in 2002 as a not-for-profit company to take over Hackney's functions as LEA and report directly to the Secretary of State. It succeeded in large part because it immediately established a strong relationship with heads, governors and teaching unions. In the words of one former head, "It did not feel that the Learning Trust was being imposed on us."

The government made it clear that the Learning Trust had a life of 10 years, signalling its intention to return education services to the council once its administrative and governance issues had been resolved. Indeed, over this period the council improved dramatically in functionality so that it could be said that schools were now improving not in spite of Hackney but alongside it. The focus of the Trust was on a commitment to high academic expectations for all children, recognition of the importance of strong leadership, and the establishment of a culture of mutual responsibility and co-operation. Federations of schools were created, linking less successful schools with those led by successful and experienced head teachers. Such federations have been criticised as over-managerial but they have been typified by a level of fluidity, with schools moving in and out of such arrangements, and benefitting through the sharing of leadership and resources. At the same time many of the educational services supporting schools, such as monitoring attendance, educational psychology and statistics provision were improving.

Schools were encouraged to find different models for improvement. For many of the stronger schools, the Trust was relatively hands-off and was described by one former head as "just so much less bad than lots of other models".

But whatever one thought of the Learning Trust, it cannot take all the credit for the turn-around in Hackney's school and pupil performance.

School funding under the Labour governments between 1997 and 2010 increased dramatically and was heavily weighted towards disadvantaged students. The coalition government continued this trend with a 'pupil premium' for all disadvantaged students. Department for Education data for funding and resources in 2011 show that Hackney schools were advantaged relative to the all-London figure and to the rest of England. On the ground this translated into more teachers and more support staff. One head reported that in her primary school staff numbers rose from 35 in 1997 to 120 in 2010.

Whilst this included bringing some services in-house the increase was still dramatic and bound to have an impact.

Another contributing factor was London Challenge; launched by the government in 2003 and targeted at improving the capital's secondary schools by changing the culture and raising expectations. Hackney, as one of the five key areas singled out for close attention, was a beneficiary from the London Challenge programme's many initiatives. One of these, the Extended School, encouraged opening buildings outside school hours. This programme, used creatively, opened the doors to many parents in new ways, increasing involvement and providing a two-way benefit.

Building Schools for the Future was another government scheme enthusiastically adopted in Hackney. As a result Hackney's school buildings, which had suffered from years of underinvestment, benefitted from a major programme of renovation and renewal, including the building of four new schools from scratch. In what became known as 'the London Effect', by 2012 gains in student achievement had been made in all inner London boroughs except one.

In Hackney, increasingly positive Ofsted reports were being matched by better than average pupil outcomes at all levels. A study of educational provision in Hackney and Tower Hamlets by two senior American academics concluded that, contrary to received wisdom, "It is possible... to provide high levels of average achievement across densely populated urban areas with large concentrations of disadvantaged students."

In the same year, the Learning Trust's 10-year contract came to an end and responsibility for education returned to the council, although the name and branding were retained along with many of the people involved. In the four years from 2012, statistics show that Hackney's schools have continued to be measured as amongst the best in the country.

The biggest challenge to continued success is in changes to the funding formula announced in December 2016, which sees London schools losing out as money shifts to those outside the capital. This was on the same day that the National Audit Office warned that schools across England were also facing an eight per cent real terms cut in funding per pupil by 2019-20. A reduction in numbers of teaching and support staff is inevitable.

At the end of 2016 the government consulted on its proposal to allow new free schools to select up to 100 per cent of pupils according to their parents' religion. This would overturn the existing rule that no new free school or academy could admit more than 50 per cent of its pupils based on faith. (Existing schools can already select up to 100 per cent of pupils based on religion.) On top of this, in November 2016, Hackney Council said it had identified 35 unregistered ultra-orthodox Jewish schools operating illegally in the borough, many failing to meet the requirements of the National Curriculum. In a borough with a rapidly increasing population, greater levels of pupil separation may threaten both educational attainment and social cohesion.

Today Hackney is a very different place to the borough of twenty years ago and finding decent affordable accommodation is a real problem for teaching and support staff. Many of those who were attracted to the borough by the opportunity to make a real difference, and who together have achieved so much, are now moving on to more senior positions or retiring, and there is a critical need to continue to attract new people to take their places.

It is ironic that the very success of Hackney's schools has been a contributing factor in the extraordinary rise in rents and house prices across the borough.

1991: The Quick Brown Fox jumps over the Lazy Dog: the reincarnation of Stoke Newington Church Street – Maureen Diffley

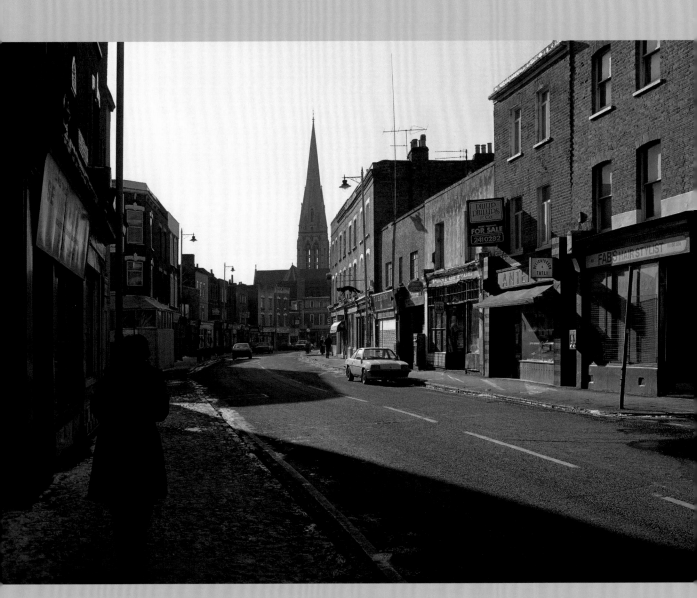

Stoke Newington Church Street in 1986. (Photo Berris Connolly)

The Fox, the Phoenix and the Festival

Stoke Newington Church Street always had charm, with its meandering medieval street pattern, its two churches, Clissold Park, the Town Hall and a legacy of eighteenth– and nineteenth–century buildings of genuine historical value. These contrast with the Roman linearity and the commercial, fast-paced nature of Stoke Newington High Street, the arterial A10. But the fabric of Church Street fell into disrepair during the 1960s and '70s. By the late 1980s, Grade 2-listed buildings survived along the street – but only just. Photos and surveys from the time show over one-third of the significant fabric at risk. This is a story about the renaissance of Church Street.

Behind the scenes, people were organising and, mainly thanks to the efforts of the Hackney Society, Church Street became one of the borough's first Conservation Areas in 1983. Funding was secured to pay for surveys of the extant fabric and schedules of remedial work were drawn up for the most at-risk buildings. Grants were made available to owners to cover essential repairs, although some saw conservation listing as more red tape preventing them from extracting maximum profit from their assets. Persuading property owners on Church Street of the value of a conservation approach was not easy.

In the late 1970s, the area gained a reputation for attracting left-leaning non-conformist types. Cheap property prices drew artists, musicians and writers. Comedians such as Alexei Sayle enjoyed parodying the 'stripped pine' politics of the new arrivals in what had been a Jewish area in the 1950s, and a predominantly Afro-Caribbean neighbourhood in the '60s and '70s. The Turkish and Kurdish refugee communities, who have contributed so much to the present character of the place, arrived in the 1970s and '80s.

The Vortex was founded in 1984 as an art gallery, and developed into a music club by owner David Mossman. It rapidly became an essential and lively part of the London jazz scene. Still in existence, it has now relocated to Dalston. Bridgewood & Neitzert set up their musical instrument shop in 1983, and are still here. Carol and Robbie Richards established Stoke Newington's first wine bar, The Fox, at 176 Church Street in 1981. Robbie was a staunch supporter of the idea of the conservation area.

By 1991, twelve years of Conservative government had delivered 17 per cent interest rates and widespread negative equity. This had the unexpected virtue of breaking the once-prevalent pattern of people moving to trendy inner-city London in their twenties, and then leaving to find decent schools for their kids in their thirties. Unable to sell up, more families were staying put. A more stable community allowed businesses to build up loyalty in their customer base.

The Richards' fortunes mirrored that of the wider community. In 1986, they upgraded their wine bar to a restaurant, La Fin de la Chasse, and bought a house on Osbaldeston Road. By 1991, however, Robbie was ill with cancer and the restaurant was struggling, so they took the decision to move back over the shop and re-open the wine bar as The Fox Reformed. This was a turning point in the fortunes of the family and the street. The venue soon became the beating heart of the community, a place of gossip, intrigue, campaigns, backgammon, food and booze. Robbie, aka the Fox, was the self-styled skipper of the good ship Church Street, at the helm behind his bar, eyes on the street. Every aspect of the street interested him and he enlisted the help of all his contacts and customers to further his aims, large and small. He persuaded the council to install Christmas lights, bike rails, new paving slabs, memorial plaques, and improve rubbish collections. He founded the Stoke Newington Business Association, campaigned for the refurbishment of Clissold Park House and planted daffodils in Old St Mary's Churchyard. Carol kept the restaurant going, focussing her skills on looking after her customers' gastronomic needs rather than their ethical and political responsibilities.

I was drawn into a net, cast by Robbie in 1994, to find organisers for the Stoke Newington Church Street Midsummer Festival, as it was originally known. A couple of years earlier, Robbie had been intensely irritated by an article in the national press, which described an evening out in Church Street as deader than a night in Abney Park Cemetery. He conceived the idea of closing the road to hold a big street festival in 1993. It was clear after the first year that a new community-based organisation was needed to run it. Kay Trainor, Fiona Fieber and I decided to get involved. As a trio we were committed to making the festival a real outpouring of the creative soul of the local community. 'Unusual conjunctions' was the catch phrase for helping local people gain access to buildings, closed for years or normally shut off to the public, or for placing artistic events in mundane places.

We were determined to ignite artistic fire in the collective belly of Stoke Newington dwellers. We held an avant-garde cinema night inside 'The Castle', the long-closed pumping station on Green Lanes, now a climbing centre. A string quartet played in the laundrette. We reopened and held the first art show for many years in the Library Gallery. Clissold Park at night was the venue for a family camping sleep-over and also featured 'Parklight', two nights of art and play to celebrate the Millennium. We renamed Stoke Newington Secondary School's theatre as the Boiler House Theatre and held the first Stoke Newington Opera Cabaret there, an event which continues to this day, run by Farquahar McKay and Wendy Weinstock (www.operacabaret.org). Bertolt Brecht's *The Caucasian Chalk Circle* was performed in William Patten School, directed by Mehmet Ergen, who went on to found Arcola Theatre.

And then there was the Street Festival!

The street was closed to traffic on the second Sunday of June, and for ten consecutive years the event was never rained off. It was tremendously difficult and time-consuming to organise, done on a shoestring budget, with support-in-kind, but miniscule funding from Hackney Council. There was genuine involvement from local businesses, and massive volunteering by local people, in particular women with school-going children. The local schools, especially William Patten and Grazebrook, were the communications conduits. It helped that the Turkish, Kurdish and Caribbean cultures really embraced the idea of Carnival, and the jumbling of high and low culture which it entailed. The street festival hosted processions and bands, street performers and artists, stalls, stages, soothsayers and lashings of food. At the end of the day, we had to clear the whole thing away and, totally exhausted, stand guarding equipment until it was picked up. Otherwise, it would be nicked! The festival was innovative, fun and profound. Ownership grew out of this diverse involvement and a receptivity in the community to experimental art. One of my abiding memories is of a site-specific performance piece by artist Tom Geoghegan, where he hung, totally still, for eight hours a day, on the gable wall of

Traymans Solicitor's office, for the entire week-long festival. In its own quiet way, it was dramatic, disturbing, and very accessible.

Brick by brick, building by building, phoenix-like, the fabric of Church Street was repaired and refurbished. The edginess of the late 1980s and early '90s grew into a friendlier atmosphere, in many ways helped by the cross-community relationships, which the festival had fostered.

Fast forward to 2017, and the problem of over-priced property creates new difficulties, empty shops and unaffordable housing. Wilmer Place, the car park site adjoining Abney Park Cemetery, remains a battleground. The idea of a very large residential development sitting on top of a supermarket, over-shadowing the cemetery and pumping additional traffic on to Church Street seems a prime example of property speculation rather than community development. Resistance to the proposals showed that local people still care and are prepared to act together for the collective good. Stoke Newington has a way of energising its residents with its long-standing non-conformism. Long may it continue.

Many of us who were involved in making the festival happen still live here. Sadly, in January 2016, we buried Robbie Richards, followed by Carol a couple of months later. Many of the new and long-standing businesses on Church Street are supportive of community and artistic activity, and regular events are held at the Old St Mary's Church (see www.theoldchurch.org). But so far, no new Fox has appeared. The new Fox, will undoubtedly be a different sort of manifestation, hopefully a person, or persons with feet on the ground, pulling people away from virtual interaction and privatised entertainment, towards something more communal, something creative, happening on the street. For the street to continue to prosper, it must be taken care of, it must be loved as the place where our special memories are laid down, and where our neighbouring lives are lived.

The Fox is dead, Long live the Fox.

Café culture on Stoke Newington Church Street. (Photo Simon Mooney)

1992: A Spiritual Home in Hackney: the journey of the Black Majority Churches – Beth Green

Members of the Redeemed Christian Church of God at prayer at the Round Chapel Clapton.
(Photos courtesy of the RCCG Kingdom of Praise and Thanksgiving Church)

Walk down any road in Hackney today and you will see shopfronts with signs announcing the presence of 'The City of Victory', 'The Lighthouse Assembly', and 'Resurrection House,' among others. These seemingly insignificant signs mark out the places of worship of Black Majority Churches. Sounds of singing and spirit-invoking prayers at vigils, running into the early hours, ring out on Friday and Saturday nights, whilst neighbours are sleeping.

These churches have been significant in turning the narrative of religious decline in Britain on its head, and tell a story of perseverance, faith, and quest for belonging. Just as the Israelites journeyed through the desert for forty years towards the promised land – as the Old Testament tells us – Black Majority Churches in Britain have had a similar journey towards finding their identity in a strange, and often hostile, land.

Up until the 1950s, the small population of West Africans living in Britain sat uncomfortably in church pews, following formal and formulaic liturgy, often facing antagonism from fellow congregants. Perhaps some of it was familiar, particularly for those who had grown up attending an Anglican or Methodist church (historically, a mission station). Perhaps some were comfortable in their new surroundings, and some attended in a deliberate attempt to be part of community. But others stopped worshipping within a formal church context. Their stories, along with the hushed but fervent prayers of the faithful as they gathered in living rooms and around kitchen tables, go quietly untold.

From the late 1950s, the spiritual tide began to change. The coming of SS Windrush in 1948 presaged the arrival of a generation of Caribbean believers who embarked on a quest for a home in a new and strange place. The so-called 'Windrush churches' – the New Testament Church of God, the Church of God of Prophecy and the First Born Church of the Living God to name a few –inherited an 'other worldly' theology. The wearing of white robes was one marker of their emphasis on holiness; on being set apart from the world and its vices. They carried expressions of religious celebration that travelled across the seas, and cemented a sense of identity within this first generation of Caribbean migrants. The small number of West Africans who joined them found refuge in a familiar way of worshipping God; in joyful, upbeat and heartfelt praise, matched by devotion to the Word of God, and a solemn seriousness to live as people 'set apart'. With community, came practical help; a network within which jobs, homes and extended family could be found.

In the 1980s, change in the spiritual realm was stirring again. The theology and expression of worship in the 'Windrush churches' felt unfamiliar to a new generation of West Africans, mostly Nigerian students. They had experienced something quite different back at home – travelling preachers filling lecture halls and stadiums, and American televangelists expressing the power of prayer to heal, and to achieve even the most ambitious dreams. Riding on the back of prophecies in a war-stricken region of West Africa, revival was spreading throughout the cities of Nigeria and Ghana, and making its way to Britain. The Holy Spirit, and those filled with it, were not to be bound by borders.

This sense of spiritual hunger among young West Africans was part of a narrative of 'reverse mission'. After decades of colonialism, the story had changed. While Europeans had first arrived to 'save' the 'Dark Continent', now it was Europe's turn to be saved. Empowered and purposeful agents of mission, such as the Ghanaian Christian Fellowship and the Overseas Fellowship of Nigerian Christians provided organisations in which like-minded and like-hearted migrants self-identified as missionaries. Church communities born in the 1980s and 1990s with this distinctive, missionising DNA at their core, such as Kingsway International Christian Centre (KICC) and the Redeemed Christian Church of God (RCCG), marked this departure.

The founding of KICC is a significant chapter in this departure and Hackney is at the centre of the story. Pastor Matthew Ashimolowo, leader of KICC, spoke to the worries and aspirations of a new generation, culturally but also more importantly, what was going on in their hearts. The beginnings of KICC are unclear. Some say there were 11 people at the first meeting in 1992 held in a school hall in Holloway, while other sources say there were over 200 people. Whatever the number, imagine the feeling of anticipation and excitement in that room. Imagine the first service, a year later, in KICC's own building in Hackney. This new church dreamed big, buying a building in Darnley Road capable of seating 1,000 worshippers and making it home. Perhaps it felt like a service in Ghana or Nigeria, but when it came to an end, people poured out of the doors into the Sunday afternoon on Mare Street, mingling with the hustle and bustle of Hackney.

By 1997, the congregation was overflowing its Darnley Road church, holding additional services in Central Hall and the Hackney Empire. Taking a giant further step, KICC bought up two warehouses by the old greyhound stadium in Hackney Wick, transforming them into a church that could seat 4,000. The growth of KICC in Hackney and other Black Majority churches in Hackney was mirrored by a growth in the borough's African population. 2011 census data record 11.4% of Hackney's population as being of Black African origin.

The annual 'Gathering of Champions' became a milestone in the life of KICC; an annual conference, led by Pastor Matthew Ashimolowo. The event quickly developed as a focal point; packed with a theology of empowerment and purpose, with emphasis on prayer and spiritual power. This language spoke to the reality of KICC's members; and word spread fast as Pastor Ashimolowo had a talent for putting his congregants' deepest fears and most ambitious dreams into words. Straddling the spiritual and the practical – the theology of 'Heaven now' – KICC's growth was remarkable. It was too often explained away by observers as down merely to pragmatic and contextual responses to the migrants' experience of living in the UK, missing the force of its message and its mission.

At KICC, and at other Black Majority churches originating from West Africa such as RCCG, a service may be heard in a mingling of English and of different West African languages. As congregants try to navigate life in Britain, the very real issues of money, of visa situations, marriage and family are dealt with as practical as well as spiritual matters. Prayer accompanies debt advice, legal counsel, and educational opportunities.

The story is not without its bumps, and a church of this scale and ambition does not go unscathed by challenge and controversy. Supporting a church financially, or 'tithing', as members are encouraged to do, while viewing their leaders as akin to prophets, often becomes murky within a culture of charitable due diligence. With a charismatic leader at the helm, the rumours of financial mismanagement at KICC and elsewhere have genuine substance, but too often they have become the main story. Elsewhere there are hundreds of quieter stories of loud prayers declared in living rooms and in rented factory buildings transformed into improvised churches.

KICC's enforced move from Hackney to make way for the Olympic Park was not the end of its story but the start of a new chapter as the congregation set up camp in Prayer City – a large campus in Kent. Leaving behind a significant spiritual imprint in Hackney, KICC is one of the fastest growing churches in Europe. But it is only one of many Black Majority churches stirring with life at a time when the narrative of religious adherence elsewhere has been one of chronic decline. While the Church of England was battling to keep churches open in the 1980s, KICC and RCCG and others, were opening their doors and overflowing with worshippers.

When the tide changes again, as it always will, the story will inevitably introduce new characters, plots and places. Black Majority churches have a challenge on their hands to adapt and change, particularly in retaining their young people whose religious and cultural experience in the UK differs from their parents and grandparents who were born in West Africa.

Black Majority churches are sharing buildings with other denominations, including long-established nonconformist churches, helping to maintain these buildings in economically viable use. The challenge in years ahead will be to work together for the Gospel; the Good News which declares that in God's house "there are many rooms".

Poster for RCCG prayer gathering. (Courtesy of the RCCG Kingdom of Praise and Thanksgiving Church)

1993: Abney Park Cemetery, trees, tombs and radicalism – Russell Miller

Abney Park Cemetery in springtime. (Photo Simon Mooney)

The history of Abney Park is fascinating and complex. As a natural historian, Abney has been my classroom for the past 20 years. Two centuries before I discovered it in 1993, Abney was the manorial garden to Abney House and Fleetwood House. The main north-south axes, Great Elm and Little Elm walks, date from that time. In 1840 the gardens were merged in a radical experiment in urban green space. The 32-acre Abney Park Garden Cemetery combined a visionary public arboretum with desperately needed space to intern the deceased of London's fast-growing population. Abney was one of seven 'magnificent' new cemeteries designed to take over from much smaller local churchyards. This was long before most of the London parks we know today were established. Uniquely, Abney was a showcase horticultural park with the world's biggest collection of exotic trees and shrubs (2,500 species) and 1,000 varieties of rose, all planted by Hackney's famous Loddiges Nursery.

Tragically the economics of the cemetery business, and the huge demand for burials, meant that most of the great Loddiges collection was felled before it matured. However 20 survivors remain hidden within the current, much younger woodland. Some of these survivors are so rare they do not have modern cultivar names. The remarkable Lucombe Oak grove is a window on to Loddiges' early Victorian tree craft. In 1890 ash, poplar and horse chestnut were planted and it is these trees that are the backbone of the site's current landscape and ecological significance. Little appears to have happened thereafter, aside from 250,000 burials, until lack of space scuppered the company's finances and natural succession took over.

The cemetery went bankrupt in the 1970s, raising the threat of development, so the Save Abney Park Campaign was born and a typically Hackney grassroots effort secured public ownership of the site. Hackney Council was able to acquire Abney for one pound; the value of the site was depressed by the responsibility of maintaining a site containing thousands of decaying graves. The council did not, however, have any clear plan for Abney, nor was it to do so for many years.

A rare shield mushroom, Orange Shield Cap, fruiting inside a hollow poplar log.

By the 1980s nature was well on its way to transforming the site into a diverse ash woodland. Scrub then woodland is the natural progression of things where grazing or mowing are excluded. Twenty years later I discovered that many of Abney's veteran trees had old basal cavities typical of fire damage. Further investigation showed there had been a perverse practice of building fires against trees in the 1980s when slash and burn passed for conservation on site. Some of these trees survive but many are dead and we continue to lose trees before their time every year as they succumb to root disease, structural failure or pollarding stress.

Fabulous Fungi

There were winners in this human interference. Fungi proliferate in Abney's decaying trees and deadwood. Local

Hoverfly, *pocota personata*, superbly mimicking a bumblebee.
(Photos Russell Miller)

mycologist Gina Rackley's 30-year study has so far recorded 300 species. Kew Gardens retains a sample from one of Abney's rare bracket fungi (*Phylloporia ribis*) and mycologists there have commented on the importance and expertise of Gina's work. Like many Abney naturalists, however, Gina is modest and unassuming.

Isolated Island

Bird life at Abney tells a different story. Although the sparrowhawks, blackcaps, goldcrests and many others continue to flourish, you will not see the lesser spotted woodpeckers or tree creepers I used to watch in the 1990s. Huge development pressure along Abney's boundary has greatly increased the site's isolation as a green island amidst hostile human infrastructure. Combined with national decline, this pressure has led to local extinctions of species that cannot now recolonise. Even Abney's tawny owls are at risk. The resident female died two years ago and the lonely male has called and called along the boundary hoping to attract a new mate to no avail. He may succeed one day: tawny owls are pretty adaptable to wooded urban islands. But equally he may not. I have been installing owl boxes in neighbouring sites in the hope of increasing the local population but there is a risk that Abney's remaining owl may die or move on before that project succeeds.

Hackney Council's engagement with Abney over the years has been mostly characterised by lack of understanding, parsimony and, for long periods, outright neglect. The 1980s, as I have mentioned, were characterised by crude and cheap management practices including indiscriminate clearance by slash and burn. In 1991, Abney Park Trust was formed as a charity by local people to protect and preserve Abney and the designation as a Local Nature Reserve in 1993 signified belated recognition by Hackney Council of Abney's importance. For many years Abney Park Trust held Abney under a management agreement with Hackney Council. The Trust did what it could to manage the woodland, mostly through volunteers, and organised guided walks and school visits. But its resources were meagre and Hackney Council's support half-hearted at best, and the Trust's efforts to raise a major lottery grant to restore the cemetery and the chapel were never successful. In 2014 Hackney Council abruptly took back control from the Trust.

But one success can be credited to the eminent tree expert Dr David Lonsdale, one of Hackney's great progeny, who before leaving Stoke Newington made it his task to secure Tree Protection Orders at Abney. On a train from the Ancient Tree Forum 2016 Summer Conference he recounted to me how, after receiving his request, Hackney Council trialled the unfamiliar legal procedure on a sycamore on the Regent's Canal before making Abney's its first group TPO *circa* 1980.

Butterflies and Biodiversity

Research on Abney's rich invertebrate community has revealed 800 species so far, including extraordinary rarities that would justify the site's designation as inner London's first Site of Special Scientific Interest (SSSI). Matthew Gandy and Tony Butler have been my companions in searching Abney for tiny wonders. White-letter and purple hairstreak butterflies are frequent and Tony sees silver washed fritillary most years. A purple emperor popped over the wall last year. Woodland moths like maiden's blush and mottled emerald are found nowhere else in North East London,

The newly restored chapel. (Photo Simon Mooney)

demonstrating Abney's importance as a wildlife refugium for locally threatened species.

Other important groups include deadwood beetles and a surprising diversity of wild bee species, but it is rare and bizarre flies that are Abney's greatest rarities. The wasp-like conopid fly *Leopoldius brevirostris* is so rare that no one knows much about its life cycle. Even more exciting is Abney's fluffy bumblebee mimic hoverfly *Pocota personata*. The species was last seen in London in 1966 before its rediscovery in an ash tree in Abney. So, despite the expensive flats all around the boundary wall and the 1980s pyromaniacs, Abney remains a diverse woodland biodome for thousands of species, including over 400 plants.

Radicals old and new

There is a lot more to Abney than its wildlife. For years people have campaigned for restoration of the listed chapel and others have researched some of the remarkable people buried at Abney.

As I write, work is finally under way to stabilise the chapel so as to remove it from Historic England's Buildings at Risk register. Designed by William Hosking, Abney's was the world's first non-denominational chapel. Combined with the unconsecrated land and the public arboretum garden, Abney has always been a place for everyone but especially dissenters, the unconventional and the radical.

In 1983 local Irish historian, the late Chris McGuire, re-discovered the grave of the great Chartist writer and journalist James Bronterre O'Brien. The discovery led to annual lectures at the graveside by the likes of Tony Benn, Arthur Scargill, historian

A. J. P. Taylor and, in 2015, Jeremy Corbyn (just prior to his election as Labour leader). McGuire uncovered a remarkable collection of nineteenth-century radicals buried at Abney. Scholar, early pamphleteer and freedom of speech campaigner William Hone was buried with Charles Dickens and George Cruikshank in attendance. Not far away, McGuire found the graves of Chartist orator Henry Vincent and publisher John Cleave. The discoveries continue and in 2006 Joanna Vassa's monument was found and resurrected. Vassa was the only child of author, enslavement survivor and anti-slavery campaigner Olaudah Equiano.

What of the future?

The original arboretum was intended to facilitate popular learning in what was a very early, deliberate, outdoor classroom. For naturalists and historians it continues to offer interest from the casual to the academic. Abney's current challenge is to become a sustainable community asset in an era of neo-liberal economic insanity. After taking back control from Abney Park Trust in 2014, Hackney Council is investing to restore the chapel and to help secure the site's future, but if that is to succeed it will require more learning. LBH parks department has come a long way from an obsession with geranium beds and amenity grass deserts. That change has been led by dedicated community groups like Park User Groups and Tree Musketeers, often against defensive resistance from Hackney's political establishment.

For Abney to continue to be the inclusive, diverse, alternative space that it always has been, Hackney's senior politicians will need to be less hostile to local wisdom than was Mayor Pipe. The future of public space itself is uncertain. Capital-intensive lottery makeovers, like the £9m Clissold Park fiasco, bring revenue demands that rarely materialise, leaving financial headaches not to mention huge ecological damage. Avoiding similar mistakes at Abney means less tolerance of lightweight consultants and greater respect for community expertise.

Further Information

Paul Joyce, *A Guide to Abney Park Cemetery*, Save Abney Park, 1984

Russell Miller, 'The Trees and Woodland of Abney Park Cemetery', *London Naturalist*, 87: 29-51. Free to download online at: www.researchgate.net

1994: Dalston City Challenge, regeneration in Hackney – Richard Simmons

Circus Space, Hoxton, one of the projects supported by Dalston City Challenge. (Circus Space)

Hipster Hoxton, Shoreditch, Haggerston and Dalston. It's easy to forget how little their potential was realised from the 1970s to the early 1990s. Despite neighbouring the City, unemployment was 26.9 per cent in 1993, thanks to outdated manufacturing firms closing in the 1960s and 1970s. With four of seven wards among the most deprived in Britain, sites were derelict, buildings vacant. Drug abuse, crime, poor health and low educational attainment persisted.

Many people lived on shabby, 'postcoded' council estates – your postcode more or less guaranteed you wouldn't get work. There were sharp racial divides between white working-class Hoxton and a growing mix of ethnicities up Kingsland Road into Dalston, where 40 per cent had roots in Asia, Africa or the Caribbean.

There was also aspiration: gentrification in De Beauvoir Town and Sandringham Road; avant-garde artists moving into cheap, vacated workspaces in Shoreditch; vibrant local arts and crafts. Mostly, though, private investors thought Hackney too risky. Government cash was needed to boost confidence and bridge the investment gap.

In 1990, John Major's Conservative government introduced City Challenge. Partnerships between councils, businesses and communities competed for government money, submitting an action plan for a tightly defined area. The prize: £7.5 million annually for five years, to be spent only within that area. The plan had to include measurable targets and attract additional resources from public, private and NGO sources. Winners signed a pledge to government to deliver.

Hackney, bidding in 1992, looked unlikely to win, given past political antagonism towards the government. Luckily, it had the right people at the right time. Pragmatic Labour Council Leader John McCafferty was aided by Jerry White, a chief executive with the skills to persuade government. McCafferty could work with lone Conservative councillor Joe Lobenstein. Lobenstein helped convince inner-cities minister Sir George Young that Hackney would deliver. Council regeneration experts Mike New and John Burrow assembled the plan, concentrating on a narrow 'Dalston Corridor' for maximum impact.

They had become experts because Hackney had used previous government regeneration funds effectively when they were allocated according to need – notably the Urban Programme (1968-1978), originally targeted at social issues, and Inner City Partnership (1979-1993), purposed more towards stimulating the local economy. City Challenge was different, though. Need alone was insufficient. Your plan had to be better than the competition from other deprived places.

Dalston's bid was promoted through the overarching Hackney 2000 Partnership, established in 1991 to build relationships between the council and other agencies. Aiming "to create a vibrant, cleaner, greener, safer, more prosperous Hackney by the year 2000", it began by working with local businesses. It grew to embrace the police, NHS, community organisations and providers of training, transport and the arts. It put Hackney in a stronger position to argue for government and EU funds. It included the Council's Comprehensive Estates Initiative (CEI) to renew Hackney's most decrepit council housing. CEI's innovation appealed to government, so its intention to redevelop the failed Holly Street Estate was a big positive in the City Challenge proposition. Later, Hackney 2000 successfully promoted bids for regeneration elsewhere, such as Mare Street and Hackney Wick.

On the City Challenge partnership, Dalston Business Forum represented local firms. Sir Stuart Lipton (developer of Broadgate in South Shoreditch) and the East London Partnership business leadership team recruited big companies, including Warburg's bank. Dalston Community Forum and an All Faiths Group spoke for residents and voluntary organisations. Several public bodies augmented the board.

Adept negotiation and strong partnership won the bid. Dalston City Partnership (DCP), a non-profit company, opened in 1993 to deliver City Challenge. I became CEO; John Burrow, deputy. Recruiting staff representative of the community, we refurbished as offices 1 Kingsland High Street. We began turning plans into action, laying foundations for success.

We faced early problems. People took time to acclimatise to City Challenge disciplines like measuring results. Government officials struggled to understand the edgy 'creative quarter' we fostered in Hoxton/Shoreditch, telling me I risked losing my job if DCP backed Circus Space in Hoxton Square. Fortunately, project sponsor Warburg's persuaded them. Circus Space went on to train performers for the Millennium Dome and London 2012, so government eventually came round.

City Challenge wasn't allowed to fully-fund projects. Its government grant was designed to catalyse other investment, encouraging partnership and local commitment. So, DCP led some projects, and partnered many led by others. A strength of City Challenge was its ability to promote regeneration holistically across physical, economic and social boundaries. Too often, governments spawn one-size-fits-all initiatives that don't adapt well to local circumstances. Complex problems don't get fixed by one form of action. It was a boon that DCP could address multiple problems simultaneously. The Action Plan had six 'Strategic Programme Areas', with 63 projects. Only a few examples can be included here:

a. Inward Investment – Running the *Dalston First* marketing agency to attract new investment; co-funding high-quality industrial units under Dalston Viaduct. We wanted to secure the railway arches for transport re-use. I chaired the East London Line Group, which promoted rebuilding the line, persuading ministers to safeguard what eventually became part of the Overground.

b. Business Support – Supporting an enterprise centre; running an investment fund for local businesses; giving grants to refurbish redundant factories and other buildings as modern work units; employing a Dalston Town Centre Manager. To develop cultural industries, DCP co-funded Circus Space, 'Hand Made in Hackney' trade fairs for designer-makers, the extension of the Geffrye Museum, new bars and restaurants and more.

c. Developing Skills – Co-funding Hackney Community College's Shoreditch Campus; numerous schemes training local people in skills like ICT, construction and media; helping Dalston schools to increase attainment.

d. Environment – Contributing to improvements for pedestrians and cyclists; public art; Ridley Road Market storage; celebrating heritage; CCTV; better business security; Community Chest for neighbourhood improvements.

e. Housing – Funding tenant involvement and training, and better design, in Holly Street's redevelopment; supporting conversion of the German Hospital for housing; other new homebuilding and estate improvements (e.g. in Haggerston).

f. Health and Care Services – Contributing to new health centres at St. Leonard's and the German Hospitals; projects to improve quality of life for disabled and older people and pre-school children.

The programme was big and complicated. With little time to get results there were bound to be projects that didn't work, though far fewer than we expected. Bishopsgate Goods Yard was not demolished because ownership complications arose from rail privatisation. Local controversy delayed redevelopment at Dalston Junction.

Yet, when its funding ended in 1998, most of DCP's projects had happened, in spite of the massive political upheaval when Hackney Labour split in 1996. Measurably one of the most successful City Challenges, it exceeded many of its targets. Its physical legacy is visible in 2016. It's harder to judge the long-term impact of DCP's people projects – improving education and employment prospects, promoting designer-makers and the like. There was no consistent research into these short-life programmes' longer term outcomes. DCP's funding for community involvement in Holly Street's renewal is one project where there is anecdotal evidence. Some years after City Challenge ended I met a tenants' representative and an academic. The academic asked how it was for the residents. The reply: "We got exactly what we asked for. To be normal Hackney streets."

The focus on the Dalston Corridor aggravated some councillors. DCP was limited, unhelpfully, by boundaries that sometimes excluded the poor on its doorstep from benefiting. McCafferty argued that it was necessary to build government confidence so more funds would follow. He was proved right when new regeneration programmes came along. The 'Heart of Hackney', Hackney Wick, Shoreditch and Hoxton did indeed benefit. So did DCP, managing the Hackney Wick and City Fringe Single Regeneration Budget partnerships.

DCP succeeded in improving properties and the cultural economy. Boosting creative industries and smartening up the area made it attractive to better-off hipsters and mainstream investors. This contributed to property price increases unimaginable in 1993, subsequently exacerbated by markets overheating for other reasons in the twenty-first century. That has undoubtedly been problematic for poorer residents who haven't shared the new prosperity. The New Deal for Communities partnership that followed City Challenge in Hoxton created a community trust to redress this balance, locking-in value for locals: not an option for DCP, but imaginatively building on its achievements.

City Challenge shared a weakness with most English regeneration programmes: they are not sustained. People-based regeneration takes longer than construction, especially in places like Dalston with high population turnover. Most funding ends too soon to effect generational change. Expertise and confidence are lost rapidly when teams who have gained the trust of local communities are dispersed.

We did manage to offset the latter problem to some extent by merging DCP and the Council's Heart of Hackney regeneration team to form Renaisi, a non-profit regeneration and inward investment agency. Renaisi passed on DCP's experience and expertise to communities in Hackney and beyond. It helped set up Hoxton New Deal and was still working in East London in 2016, so lessons learnt from 1993 to1998 continued to play a part in shaping the borough after City Challenge had ended.

1995: Ralph Fiennes appears as Hamlet in Mare Street: the rebirth of the Hackney Empire
– Simon Thomsett

Determined to make it happen: Roland Muldoon (second from left on front row) and supporters stare at the camera on the opening night in 1986. (Courtesy of Roland Muldoon)

When, some time in 1985, Roland Muldoon put on a posh voice (he was an actor so this wasn't too hard) and bluffed his way into the Hackney Empire Theatre, then functioning as a bingo hall, claiming to be from Mecca HQ, he could hardly have dreamt that in 10 years' time a genuine movie A-lister would be gracing its stage as Hamlet and playing to an official 104 per cent of its seating capacity.

The Edwardian Empire had been unloved through the 1960s and 1970s, was almost demolished to make way for a car park, and was rescued by bingo. Mecca kept it open and in use by the public and avoided irreversible destruction of its extraordinary, lavish interior decor. It was only when Muldoon and his touring company (CAST) walked in to case the joint that its rebirth as a palace of popular performance began; they and later others saw it for what it was, one of architect Frank Matcham's masterpieces with a magical connection between audience and stage.

There was something of a contradiction about CAST being there at all. Famously class conscious and driven by a romantic sense of Socialism (Muldoon's description), they suddenly had to run a business and make the hard decisions. The Empire's survival today is a testament to their tenacity but it came at a price. They had to deal with officialdom, with 'odious funding officers' (©R Muldoon) and later a plague of management consultants as the establishment slowly caught up and saw for themselves what a jewel in Hackney's crown the Empire was. Their shocked realisation that a self-styled bunch of pirates had nipped in and occupied it under their noses must have hurt.

After countless bills of 'New Variety', it was the Almeida Theatre under the guidance of co-directors Ian McDiarmid and Jonathan Kent who came along and suggested they bring their forthcoming *Hamlet*, starring Ralph Fiennes, to Hackney. McDiarmid and Kent had been at the helm of Islington's Almeida Theatre for five years and had built up considerable artistic capital in that time. Their plans for a definitive *Hamlet* were hatched with a major US co-producing partner and the target was Broadway; gloriously, the start of the journey would be in Hackney. The concept was a great compliment to Muldoon and his team and demonstrated just how desirable the Empire had become. Of course, in time this desirability had a downside; others had started to take notice of what was going on in Hackney.

I arrived at the Empire as General Manager in early January 1995. *Hamlet* was due to open on 17 February. It was one heck of a probation. There was a constant low level hysteria as the clock ticked down to the first performance. The Empire team braced itself, aware that this was a pivotal moment. The Almeida people arrived in waves, there seemed to be armies of them, all there to insure against anything that might happen now they were in the East End. They brought top creative talent, they had serious sponsors who needed looking after, commercial backers and huge expectation. There was a cast of 29 that were somehow crammed into the handful of dressing rooms behind the stage, all sharing one wonky shower ("we're planning to build another one soon..."). Ralph Fiennes headlined of course but it was an outstanding cast overall, including Francesca Annis, Tara Fitzgerald, Terence Rigby, a young Rupert Penry-Jones and an upstart less than two years out of drama school by the name of Damian Lewis.

People who had never set foot in Hackney before took on our aging telephone system and tried to buy tickets, sometimes successfully. Shortly after my arrival I found out we were selling from more than one seating plan. No-one was completely sure how many actual seats there were in the theatre (a detail perhaps, but it was becoming important), so the Almeida's not-to-be-beaten marketing officer Jacqui Gellman and I did the obvious thing and went into the auditorium and counted them; even then we ultimately seemed to sell more seats than we thought existed; a mystery to this day. People I had never heard of called me up to enquire after my health, casually asking whether there might be any spare tickets going, possibly…?

Hamlet became the hottest ticket in town for its five-week run., With the Almeida's agreement there was a special performance at the end of the run for Hackney people only., Tickets were free but you had to prove you were a resident. It was a way to say thank you and it produced a queue that circled the building.

There was already talk of Lottery money for the Empire and it was our priority to put together a coherent scheme that would sort the building's problems out once and for all and find a way to pay for it. The need to rescue the fabric of the theatre was obvious, as was the requirement for modernisation here and there (those new showers really were quite important if we were to attract top names) so we were able to make a strong case for support. It was also a time when the council had ambitious plans for regeneration and on a good day they agreed that the Empire was one of the borough's priorities. On a less good day, there was palpable anxiety over who controlled the theatre and who would do so after the money had been spent. Everyone who was getting involved had some kind of agenda. Hackney Council's regeneration arm, called Renaisi, had a grandiose scheme to create a 'Cultural Quarter', intended to spearhead the economic rebirth of Hackney Central. The jewel in the crown of this project was not to be the Empire, but their own project, a music venue to be called Ocean, fashioned out of the old Methodist Central Hall and the Carnegie Library just over the road from the Empire. Ocean pressed all the buttons of Hackney Council and the funding agencies, and swallowed an inordinate amount of funding, some £23 million, before going bust. (The building is now the site of the Picture House.) It helped Ocean's cause that Hackney Council owned the building and invented the project, and its management team were always funder-friendly. The Empire was emphatically 'Not Invented Here' and Roland was never the most biddable of leaders.

Nevertheless, the sheer volume and variety of funding sources played to our advantage. No one body, including Hackney Council, could lay claim to being the prime mover and so, to a large degree the Empire's independence was safe, at least for a time.

The Empire had been in constant use for nearly a century and it was a bit worn out and needed some love. A brilliant design team, led by architect Tim Ronalds, worked closely and tirelessly with the Empire management to create a scheme that would fix the theatre's problems. We were well aware that this was a once in a lifetime opportunity. We spent many hours getting the brief right and many more working to get the money. The budget was initially £15m and relied on Lottery funding to open up all the other sources. Eventually that was forthcoming (at the second attempt) but the proportion was smaller than we'd hoped. Yet more applications were made, more rich people found us bothering them as part of a sustained and ultimately successful appeal campaign led by the limitless bundle of energy that is Griff Rhys Jones.

And so another countdown began, this one to a closure for a full-scale refurbishment. It would take almost three years in the end. Commercial necessity meant working right up to the closure and the main strip-out of the theatre prior to the works took just over a week. When you empty a theatre out, it quickly looks forlorn. The wear and tear and history is revealed. As the handover day drew near, staff would often wander in for a last look.

The front of house crew had left a bucket of small change, mostly one and two pence pieces that they couldn't be bothered with counting up and banking. The strip-out crew could though and they took it to the bank across the road where it was added up to over £50 which immediately went behind the bar at the Old Ship Pub nearby for all and any who may pass by to drink a toast to the Empire. And they did, of course.

On 28 May 2001, the keys were handed over to the main contractor and the serious work began. The story of the refurbishment is a longer tale for another day but after many twists and turns the theatre finally re-opened to the public in January 2004, 19 or so years after it was rescued from bingo and just over 102 years since it first offered entertainment to the good people of Hackney. The new age of the Empire began.

Further Information

Roland Muldoon, *Taking on the Empire: How We Saved the Hackney Empire for Popular Theatre*, Just Press, 2013

An early variety playbill, 1987.
(Courtesy of the Hackney Empire)

1996: Wick Woodland takes Root: the greening of the Lea Valley – Anne Woollett

Hackney Marshes in 1962. Wick Field (now Wick Woodland) is in the foreground below the road. (Getty Images)

The River Lea (or Lee – both spellings are used) forms the eastern boundary of Hackney. For most of its length the Lea runs alongside open space: Springfield Park, Millfields, Middlesex Filter Beds and, in the south, Hackney Marshes. These open spaces are valuable for people and wildlife in a densely populated borough. Professor Patrick Abercrombie, in his visionary *Greater London Plan* published in 1944, envisaged the Lea Valley as a green lung – a 'great regional reservation' linking the countryside around London to the teeming millions of the East End. This vision was turned into a Regional Park by Lou Sherman, leader of Hackney Council in the 1960s. He persuaded the riparian boroughs in London, Essex and Hertfordshire to support a Parliamentary Bill to establish a Park Authority and to club together to pay for it through a precept on the rates. The Lee Valley Regional Park Authority came into being on 1 January 1967.

Despite the very green nature of Professor Abercrombie's vision, the Park Authority's primary focus turned out to be the provision of organised sporting and leisure facilities. The first blueprint, the 1969 Park Plan, focused on regional leisure facilities on a vast scale including centres just outside Hackney at Eastway and Lea Bridge. The Park Authority (most would say fortunately) lacked the resources to achieve these grandiose ambitions but organised leisure and the income it might generate remained, and still remain, at the top of its agenda.

As green critics became more vocal, the Authority's plans were increasingly resisted, and arguments were made for a wider view of the Lea Valley and its Park. In the 1970s the Park Authority proposed to extract gravel from Walthamstow Marshes, with the promise of a boating lake after the gravel had been removed. Although Walthamstow Marshes are in Waltham Forest, it is very much Hackney's countryside and a group of Hackney people, led by Clapton residents John and Jane Nash and Mike Knowles, formed Save the Marshes to fight the Authority's plans. Save the Marshes documented the exceptional ecological importance of Walthamstow Marshes leading eventually to their designation as a Site of Special Scientific Interest. After a long struggle the Park Authority conceded defeat and the Marshes have since been managed as a nature reserve. In the 1990s cattle were brought in as a way of ensuring that the Marshes retained their marshy character.

In 1969 the Middlesex Filter Beds ceased to be used for purifying London's drinking water. By the 1980s, when Thames Water (then a public body) sought to dispose of them, the Filter Beds had been marvellously reclaimed by nature. In line with its sports agenda, the Park Authority's first crackpot scheme was to fill the beds and create football pitches to supplement those on Hackney Marshes. A Hackney-based group, the Lee Valley Forum, persuaded the Park Authority that the Middlesex Filter Beds (and later the nearby Essex Beds in Waltham Forest) should be managed as a nature reserve based on their value for nesting and migratory birds, not to mention their seclusion and beauty.

Hackney Marshes form by far the largest area of green space in Hackney. They were traditionally managed as Lammas Land, which meant that commoners were entitled to graze their animals on the marshes after Lammas Day – 12 August – each year. In 1894 they came into public ownership following an outcry at proposals for their development. Purchased at the (then) huge cost of £75,000, the Marshes were dedicated as open space for the people of Hackney and neighbouring boroughs, thanks to the commitment of Mr G.B. Holmes, the local member of the LCC. (Much later, an unknown GLC employee performed an heroic service by ensuring that the Marshes were added to the Common

Land Register.) The purchase was celebrated with a procession from Hackney Town Hall to the Marshes. As well as marking out football pitches, the LCC planted trees along the river and the Lea Navigation canal (known locally as the Hackney Cut). The trees were native black poplars – a rare English tree – and London plane trees, a few of which survive.

The Marshes have been gradually reduced in area. Parts were taken for railways and the railway yards and engineering works at Temple Mills (most of which has become the site of Spitalfields Fruit and Vegetable Market); for roads (including M11 Link Road); industrial use (including the old Lesney Factory on Homerton Road); and housing development (Kingsmead Estate in the 1930s and Lee Conservancy Road in the 1990s).

The character has also changed: during and after the Second World War, bomb rubble from the City of London was dumped on large areas of the Marshes. The Marshes ceased to be marshy and an occasional reservoir for the overflowing river in times of flood. Rubble was never dumped on the southern section, known as Wick Field, and this remains at a lower level than the rest of the Marshes.

Yet more open space was lost to the Olympics when Arena Field became the site of the Olympic Media Centre, whilst East Marsh became the Olympic coach park (though later returned to grassland). And next to Hackney Marshes, the wonderful (and rather secret) Bully Fen nature reserve became the Velodrome and Olympics Village. Since the Olympics, the pressure for sports facilities has continued. The Hackney Marsh Community Hub has been built at the south end of the Marshes. This has provided much-needed up to date facilities for the footballers but the 'stunning contemporary architecture' of concrete and weathered steel is by no means to everybody's taste. Now Hackney Council has plans for a cricket hub at the north end. Hackney Marsh User Group (HMUG) and others consider that the centre (and especially the large hard surface car park) are overscale and impinge unduly. They have attempted to persuade Hackney Council to modify these plans but without conspicuous success.

The Marshes are probably best known as the home of park football with over 100 pitches laid out in its heyday, the footballing nursery of David Beckham among many others. The Greater London Council (GLC) planted trees adding to the collection of rare black poplars and London planes – an interesting selection from the GLC Tree Nursery. These were planted around the periphery of the Main Marsh, East Marsh and Arena Field so they did not intrude on the football pitches. However, the attached photo from 1962 shows that the Marshes were then comparatively bare. In 1986 Hackney Council took over responsibility for Hackney Marshes and HMUG was formed. HMUG has worked with the council, Groundwork Hackney and Tree Musketeers to continue adding vast numbers of mainly young trees planted by volunteers and children from local schools. These trees are now maturing, creating a dense ecological margin and changing the often windswept character of the Marshes.

Wick Woodland is a particular success. As the demand for football pitches on Sunday mornings diminished, Wick Field – a triangular section of the Marsh at the southern end – ceased to be marked out for football. Between 1996 and 2000 it was planted with trees, mostly by volunteers. It now includes many young black poplars specially grown for Wick Woodland. The Woodland has become a forest. No other word will do. Its previous incarnation as football pitches seems unimaginable. As the trees mature,

Wick Woodland today. (Photo Glory Hall)

volunteers led by Tree Musketeers coppice and thin them to ensure that light reaches the woodland floor and the diversity of habitats is maintained.

In 2000 the Community Tree Nursery and Forest Garden were established on the Marshes by local volunteers, supported by Groundwork Hackney and Hackney Council. The Tree Musketeers work with local volunteers to grow trees including fruit trees for planting on the Marshes and in other Hackney parks and care for them as they settle into their new homes. Trees are chosen to provide a year-round food resource, and roosting and nesting sites for birds, small mammals and insects. In recognition of their contribution to the greening of the Lea Valley and Hackney parks, the Tree Musketeers have won numerous tree 'Oscars' at the London Tree and Woodland Awards including best community tree project in 2008 and 2015.

The value of Hackney Marshes and the Lea Valley for wildlife is recognised in their designations as sites of Importance for Nature Conservation because they provide an important north-south route for migrating birds and a variety of habitats including open water habitat. We still, fortunately, have a vast space to wander, with surprisingly secret-feeling retreats in Wick Woodland, the Filter Beds and beside the old course of the River Lea on the east side of the Marshes. However, there is still intense pressure for construction of organised sports and leisure facilities and the car parks now accompanying such developments. Arguing the case for the green open spaces of the Lea Valley continues to be a struggle.

Further Information

Information about the Tree Nursery can be found on Sustainable Hackney website: http://sustainablehackney.org.uk/tm

1997: The Strange Story of Murder Mile – Julia Lafferty

Palace Pavilion in Lower Clapton Road. The former Chimes Nightclub (now the Clapton Hart pub) is to be seen next door. (Photo Emily Webber)

A book published in 2004 with the damning title, *Crap Towns II*, reflected the media view of the London Borough of Hackney, and in particular the Clapton neighbourhood, at the dawn of the twenty-first century:

> The metropolitan bourgeoisie, after a few glasses of red, might roll their eyes at one another and mutter darkly about living close to "the front line", but the north-eastern corner of the borough, Clapton, is worse than that. It is interzone: it is down the rabbit-hole wrong…. The press dubbed the area "Murder Mile" but that's incidental. You don't need media scare stories, you can just walk around it for ten minutes to be terrified.

Hackney was (as it still is) a multi-racial inner city area of London, and recognised as one of the poorest boroughs, suffering from high unemployment, homelessness and dilapidated housing stock. In the 1960s, Clapton had been the home of the infamous Kray twins who ran their criminal empire from a block of flats off Upper Clapton Road, and knifed Jack 'the Hat' McVitie to death in a house in Evering Road in 1967. The criminals of the area tended to be home-grown, with many police and villains sharing a similar social background. This began to change with an influx of what were termed 'Yardie' gangsters from the Caribbean, fleeing from justice in their home countries.

The situation was particularly acute in Jamaica where, in the slums of West Kingston, the island's unemployed youth had armed themselves with handguns and ratchet knives so that the streets increasingly came to resemble a war zone. The general election in October 1980 proved the bloodiest in Jamaican history, with over 800 killed by rival gangs sponsored by political bosses. Two years earlier, Errol 'Rankin' Dread, wanted by police for a number of murders, fled to the United Kingdom and lived under various aliases, including Errol Codling. He set up base in Darenth Road, a street leading off Clapton Common. 'Rankin' Dread had been a DJ in Jamaica and had a minor UK chart success in the 1980s with the song 'Fatty Boom Boom', but soon became notorious for his criminal activities involving drug-dealing, armed robbery and prostitution, as well as murder. He was branded the most dangerous foreign national living in Britain.

By 1981, London's inner cities areas with large Afro-Caribbean communities, such as Hackney, Tottenham and Brixton, were in economic and social decline, with high unemployment, and a large proportion of low income households and one-parent families living in poor quality housing. That April, a serious riot erupted in Brixton in reaction to a Metropolitan Police operation aimed at reducing street crime, principally through use of the so-called 'Sus Law' which gave police the power to stop and search individuals on the basis of mere suspicion of wrongdoing. Feeling that they were being unfairly targeted, the black community rioted, resulting in widespread looting and damage to property. Similar unrest erupted that summer in Toxteth in Liverpool and Moss Side in Manchester. In response to this civil disorder, Lord Scarman in a report recognised the importance of community involvement in policing and called for a policy of "Direct coordinated attack on racial discrimination". He pointed out that "without close parental support, with no job to go to, and with few recreational facilities available, the young Black person makes his life the streets and the seedy, commercially-run clubs of Brixton. There he meets criminals, who appear to have no difficulty obtaining the benefits of a materialist society."

Errol 'Rankin' Dread was just such a criminal, with his drugs empire. In the late 1980s, the Metropolitan Police set up an intelligence unit in response to a warning from the US Drug Enforcement Agency about the highly addictive cocaine derivative known as 'crack'. However, when big crack seizures failed to materialise, the unit was disbanded by the summer of 1990. This was a very unfortunate decision, given the exponential rise in the use of crack in the following years, and consequent rise in violence allied to turf wars amongst the gangs involved in distribution of the dr

Kenneth Edwards, proprietor of the Palace Pavilion. (*Hackney Gazette*)

Looking back at how the police viewed the spiral of violence, the *Economist* wrote in 2002: "Drugs are part of the explanation: rival gangs are vying for control of the trade, occasionally kidnapping each other's mules… . But much of the violence arises from personal vendettas and petty slights: a quarrel at a New Year's Eve party at Hackney, which ended with a single bullet killing two people, is said to have started when someone trod on the wrong foot." The fatal shooting of 16-year-old Guy-Dance Dacres took place on 5 January 1997 at Chimes, one of two adjacent music venues favoured by black youth at the junction of Lower Clapton Road and Lea Bridge Roundabout. Chimes was owned by music producer Anthony Brightly, who had been co-founder of the British reggae group Black Slate in 1974. The owner of the Palace Pavilion next door was Admiral Ken, aka Kenneth Edwards, who had been resident DJ at the Bouncing Ball Club in Peckham, and whose sound system was regarded as one of the best in London.

Palace Pavilion playbill.

John Heale in his book, *One Blood: Inside Britain's Gang Culture,* makes clear that the shooting of Dacres was the result of a murderous feud between two gangs, Mandem from Tottenham and London Fields from Hackney. Heale describes how Dacres was accidentally shot by two Tottenham men who fired into a crowd of partygoers as a display of force. "The bullet passed through his head and hit a girl standing behind him who was lucky to survive. In response, another youth whose street name was Popcorn, was chased down by six men who beat him half to death and then shot him in the stomach.

The tit-for-tat killings escalated – two of the six convicted would themselves be shot dead in years to come."

The area surrounding Chimes and the Palace Pavilion emerged as the epicentre of what became known as the 'postcode wars' as gang members pursued their deadly vendettas against rivals. The litany of shootings and knife attacks attracted the attention of the national press, for whom the tag 'Murder Mile' was irresistible. Moreover, the conspiracy of silence in the black community often made it difficult for the police to identify the killer or secure a conviction. Warren Graham was stabbed to death on the dance floor of the Palace Pavilion in October 2004 in front of hundreds of clubbers. Graham's mother was still issuing an appeal for witnesses to his murder in the pages of the *Hackney Gazette* in 2012.

Chimes was shut down in 1997 when Anthony Brightly relocated to Antigua but it would be nine years after Dacres' murder that the police and Hackney Council finally took action to secure the closure of the Palace Pavilion. This followed the death of 19-year-old Barrington Williams-Samuels, who was machine-gunned as he sat in his parked car outside the club in January 2006. Cynics in the local community commented on the remarkable coincidence that Britain's successful bid for the 2012 Olympic Games had been announced only months before. Clapton's proximity to the site of the Olympic Park and the legacy resources channelled into Hackney were an important factor in the changes that the neighbourhood has undergone. Demographic change has produced a cluster of creperies, gastropubs, upmarket bars and coffee shops amongst what remains of the greasy spoon cafés, dingy drinking dens and massage parlours.

However, even where eggs and chips have given way to eggs benedict, there are indications in the media that Clapton's reputation as 'Murder Mile' will be difficult to shake off. Post-Olympics, the *Sunday Telegraph* of 17 February 2013 ran the headline 'Teenager Shot Dead in London's Murder Mile', as the fatal shooting of black teenager Joseph Burke-Monerville on Pembury Estate recalled the gangland savagery that had blighted Clapton. More recently, in September 2015, local residents were in a state of shock when Moses Fadairo was pursued by three men along busy Chatsworth Road on a Saturday afternoon and shot dead in front of horrified shoppers.

So, what of the future? Jules Pipe, whose term of office as Mayor of Hackney ended in 2016, delivered a message of optimism in his valedictory column in the council's newspaper, *Hackney Today*, but also indicated that there were challenges ahead: "Now every child has access to good and outstanding schools. It is this that will have the biggest effect on the life chances of children growing up here. It is access to a high quality education for all that will most effectively tackle entrenched inequality, and issues like gang crime. The big challenge for Hackney now, is to ensure that its growing prosperity can benefit everyone who lives here."

And yet… despite the official rhetoric of 'trickle-down' regeneration, the polarised nature of Clapton's gentrification has become increasingly apparent, with the growth of gastropubs going hand-in-hand with an increase in pawnshops catering for local people affected by child poverty, unemployment and welfare dependency. As long as these entrenched inequalities continue, a rise in academic achievement alone is unlikely to overcome the social problems arising from drugs and gang culture.

1998: The Four Aces Club is Condemned: last days of a musical legend – Winstan Whitter

The entrance to the Four Aces Club (under-age drinkers entered by the drainpipe and the ladies toilet window). (Photo David Corio)

So, it must have been around 1982 when I first went to the club, I was eight years old and bold! My father Mr Glenford Whitter, who was from a town called Kingston in Jamaica, was working at the Four Aces Club down the road from Stamford Hill where we lived. My father must of realised I was strong because it was hard work being a caterer and DJ at the club. This was my weekend's work; I was little Mr Removal Boy.

It all starts around 4.30pm in the hustle and bustle of West Green Road in Seven Sisters. First stop the butcher shop, lots of chicken is ordered. As it is being chopped up we would head down to the off licence to buy crates of soft drinks, beers, spirits and mixers to top up the bar. We stop at home to prepare the food and round 8pm we head to the club on Dalston Lane in my Dad's old classic Mercedes 280 and load in through the double doors. It was always very dark in there. I would have to feel my way to the stairs and down into the Hideaway in the basement.

Now, this building was a real labyrinth. Originally built as a circus in 1886, the great Dalston Coliseum, it later became the Dalston Theatre, Dalston Cinema, then a whole string of nightclubs with the New Four Aces being the last. It was also a poorhouse during the Great War and a used car showroom at one time.

Mr Newton Dunbar, Winston Wellington, Norman Mattis and Jimmy Nelson all fresh from Jamaica they created the Four Aces Club in 1966 in Highbury. It quickly became very popular as there weren't many places for the West Indian community to gather together at night like back home in the West Indies.

In 1967 Mr Dunbar and his colleagues needed to expand the club into a bigger venue, which is when they moved down to Dalston. The club only occupied the entrance hall at that time but that was big enough to hold over 1,000 people. Apparently this entrance hall was designed for Professor Collier's circus elephants in 1886 to enter backstage; hence the white curved arches which gave the venue its architectural character.

The year is still 1982 and at this time the Four Aces was split into two areas, the main floor with the big sound system and stage and bar and the basement called the Hideaway. This was a more mellow chill-out area where you could order food and drink and play dominoes.

It was a bit of a family business because my two older brothers Glen Jnr and Stanley would work there also. They would work the door, bar and help prepare and clean up the place. Glen Snr would manage the kitchen and DJ. So Dad, me and the squad would set up the club every Friday and Saturday night for years. Most times Dad would drop me home around 11/12pm-ish. For an eight-year-old it was pretty cool!

At that time the mainstream music that was being played was roots reggae, dub and lovers rock. Around 11pm the crowd began to arrive, the music sounded so heavy that I could lean against the bass lines. I mean, talk about vibration! I witnessed many times people's drinks jumping around, as did the people who were skanking to the grooves. At that time I was half the size of most people there. Visually everyone appeared pure silhouettes as described by Dennis Brown in his famous song 'Silhouette'. I'm sure he was talking about the Aces because there would be the maximum of two table lamps down there, people would be towering over me whilst clouds of smoke floated by, this made visibility even more misty in roots. I remember lovers rock music would be playing and it would just be couples dancing very slowly, locked in a permanent hug, some couples were literally up against a wall.

The other place I would go and hang out when the work was done would be up in Mr Newton's office/living room. It was like another club with a backstage vibe about it. Again, only one very low table light, CCTV screens, paintings, sculptures, TV, hi-fi system, smoke. People coming and going: young, old, men and women with me, the youngest member of the club, rubbing shoulders with all kinds of characters and getting ire from all the second-hand smoke.

Every now and again Mr Newton would be on his walkie-talkie giving instructions or telling someone off in his team, throwing people out that were too young to enter. Apparently the way in to the club was to climb up the drainpipe on Beechwood Road and enter through the ladies toilet window!

All the elders would be reminiscing about the West Indies, reflecting on their situation in England, music, politics, spiritual, food, conspiracies, sports, police and gal (women). I didn't really understand at the time but I sure do now!

Mr Newton also lived there and had his kitchen next door and lots of doorways with little rooms; looking back it kinda had the Alice in Wonderland vibe about it. There would be doorways that were half the width of a normal door, rooms that were only a couple of metres wide with an almost vertical stairway that led to a single bed. Under the table in Mr Newton's kitchen was a trap door with vertical stairs leading down like something out of a James Bond movie escape scene.

The year is now 1987, the year of doom and change for me. My father sadly passed away and my job came to an end, as did my time at the Four Aces.

It was in 1992 when friends of mine said we should go to this amazing Drum & Bass Club called Labyrinth. When we got off the bus at Dalston Junction I realised it was the same club. How bizarre it was to see the same old club with a completely different set of people and music. It was rammed – I mean at least 1,500 people in there!

I hit the buzzer and went backstage into what was such familiar territory; nothing had changed. Again, Mr Newton was hosting many cool characters – friends, artists, colleagues. I sat up there chatting and catching up with Newton and others and completely forgot about the friends I'd come with. I went back into the main dance floor to find them in the mayhem of white gloves, strobes, sweat dripping like rain, fluorescent backdrops, smoke machines, gurning faces, bottles of water, lots of whistles around necks and horn blowing.

By this time, the club used all three floors; there were various rooms all over the place with different styles of acid house playing. Some rooms just had a strobe light. And there was the garden, which was the real chill-out area where you could recover from the smoke.

We went many times over the years. I think it was 1993 or 1994 when we were sitting in the attic about 5am, cooling out to the music and rolling a joint, when all of a sudden the door gets kicked in by about 10 policemen in riot gear. We were so mellow that we didn't even flinch. About five of them jumped on top of this really big man like he had a rugby ball in his hands that the police were scrambling for and dragged the poor, battered bloke out. Apparently he was a drug dealer of some sort, but he was dealt with like some kind of terrorist. We were kinda in shock but continued to roll our joint before we left.

Leaving the club was always a good run for your money. It's bright and sunny and there was an ice-cream van directly outside at 5am serving fried fish and dumplings. Dalston Lane at that point had huge traffic jams due to the amount of people trying to leave the club, most of whom are lost 10 feet away from the club.

Back in 1996 I revisited the club which had changed direction once again from acid house back to dub, soul and hip-hop. My brother Stanley was still working there and that was when he told me about the history of the club and the big artists performing there in the 1960s. I was now studying film-making at college and he suggested that I make a film about the club. That was when the history of the club and the history of my life combined.

Sometime in 1998 Newton received a notice to leave the club under a compulsory purchase order. We had no idea what was really going to happen, so I continued to document everything going on. I filmed the last two years of the Four Aces Club until it closed in 1999. I still had a feeling that this building was special, so continued even when it was falling into a terrible condition. We found out that the whole theatre was earmarked for demolition in 2005. So, we the people of Hackney, through the organisation called Open Dalston, fought this decision, but it was too late. In early 2007, the council began to demolish the building. Now there is a place called Dalston Square where the Four Aces used to be and there are a lot of new venues opening up, but none of them can compare with the Four Aces.

Playbills for The Four Aces Club.

Fortunately, though the venue has disappeared, Newton Dunbar and myself have managed to help keep its history alive through the films that I have made: *Legacy in the Dust: The Four Aces Story* and *Save Our History*, as well as through Newton sharing his story. We still laugh and reminisce on those good times. One of Newton's classic quotes is, "The club for what it was is a one off, and there will never be another place like The Four Aces."

1999: The Restoration of the Aziziye Mosque: the Turkish community in Hackney – Muttalip Unluer

The restored Azizye Mosque, Stoke Newington Road. (Photo Simon Mooney)

Although it was a warm and balmy night, all was momentarily deathly quiet in Dalston on 20 June 2008. The reason – a penalty shoot-out in the Euro quarter finals between Croatia and Turkey with the winner progressing to face mighty Germany in the semi-finals. As Mladan Petric stepped up to take the decisive kick the Turkish goalkeeper Rü tü dived to save it and Turkey were through. Kingsland High Street erupted at once with joy. From every doorway, pub, restaurant and basement jubilant supporters streamed out and Dalston became a cavalcade of blaring horns and waving flags. Hackney's Turkish community was in celebration.

This community – my community – is an important and settled part of Hackney today. Census figures for 2011 show that 4.5 per cent of Hackney's residents gave Turkish as their mother tongue, making it the borough's second language. How did we get here, and how have we fared since we arrived?

The first to arrive in Hackney after the Second World War were Cypriot Turks. As British subjects, they could come without restriction and immigration of manual workers from Commonwealth countries was actively encouraged by the government to overcome labour shortages in the 1950s. At the same time, friction between Greek and Turkish communities in Cyprus contributed to an exodus from the island of younger people seeking a more certain future elsewhere.

Hackney was an attractive destination, having an established diverse community with a long tradition of welcoming immigrants and (at that time) plenty of cheap accommodation to rent or buy. Most importantly, it was a major centre for clothing and footwear manufacture with a large number of small manufacturers, mostly Jewish-owned, in constant need of workers. Although there were some large clothing businesses, including Simpson's and Burberry, the industry consisted mainly of small enterprises with significant numbers employed as pieceworkers in their own homes. It has been estimated that in 1979 60 per cent of Cypriot women (Turkish and Greek) in London were employed in the textile and clothing industry, many as home workers.

The second wave of immigration, beginning in the early 1970s, was predominantly from mainland Turkey. Although immigration policies were becoming more restrictive, permits were available to bring in qualified workers in trades with labour shortages. At this time, strange as it may seem today, high street stores sold mainly British-made clothing, much of it produced in Hackney. Every week, the *Hackney Gazette* carried up to 12 pages of advertisements for employment in the clothing trade: machinists, lining-makers, piecers-up, felling hands, underpressers, Hoffman Pressers and others; all were in demand and there was more work to do than people to do it. By this time, significant numbers of first-wave arrivals had become employers themselves and could arrange permits for the workers they needed. Typically, everything was arranged – flights, permits, accommodation (often in cramped conditions) and employment at the lowest wages.

Fortunately, there was no system of bonded labour and the new arrivals soon saw that they could jump ship to better-paid work. The most enterprising (and Turks have always been entrepreneurial) could see that they could improve their income by dealing with the makers of finished garments at the top of the chain, cutting out the middleman. This could be the first step to becoming an employer – taking on workers, generally on a sub-contract basis, to supply the pieces to make up the garments. This pattern of upward mobility was uncannily similar to the pattern of Jewish workers arriving in London two or three generations earlier. Many of the most successful followed the Jewish example in another respect, fanning out from Hackney to leafier suburbs such as Southgate and Palmers Green.

This thriving business sector unfortunately collapsed in the 1980s and 1990s as the dismantling of import restrictions and competition between high street chains wiped out the British supply chain. The response of the community has been strongly directed to self-employment. Turkish-owned businesses predominate in many sectors of the local economy, including retailing (particularly food), restaurants, dry-cleaning, motor repair, minicab offices, nightclubs, off-licences and entertaining. Our great road artery, Kingsland High Street, which becomes Stoke Newington High Street, is dominated by Turkish businesses and the braziers of our restaurants, grilling healthy lean meat, attract visitors from far and wide.

Meanwhile, what of our religious and cultural institutions? Turkish people are predominantly Sunni Muslims and, whilst many are non-practising, they define themselves as Muslims and the leading Turkish community organisations are mostly Islamic in character.

The first Turkish mosque was opened by the UK Turkish Islamic Trust in Green Lanes in 1974. It served a small number of people for daily and Friday prayers and it soon became clear that a larger place of worship was needed. In 1977 the Trust bought a redundant synagogue on Shacklewell Lane to convert to a fully functional mosque which served nearly 600 worshippers at any given time.

In 1979 a new charity was set up, the UK Turkish Islamic Association, with the objective of establishing an additional mosque to serve the needs of the growing community with services provided in the Turkish language. In 1983 the association bought the Astra Cinema in Stoke Newington Road, a 'fleapit' which had seen better days and was by this time serving up a programme of martial arts and sex films. The work of raising funds and conversion was to take another 15 years.

The result has been a fantastic and gorgeous building in the Ottoman style. The façades have blue, turquoise and white tiles, gold cupolas and mosaic columns, bronze window frames and a great dark green dome, together making a great landmark. Non-worshippers can experience some of the ambience of the building in the exquisite blue-tiled restaurant at the front of the building. The newly restored mosque finally opened its doors to worshippers in 1999.

Over the same period, another group, the UK Turkish Islamic Cultural Centre, first opened the Suleymaniye Mosque and cultural centre in a flat above a supermarket in Kingsland Road. Determined fundraising (with support from Turkish associations in Germany) enabled the centre to build the remarkable mosque which opened in 1999 and is now headquarters of a nationwide charity focusing on education and social welfare. It is built over six floors with a dramatic double height worship space.

Self-expression is found in other ways too. There are several Turkish language London-based newspapers and, until recently, London Turkish Radio broadcast 24 hours a day. Two annual festivals of Turkish culture are held in Clissold Park. The Anatolian Cultural Festival in May celebrates traditional and conservative cultural practices, including Ottoman marching bands and whirling dervishes. The Daymer Festival in June or July is more political and left-wing with strong involvement of the Turkish Kurdish community.

And then there is football. The Turkish Community Football Federation organises a league of two divisions, many teams representing players from their area of origin in Turkey. At a time when grassroots football is declining, there are games of high standard between these teams down at Hackney Marshes. As for the many shop premises bearing the name of leading Turkish teams, they too combine enthusiasm for the game, but often admixed with gambling.

I have made a brief reference to the Kurdish community. This was established in Hackney mainly in the early 1980s at a time when there was a great deal of tension between the Turkish government and Kurdish separatists. Many of these Kurdish refugees were from a more educated background than other Turkish arrivals. Kurdish is a wholly separate language but Kurds originating from Turkey also speak Turkish and there are considerable numbers of Kurds worshipping at Aziziye and other mosques. There are also community organisations including Halkevi and Daymer to which many Kurds belong. Inevitably, the recurrence of tension between the Turkish government and separatists is also reflected in differing views here in Hackney.

So our community is in good – but not yet in perfect – shape. Whilst there has been some progress towards the professions in our younger generation, this has not been as fast or as widespread as hoped. The cost of university education has often been regarded as prohibitive and rising fees can only make this worse. Very few members of our community have made their way in the financial services industry on our doorstep, and it is probably fair to say that unacknowledged discrimination works against our young people. And the predominance of older people who work on their own, or in Turkish family-owned businesses, means that too many have poor English-language skills. Like any community, at any time, we are still a work in progress.

A Turkish machinist pictured in 1981. (Photo Neil Martinson)

2000: The Arcola Theatre, Sweet Smell of Success – Mehmet Ergen

An Arcola Theatre production, 2012. (Courtesy Arcola Theatre. Photo Simon Annand)

I arrived in London in 1987 from Turkey, as a young man of 22, with very little English. I was instantly taken with the city, and began to expand my vocabulary by cycling around, listening to Shakespeare audiobooks and trying to remember the lyrics to English songs I had played in Istanbul, during a brief stint as a nightclub DJ. I had, however, brought with me a great love of theatre, nurtured by a nine-month acting course and, with little more than that, I declared myself a director. I placed ads in the *Stage*, inviting actors to join my 'company', and we began to put on plays anywhere that would have us!

The fringe theatre tradition was in full swing, but held mainly in basements or former pool rooms at the back of pubs and cafés, which meant working within the hours and conditions set by the primary business. Actors, for example, were obliged to apply make-up in the same toilets used by pub customers. I found myself watching my own productions to the unexpected soundtrack of live football, a live band or – if I was really unlucky – karaoke. We could try to improve things, but invariably would be told that "this is a pub first". We were also very limited in terms of what to do on the stage itself: no nails, no screws, no water, no sand, no soil. If we could paint, it was always with the dreaded caveat: "paint back to black".

When at last I decided to open a theatre, Southwark Playhouse, I made sure the contract stated: "Do what you like, but do NOT paint it back to black". To this day, badly-hung black drapes and gaffer tape trying to cover staple marks upset me as much as a boring set. If there's no room for creativity, there's no room for theatre. You need a different room.

Southwark was a success, and I developed a habit of spotting light industrial spaces and imagining them as theatres. While I was teaching in Dalston in early 2000, I discovered the building that was to become the Arcola Theatre, an old clothing factory down a small dark street off Stoke Newington High Street. The rag trade in Hackney was in decline, but during our first years of operation there was still a working factory upstairs. Göknur, who ran it, told us that in days gone by you could hear the bells and horns of dozens of factories in the area, announcing lunch breaks for hundreds of local workers. By the time we arrived there were far fewer workers, but the building had that something special that makes the imagination light up, a promise of endless possibilities. There were others who had their eyes on the property, either for a snooker hall or a cash'n'carry, but together with my co-founder Leyla Nazli, we took out a £5,000 credit card debt, and secured the lease.

Now we needed to turn it into a theatre. An actor I had worked with previously, Rebecca Lenkiewicz, had just written a play which I very much admired. I called her immediately and said I had a new space. She arrived the next day to be greeted by an empty warehouse, with all the remnants of its former life as a shirt factory – sewing machines, rolls of fabric and empty boxes – still scattered about.

So, along, with Leyla, Rebecca, and the great Jack Shepherd, we sent invitations to all the theatre people that we knew to join us for a paint party. Arcola's first seating system was made up from the factory's former cutting tables. There was no money for steel decks, so the wooden levels were furnished with benches sourced from a recently-closed Indian restaurant.

Our first season show-cased Rebecca's new play, and works by and influenced by Shakespeare, all with a distinct smell of curry in the air.

The Arcola Theatre and Café Oto, Ashwin Street: the hub of hip Dalston. (Photos Simon Mooney)

There were, in theory, no limits on the shows we could stage or the ways we could stage them. In reality, however, managing an independent space meant overcoming practical and financial challenges of a totally different order; challenges that were also going to require some creative thinking.

People were not necessarily sold on the concept. The *Evening Standard* in 2001 observed:

Only a truly creative man, or a lunatic, would pass by a deserted sewing machine factory in a Dalston side-street and immediately see its potential as a theatre.... . Mehmet Ergen may be a mixture of the two, but the case against locking him up is strengthened by the fact that the Arcola Theatre has just opened its second studio space, while his co-director on the new main-stage production of *A Midsummer Night's Dream* is Jack Shepherd. An actor, writer and director as eminent as Shepherd wouldn't get involved with a madman. Would he?.

Over the next decade, I managed to avoid being locked up and – gradually – we built a theatre. By 'we', I mean the Arcola's small staff and, crucially, a legion of extraordinary volunteers. We all painted walls, carried planks, tore tickets, served drinks and kept the shows going night after night. In time we developed better seating, better lighting, better everything. Most importantly of all, we developed an audience. Emboldened by the warm embrace of our audience, and the calibre of artists who were now approaching us to present work, we grew, eventually to four studios, all built and un-built by passionate volunteers and friends, and still with the rule – never paint back to black.

The theatre establishment continued with their reservations. Charles Spencer, then lead theatre critic for the *Telegraph*, wrote in a review for our 2009 production of Timberlake Wertenbaker's *The Line*, starring Henry Goodman:

Reviewers should be honest about their prejudices and one of mine is a great dislike for the Arcola Theatre in darkest Dalston. It's a nightmare to get to, and when you finally arrive in the neighborhood you find yourself on a menacing main street, often patrolled by terrifying hooded youths, and with shops that seem to consist entirely of cut-price supermarkets, kebab establishments and, rather bizarrely, gentlemen's hairdressers. A colleague had his pocket picked and his wallet removed on his way to *The Line*, and seemed to regard it as par for the course. The foyer is warm and welcoming but the auditorium is cramped and stuffy with a claustrophobically low ceiling. It was once a garment-trade sweatshop. Now it's a sweatshop for out-of-sorts theatre critics.

Until recently, this review hung proudly in the bar of our new space, a reminder of where we, and Hackney more widely, have come from. It also represented a reminder to the press, industry and London more widely, not to discount the ingenuity and ambition of this borough.

By 2011, when the landlord told us that the theatre would need to leave Arcola Street so that the factory could be turned into private flats, we had staged hundreds of shows and welcomed thousands of people, many of them first-time theatregoers. The journey couldn't end here, and with the generous support of Hackney Council, we were offered another former factory – Colourworks Paint – just down the road on Ashwin Street. It meant that we could keep our place in the community, and – in the bigger and better space – aspire to making bigger and better shows.

At our new location, we were determined to recreate the buzz and atmosphere of the first Arcola, a place to hang out, and as different as possible from the formal, pre-meditated spaces of the commercial theatre. This building brought challenges of its own. Heavily damaged in the Second World War, it had been used since as an office for various community and political organisations, as a squat, and as a venue for illegal raves and parties.

Our Executive Director, Dr Ben Todd, who started as a volunteer, brought all his previous experience working to develop low emission, environmentally friendly, hydrogen fuel cells for companies such as Rolls-Royce. We were aiming to create the world's first Carbon Neutral Theatre. The press called this ambition, "The Theatre of Dreams". With financial support from Arts Council England, Hackney Council, and thousands of individuals, we raised the capital to begin the transformation. In a building process that lasted little more than two months, we recreated two professional studio theatres, a workshop and rehearsal space, café/bar and green technology incubator. We also added a second workshop/rehearsal space to accommodate a burgeoning youth and community programme. All of it retains the industrial, 'found-space' atmosphere of our former building.

What was most heart-warming was that the majority of building work was achieved by mobilising nearly a thousand volunteers supervised by an in-house foreman and a site manager seconded from Hackney Council. The final step was to move all the furniture, costume and props to Ashwin Street. Drawing inspiration from a Filipino tradition, a Bayanihan (where the whole village join to help a family move house), we formed a procession of over a hundred staff and volunteers, led by a brass band, that weaved its way down Kingsland Road to carry the 'old' Arcola to the 'new'.

Our new building has given us the scope to extend our engagement with the local community. We offer free rehearsal space to local groups; stage works by new writers and the opportunity for performance both to experienced actors and to complete novices. The entire process has also spun off a sister company, Arcola Energy, providing support to companies in the energy, transport and construction sectors who want to explore, develop and deploy fuel-cell systems and products.

And as we have developed, Dalston has developed around us. An early visit to Arcola Street was seen as an 'adventure' by many of our audiences. Now our new home in Ashwin Street is at the very heart of the 'Dalston Quarter'. With our neighbours at Café Oto, Bootstrap, Shiloh Pentecostal Church, the Eastern Curve Garden, and others, Ashwin Street is a hive of activity, especially on warm summer evenings.

A *Guardian* article noted that "The Arcola's independence means it can treat drama more seriously than pub fringe, while not forgetting it's part of a poor and mixed community." We are still a part of that community, and we still take drama seriously, commissioning and producing new work from major artists as well as from some of the most exciting up-and-coming talent. And best of all, you can watch an entire production with 0% risk of karaoke.

2001: Gardening Communities go Organic: horticulture in Hackney – Margaret Willes

Members of Growing Communities harvesting lettuces in the backlands of Stoke Newington.
(Courtesy of Growing Communities)

Furniture-making and garment-making are often described as the traditional industries of Hackney, but horticulture can claim a much longer tradition. Market gardening in all parts of what now constitutes the borough has over the centuries supplied the capital with vital food, while the nurserymen of Hoxton made this area a horticultural hub long before high-tech businesses moved in.

Today, these market gardens and nurseries are just memories, submerged under bricks and mortar, though occasionally recalled in street names. The borough is, in fact, well provided with green open spaces including Victoria Park, Clissold Park, London Fields, and Abney Park Cemetery. The gardens attached to the Geffrye, echoing the theme of the period rooms of the museum, show the various styles of domestic garden history. But the horticultural desire lives on, and while some residents have their own gardens, many do not. The answer would seem to lie in gardening communities and community gardens.

The Hackney Allotment Society, founded in 1979, has nine sites across the borough, with one group in Clapton by the River Lea and another in Stoke Newington. It seems extraordinary now to realise that in the 1960s the future for allotments looked bleak. The Thorpe Report commissioned by the Wilson government recommended that the word 'allotment' carried the stigma of charity and needed to be replaced by the concept of the leisure garden with sites improved to become recreational facilities for the whole family following examples in other European countries. In addition, the report declared "There is certainly no evidence to suggest that many immigrants from Africa, Asia or the West Indies have taken to allotment gardening; it remains essentially a British pursuit." The report's creator, Harry Thorpe, professor of geography at Birmingham University, was wildly wrong on both counts, and in the 1970s a social revolution took place, with the middle classes discovering the joy of allotments, taking them up alongside the immigrant communities who had always recognised the opportunity to cultivate their fruit and vegetables. The demand for allotments shot up in urban areas all over the country.

Meeting this demand was particularly difficult in Hackney with the prospect of the Wick becoming one of the major sites of the Olympic Games. The Manor Garden Allotments had been bequeathed to East End families 'in perpetuity' by the Hon. Arthur Villiers in 1900. These eighty-one plots occupied a secluded site between the River Lea and the Lead Mill Stream, and were until 2007 cultivated by a multi-national community, as celebrated in a cookery book, *Moro East*, by the restaurateurs Sam and Sam Clark. But this book serves as memorial, for despite a vociferous campaign, the site was compulsorily purchased, bull-dozed and buried under the Olympic Park. Although the allotment holders were compensated by being given replacement plots outside the borough, the unmet demand for plots continued to rise, so that the Hackney Allotment Society took the decision in 2008 to close their waiting list. I have heard the quip that it is easier to become the member of an exclusive gentleman's club in St James's than to acquire an allotment in Hackney. At a recent annual general meeting of the Society an anxious discussion took place on how to bring down the waiting time, and the search for new sites was reported.

One alternative for frustrated allotmenteers is offered by Growing Communities. This project, set up in 1996 by Julie Brown and a group of friends, was ambitious: community-supported agriculture, harnessing local buying power to help make small-scale farming once again economically viable, while also providing people in the city with better, fresher food. Initially the scheme linked thirty families up with a farm in Buckinghamshire, with Julie bringing back fresh vegetables to her neighbours at an early hour, "right under the nose of the local Sainsburys". These same neighbours could join weekend working trips on the farm to help with the watercress harvest, plant plum trees and pick caterpillars off Brussels sprouts.

Such was the success of these trips that sites were found in Hackney to be transformed into plots. The first was acquired in 1997, a tiny piece of land by the old butterfly tunnel in Clissold Park, followed by the Oak Tree site in Bethune Road, alas lost seven years later due to building development. Several small market gardens have now been established in Clissold Park, Springfield Park, Allen's Gardens in Stoke Newington, and other patches on estates, church land and private gardens, appropriately known as the Patchwork Farm. A significant development took place in 2001, when Growing Communities applied to get three of the 'patches' organically certified, the first to be so designated in London. The following year, the first fully organic 'Hackney salads' were included in the vegetable bags. In addition to the vegetable bag scheme, the produce is sold at farmers' markets and plant sales are held annually in Springfield Park.

Volunteers help the growers on the different plots, but the scheme has also trained up young people in the skills of organic gardening. By 2016 the total reached 42, some trained at the scheme's organic farm in Dagenham, on the site of a derelict council plant nursery. Here too the trainees, previously unemployed lone parents, were also taught cooking and food selling skills. Some graduates now have jobs as growers in various parts of London and elsewhere, including Zimbabwe.

Another communal scheme is the charity, the Urban Orchard Project. The orchards of Stoke Newington were particularly known for the quality of their fruit during the eighteenth century, so it is appropriate that the project was originally based in Hackney, although the programme is spreading northwards to Birmingham, Manchester and Scotland. One of the people who helped to set up the scheme was Russell Miller. Russell was also responsible for the creation of the Tree Musketeers, a Hackney-based volunteer group that plants and cares for trees. Tucked away behind the changing rooms on Hackney Marsh is Hackney Community Tree Nursery, provided with the support of the council. Here trees are raised from seeds in pots by volunteers and potted on from year to year until ready to be planted out in autumn in parks around the borough.

London, in common with other cities, was once full of orchards, both in private gardens and in parks and institutions, but these have largely been neglected or built over. As a result, many rare fruit varieties have been lost, along with the skills in nurturing and maintaining the orchards. The Orchard Project, with help from the Heritage Lottery, corporate partnerships and trust funding, has brought people together and trained them to prune and look after trees planted on Hackney housing estates and in Haggerston Park. England is particularly rich in cultivars of apples, and the project aims to revive interest in these, and even in 2012 developed its own new London cultivar, named 'Core Blimey' as a result of a competition.

In addition, there are several community gardens in the borough. In Pearson Street in Haggerston is St Mary's Secret Garden. This was established in 1986 when local volunteers started to clear a disused green space and to engage with the local community and disabled groups. The garden has four linked sections: natural woodland; an area for growing food, including vegetable beds, soft fruit bushes and fruit trees; a herb and sensory garden; and an area of herbaceous borders. It is also home to The Golden Company's honey bees. The watchword at St Mary's is well-being, with the garden offering work and volunteering experience, educational outreach and therapeutic sessions.

While St Mary's Secret Garden is in a comparatively peaceful spot, the Eastern Curve Garden is right in the busiest heart of Dalston. Created from unused land that was once part of a railway line, the Eastern Curve has been planted with trees, such as birch and hazel, shrubs friendly to wild life, and raised beds for plants and vegetables. A glasshouse, the Pineapple House, has also been erected. The garden has become a great favourite with children, particularly on special nights, such as Halloween, when it is adorned with thousands of illuminated pumpkins. The days of the Eastern Curve Garden, however, may be numbered, for this is a prime area for redevelopment.

As I write this, the Eastern Curve Garden is still with us, but the threat hanging over it is a reminder that, like the Manor Gardens allotments and sites cultivated by Growing Communities, green spaces in Hackney are very vulnerable at a time when real estate has become so prodigiously profitable.

Pumpkins in St Mary's Secret Garden in deepest Haggerston. (Photo The Gentle Author)

Ready for potting on: trees raised from seed by volunteers at Hackney Community Tree Nursery. (Photo Glory Hall)

2002: A Pivotal Year for Hackney: from bleak place to beacon status
– Jessica Webb

I accidentally became a councilor in 2000 due to a surprise by-election in the ward of Wick. (Now re-named 'Hackney Wick'. Why? Who knows? Was anyone confused?) It was not a career choice, particularly given that the council of the London Borough of Hackney did not have a great reputation. In fact it deserved the really bad reputation it had, as by all accounts it was very poor at what it did. Let us take two key indicators: finance and education.

Finances

Hackney had the highest property tax in London despite having the greatest support from central funding and it only managed to collect 65 per cent of the tax due.

Overspending was 10-20 per cent of budget each year but there was no financial monitoring to understand how this occurred.

Education

Parents of more than 40 per cent of the borough's children sent their children to schools outside the borough due to lack of places and/or the quality of provision that existed.

I could mention that health indicators were worrying, crime was high and that there were no Tubes, a dismal train service and unreliable buses (so bad I had to take up cycling). In the *Guardian*, Jay Rayner wrote about "The worst run place in Britain?" Even *Hackney Today* has described it as a time of "managerial, political and financial breakdown that led to the near collapse of many Council services".

The council had been hung since 1996 and there had been no coalition between councillors or an identifiable leader of the authority up to 2002. This failure resulted in no political direction and poor or non-existent decision-making. One notable disaster was the out-sourcing of the housing revenues and benefits function to the company ITNet. Hackney had signed a contract with ITNet to sort out the delays in payment of housing benefits, but within two years the consequence was even more unpaid benefit, rent arrears, evictions, and snaking queues of desperate people outside the housing benefit office. A failing council has a human cost. My election manifesto could be boiled down to one line: get rid of ITNet.

My election slightly moved the political balance of the council towards Labour, but meetings were fraught affairs trying to agree 'vital signs' of functionality with the other parties. Votes were often 'recorded' which necessitated all councillors' surnames being read out like a school roll so we could state whether we were 'for' or 'against'. Being a 'W' did not help. In this way, the council managed to terminate the contract with ITNet, but so much remained in disarray. Budgets were frozen and streets got darker as there was no money to replace light bulbs. There were demonstrators outside the Town Hall as we sat shivering in the council chamber. The heating had broken and we could not afford to mend that either.

So, what happened to turn Hackney Council around from being extraordinarily poor to become rather good? It must be a combination of factors, but I have to give credit to the first directly elected mayor of Hackney and his role in Hackney's improvement.

In 2002 the government insisted that a referendum be held to decide whether Hackney should have a directly elected mayor. It was an attempt to get locally elected representatives to run a better service, failing which central government would take control of the council. It was a drastic step into the unknown, promoting a new political fashion for a mayoral system.

I wondered, would having a mayor improve the situation? Could it get worse? What if we got the comedy candidate (like the football mascot H'Angus the Monkey who became mayor of Hartlepool in 2002) or a media personality (like Eastender Barbara Windsor)? The people of Hackney in the referendum of May 2002 voted to have a mayor. The council election was held at the same time and brought in a large Labour majority (45 out of 57 seats). And in October 2002 we had our first directly elected mayor, Jules Pipe (Labour too). So, what were we going to do?

Jules Pipe set out priorities including improving services for all, raising the life chances of the most disadvantaged, and making sure that the council was high performing and efficient. But he could not do anything without money. Hackney's financial situation could not have been worse: insufficient tax collected to fund the planned budget; unmonitored overspending; reactive emergency measures, which included the sale of property assets; and little scope for long-term planning.

To sort this out, Jules brought in comprehensive financial monitoring across the entire organisation. Exact revenue spend on services and capital spend on large projects were reported every month, with projected full-year spend reported to cabinet meetings chaired by the mayor. Qualified finance staff were placed within directorates to oversee financial practices. Robust systems were introduced regarding the buying of goods and services. Such processes formed the foundation on which the future success of Hackney Council's transformation was based. It enabled the authority to be stable and not get knocked off course by unexpected cash flow problems or shortfalls.

At the same time, governance and management had to be established. There needed to be clarity as to how decisions were made and staff were pulled into a performance culture where indicators needed to be relevant, understood and achievable. These processes were not important for their own sakes, but to make the council functional again so it could serve the people of Hackney.

Making Hackney a great place to live, epitomised by the 'I ♥ Hackney' campaign, was ultimately about service improvement. Not just looking after families through welfare services, but doing other things like keeping the streets clean and replacing light bulbs. The list could go on, with such things as having pleasant parks, leisure centres and libraries. So, by most ways of measuring, 2002 was a year when Hackney Council started to turn itself around and walk towards financial stability and good public services.

Taking things to 2016 the two indicators have changed:

Finances

- 10 years of council tax freeze
- No cuts to the most important council services such as social services; £120 million in austerity cuts imposed by central government have been absorbed

Education

- Families want to send their children here!
- All existing secondary schools rebuilt or refurbished

- Six new secondary schools built
- Almost every school in the borough now rated 'good' or 'outstanding'

Also, as we have become a sane and sensible borough, other bodies have felt more comfortable talking to us. Our transport links have vastly improved and we fully participated as one of the host boroughs for the Olympics. Hackney Council has won many awards and can point to plenty of statistics to show how it has improved across the board. I asked Jules Pipe which was his favourite one. It was 'Council of the Last 20 Years' from the 2016 Local Government Chronicle Awards.

It would be wrong to say that all is rosy with Hackney Council. Whilst I acknowledge that the council works within huge financial constraints, there are plenty of examples where I feel it has and still does fail. Poor response and service by Hackney Homes for the most urgent and obvious faults within our housing stock come to mind. This department has recently been returned in-house and I look forward to a major culture change there. In addition, I appreciate that our Planning Department can be infuriating and that Parking Control officers' view of what constitutes consultation is sometimes skew-whiff.

However, even the hardiest Tory commentators have credited Jules Pipe as mayor for being a major player in turning Hackney around and making it a place where people really do want to live and work. Certainly there were pockets of artistic creatives and residents of wealth who weathered Hackney's bleaker days. These have been able to enlarge and consolidate. However despite 'gentrification' and an influx of hipsters, Hackney still has much poverty and the needs of our community remain pressing, particularly in these times of austerity.

At the time of writing, we have a new mayor, Phil Glanville, and I look forward to seeing him continue to maintain Hackney's rather good reputation. He has been a stalwart campaigner for affordable housing within Hackney's cabinet over many years, and this has to be our greatest challenge. I could not have predicted the transformation that has occurred in Hackney since I joined the council, but let us agree that much has been accomplished and there is much still to do. Good luck Phil.

2003: The Save the Reservoirs Campaign – Monica Blake

The former prosaically named East Reservoir, now the Woodberry Wetlands nature reserve.
(Photo Simon Mooney)

The Stoke Newington reservoirs are an oasis in the heart of a densely built-up area and a haven for birds and other wildlife. This is the story of a campaign that lasted almost 20 years to save them from development.

The site is of historic importance. The reservoirs were fed by the New River, an artificial waterway built to supply London with clean drinking water from springs in Hertfordshire. Completed in 1613 by Sir Hugh Myddelton, the New River was one of the greatest engineering works of its time, and the New River Company was one of the world's first companies. The reservoirs were constructed by the Company's engineer, William Chadwell Mylne, between 1830 and 1833, with banks faced with stone from Old London Bridge. Filter beds were added to ensure the cleanliness of the water following a cholera outbreak in 1850. Two of these were the first to be built in England.

In 1856 Mylne built a pumping station to house three steam engines. It was in the style of a castle because local residents (in what was then a very affluent area) objected to an industrial-looking building and insisted on a construction that would enhance their neighbourhood and be a source of civic pride. It was listed Grade II* in 1972. The West Reservoir Centre, built in 1936, Newnton Close Bridge, dating from the eighteenth century, and the mid-nineteenth-century Ivy Sluice House are Grade II listed, as is the nineteenth-century Gas House, which once produced the chlorine gas used to treat the reservoir water. The latter is now known as the Coal House as it has also served as a kitchen for the New River Company directors' dining hall and as a coal store for a nearby boiler house. The waterman's house of 1911 is locally-listed.

In 1985 Thames Water Authority announced that the soon-to-be-completed London Water Ring Main (an aquatic equivalent of the M25) would make the southern portion of the New River redundant, and along with it the Stoke Newington Reservoirs and filter beds. The company proposed to decommission them and sell the site for development. Local people were outraged. They came together to form the Save the Reservoirs, New River and Filter Beds Campaign. In a parallel campaign, people living along the beloved New River formed the New River Action Group to prevent its closure.

Save the Reservoirs aimed to preserve the reservoirs and filter beds for amenity, recreation and education. For more than a decade, Campaign members met as a management committee on an almost monthly basis. Although membership changed over time, there were generally some 20-30 active members plus many more supporters. The Campaign organised public meetings, issued press releases, fundraised, had a presence at local events and produced a newsletter. It responded to the successive proposals put forward by Thames Water and developed its own ideas for the site. Initially Thames Water wanted to concrete over the entire site and sell it to developers. Campaigners wanted to use the East Reservoir as a nature reserve and the West Reservoir as a boating and water sports centre. Ideas for the filter beds included swimming pools, a fish farm, garden centre, children's play area and allotments.

A breakthrough came in 1986 when Hackney Council, supported by the Campaign, recommended that the site become a Conservation Area, giving a degree of protection. Local planning guidance from the council emphasised the importance of preserving the open character of the site. Thames Water's objections to Hackney's planning policy for the site were rejected by a Government Planning Inspector in 1994.

In 1987 Thames Water came back proposing to build housing on the East Reservoir, with mixed housing and leisure use on the West Reservoir and a retail park on the filter beds. However, a year later, the company announced a scheme to retain the New River and the East Reservoir at Stoke Newington, but proposed extensive development of the filter beds and West Reservoir.

With the success of saving the East Reservoir and New River, the Campaign focused its attention on the West Reservoir and filter beds. In 1992 it published a consultation report, *Local Voices, Local Views*, showing that 75 per cent of local people were in favour of retaining water in the West Reservoir. There was very strong support for a nature reserve on the East Reservoir, with at least some public access, and educational facilities for schools. People were overwhelmingly opposed to any built development on the filter beds. Meanwhile Thames Water unveiled plans to drain the West Reservoir.

The Campaign broke off talks with Thames Water over its refusal to discuss the future of the whole site. It launched a sub-campaign, *Stop Thames Water Pulling the Plug*, to focus public attention on the continuing threat to the West Reservoir. The Campaign bought 100 Thames Water shares and transferred them to individual supporters, enabling them to attend the company's Annual General Meeting. In July 1993, the Campaign presented a petition with over 3,000 signatures to the AGM, and many supporters asked questions at this meeting. The council pressed Thames Water for details of the costs of keeping water in the West Reservoir. Education and Leisure staff explored the scope for sailing at Stoke Newington.

In 1995 Thames Water finally buckled in the face of this sustained campaigning. It handed over the West Reservoir to Hackney Council to develop as a leisure facility. In return, the company was allowed to build houses on the site of the filter beds. Whilst this was a great disappointment to campaigners, the outcome represented a success for sustained and dogged resistance. In that same year the Castle Pumping Station opened as a climbing centre. Suggestions for this building had included conversion to an industrial museum, a community centre or an arts centre. However, its development for climbing has proved a great success. Not only is climbing an innovative use of an unusual building, but income from the venture ensures a financially sound future.

On 26 June 2003, the Rt Hon. Richard Caborn MP (Minister for Sport) officially opened the art deco former filtration plant, with its magnificent engineering hall, as the Stoke Newington West Reservoir Centre providing a venue for water sports – a further success story for the Campaign. With the aid of National Lottery funding, the restoration and refurbishment of the building were carried out by Marks Barfield Architects.

The last newsletter of the Campaign was published in May 1999. Campaign meetings ceased until briefly revived in 2004 when there was a danger of new developments on the East Reservoir. This concern finally proved to be groundless. The Campaign then decided to dissolve itself and donated the remaining funds to the charities London Wildlife Trust and Friends of Hackney Archives. A meeting to hand over cheques and unveil a plaque commemorating the Campaign was held at the West Reservoir Centre in 2006.

Woodberry Wetlands on the East Reservoir is the latest legacy of the Campaign. Created by the London Wildlife Trust, the site, closed to the general public since 1833, was officially opened by Sir David Attenborough on 30 April 2016. New boardwalks allow public access at a safe distance from reed beds and other important habitats. Screening

The former West Reservoir, now a sailing centre. The former engineering hall can be seen behind the reservoir. (Photo Monica Blake)

and hides allow closer access (though some paths are closed to the public during the nesting season). The Coal House has been renovated as a café with a new roof terrace allowing spectacular views of both reservoirs. Funding for the project was provided by the Heritage Lottery Fund, Thames Water, Hackney Council and Berkeley Homes.

The Campaign's success owed a great deal to the solid support of the local community: from the residents of Lincoln Court and the vast Woodberry Down Estate, through to people living in surrounding streets, and to local businesses who funded leaflets and other campaign activities. It helped that Campaign supporters – who included lawyers, journalists, photographers and artists – offered their skills for free. In addition, MPs Diane Abbott and Jeremy Corbyn made speeches in support of the Campaign in the House of Commons, with the former describing the site as "a secret garden" in her constituency; Barbara Windsor unveiled a mural by local artist John Allman; and John Hegley wrote a poem about the reservoirs and allowed the Campaign to reproduce it on a postcard to raise funds.

It is ironic that the reservoirs are now celebrated by a new generation of property developers. The sales literature of Berkeley Homes, advertising the new Woodberry Park Estate, boast that their "Nature Collection" of waterside apartments invites residents to enjoy the harmony of living "beside a tranquil nature reserve... with stunning views of the London skyline and beyond". It is unlikely that the investors snapping up these apartments will ever know that this beautiful waterside was preserved from development by the persistent efforts of a small group of campaigners who were prepared to fight to save our natural environment.

Further Information

Monica Blake, 'Stoke Newington West Reservoir Centre' In *Hackney: Modern, Restored, Forgotten, Ignored – 40 Buildings to mark 40 Years of the Hackney Society* (ed. Lisa Rigg) Hackney Society, 2009, pp.78-80

2004: Broadway Market Reopens
– Ann Robey

Broadway Market in 1985. (Photo Berris Connolly)

"And of course sourdough": one of the stalls in the Broadway Market revived.
(Courtesy of the London Borough of Hackney. Photo Sean Pollock)

Broadway Market is one of the most visible signs of the gentrification of Hackney. In 2000 it was a run-down shopping street with a single surviving fruit and vegetable stall. Today it has become a go-to destination market that attracts both locals and visitors. Every Saturday more than 20,000 people visit this successful food market, which, as its slogan announces, promotes quality, specialty, variety. And what abundance! What choice and plenty there is to be found here! From the stall that sells over a dozen varieties of Scotch egg, to the shucked oysters from Oyster Boy, to barrows laden with brownies and cakes, and enough loaves to feed five thousand – made from sunflower, spelt, walnuts and, of course, sourdough. Broadway Market has expanded from the street into a nearby school playground, and is now joined by another market, Netil, with vintage stalls and designer-makers, as well as food.

Whether this is good or bad depends on your political and social persuasion. In the first decade of the century, local activists saw Broadway Market as a scene of social cleansing by the council, forcing long-term working-class occupants to leave their shops and cafés. Traders like Tony Platia, who ran Francesca's café at number 34 for 30 years, and Spirit, who sold Caribbean fruit, food and spices at his Nutritious Food Galley at number 71 from the early 1990s, were forced out. This happened in spite of sit-ins and extensive support from local people, and even from town councils in Italy. In their place more specialist and niche shops opened, encouraged by the large crowds who had begun to frequent the food market established in 2004. The market has transformed the character of the street and still the number of specialist and designer shops continues to grow. Almost every week a new artisan food producer or independent café seems to appear, and the street is definitely becoming more touristy.

But the story of the revival of Broadway Market is much more than the tale of the incoming middle classes, the affluent hipster and the exclusion of traditional Hackney residents. Broadway Market could have been, and nearly was, lost forever.

Originally it lay on the course of the Market Porter's Path, an ancient route for transporting produce and animals from the fields and gardens of Essex and Hackney to the markets of the City. Building began along its fringes in the early nineteenth century, especially after the arrival of the Regent's Canal. It was lined by small-scale late Georgian and early Victorian brick buildings, some of which still survive. Historically, Broadway Market has always been a commercial street, and a market has existed there since 1835. It was originally held on several days of the week to allow frequent food trading in the days before refrigeration. Its heyday stretched from the 1890s to the 1930s, and as photographs from the Edwardian era and the 1930s show, it was hugely successful. Broadway Market was the most important food and general market in South Hackney before World War Two.

Broadway Market declined in popularity for shopping after the war, as people moved out of Hackney and many nearby streets were demolished with the development of new housing estates and tower blocks by the London County Council and its successor, the Greater London Council (GLC). The market declined and parts of the shopping parades saw compulsory purchase by the GLC. In 1973 and 1975 a number of properties in Broadway Market were listed Grade II, most likely as a response to that threat.

In 1975, a report by the London Borough of Hackney stated that "Broadway Market is a traditional shopping centre for South Hackney. It consists of approximately 60 shops in Broadway Market itself". In addition, there were said to be stalls along most of its length on market days selling food, clothing, electrical goods and hardware. This may have painted an unduly rosy picture as local residents have recalled that the market was already by that time extremely run down – and getting more so. In the late 1970s, the Area Improvement and Programme Implementation Team of the council identified Broadway Market as an area for general improvement, and in the early 1980s it received an Urban Development Grant.

In 1982 Ralph Ward, a young planner, wrote in a report on the former London Transport bus garage in Shrubland Road, that it was imperative to promote confidence in the street. Broadway Market became one of Hackney Council's initiatives for area improvement. The four shops in Broadway Market that were listed (numbers 75-77 and 79-81) were earmarked for rehabilitation as part of the market improvement scheme. Other properties were upgraded, and parts of the east side were rebuilt. Soon afterwards a few shoots of recovery appeared. But successive attempts by Hackney Council to revive the market failed, although a locally famous piece of 1970s graffiti quipped: "Broadway Market is not a sinking ship – it's a submarine".

In 1982, *The Times* noted that though there was not much to draw shoppers to Broadway Market as yet, it was "a market to watch". The cleaned up and revitalised Regent's Canal, with its canal boats and towpath, was a sign of potential rebirth, while the council also started to do up some houses. Yet the 1830s building occupied by picture framer and print seller Stephen Selby still looked the same, "but for a coat of paint".

Broadway Market Conservation Area was originally designated in 1995, a formal recognition of the special architectural character of the area. But it was not until a major refurbishment of the shops in the late 1990s that any real regeneration took place. In 1996, at least 10 of Broadway Market's shops were empty and neglected, and in 2000 the market itself was down to just one stall. A not-for-profit social enterprise, Broadway Market Traders and Residents Association Community Interest Company, then got involved, reviving the Saturday market with the goal of repopulating the street. The market was officially launched in 2004 with 40 stalls, and it was soon obvious that it was going to be a success.

Writing in 2013, shopping and high streets champion Mary Portas said that it was her favourite London market and proclaimed: "I feel that it sums up what I envisaged when I talked about the regenerative power of street markets in my Portas Review for the Government". A lively public realm emerged in tandem with the re-use of once empty and derelict shops as thriving independent retailers and cafés. At the same time a very active traders' association, the Community Interest Company, worked to ensure that the market was still about the community. But many people now feel Broadway Market is overpriced and excludes the poorer residents of Hackney. Still, its customers seem very satisfied, and it continues to grow.

Elsewhere in Hackney, there are three other council-run markets: highly successful Ridley Road, and smaller sites at Hoxton and Well Street. Each serves a different clientele, helping to cater for the wide social and ethnic mix of Hackney. But in 2015 the market at Kingsland Waste closed. This was a long-standing market that originally specialised in tools but developed into a site selling all kinds of goods. At its height in the 1970s the market held 150 stalls, two rows deep, every Saturday.

Broadway Market may not be a traditional market, but it is a market of its time, geared to the demands of the young, independent and wealthy population of Hackney. For East London food-lovers, there is no better destination on a Saturday.

Ridley Road Market. (Photos Simon Mooney)

2005: The Comprehensive Estates Initiative – Patrick Hammill

Tall and lowering: the four Holly Street tower blocks. Three have now been demolished.
(Photo Chris Dorley-Brown)

2005 was a landmark year for council housing development in Hackney. One of the country's largest regeneration schemes, Hackney's Comprehensive Estates Initiative (CEI), was coming to an end. And after a virtual hiatus in council-house building over many years, new homes were approaching handover in the last phase of the Holly Street Estate.

Apart from those directly affected, CEI has now been largely forgotten. But the scale, bringing together the regeneration of five troubled estates into one focused project, was hugely significant.

Why Oh Why?

In spite of all the effort following the Second World War, including the very extensive house-building programmes described in John Finn's article, many people still lived in old, unimproved terraced housing, sharing bathrooms and kitchens. In 1964, the Wilson government set ambitious targets for council house building, with high-rise, system-built blocks a key part of the solution. Both Hackney Council and the GLC responded enthusiastically to these initiatives, and within a few years new system-built estates appeared in every part of the borough

By the 1980s, however, it was clear that the bright new dawn of municipalised housing, the dream of the Hackney Labour Council, was in serious disarray. Problems affected virtually the whole of its housing estate. The older estates were mostly soundly built but in need of systematic maintenance. Poor repair and problems such as condensation and rotting sash windows could spell

Residents did not wish to be experimented on by architects again. They wanted the same simple street patterns and straightforward housing that others enjoyed. (Levitt Bernstein)

misery for tenants. Many older estates had fallen under the stigma of 'hard to let' and were tenanted by families with social problems. Hackney Council's managerial competence was afflicted both by declining skills in project management of large capital programmes, and by general organisational malaise. The transfer of the GLC housing stock, including many of the oldest estates and three of the CEI estates, to a profoundly unwilling Hackney Council in 1982 could not have come at a worse time.

Our Homes, a publication issued by the council in January 2017, describes the situation in Gascoyne Estate with its five-storey blocks, opened in 1948, fringing Well Street Common: "Gascoyne had come to embody everything viewed wrong with inner city living, social housing, and Hackney, the pariah borough ..., itself: crack dens; burnt-out cars; crime; gangs. ...Gascoyne had become a living, breathing sink estate cliché."

A burglar's dream: the dreaded snake blocks. (Levitt Bernstein)

This was a story that was replicated throughout the borough. But problems were most acute in the newest tower block estates. Five of these, Trowbridge, Nightingale, New Kingshold, Holly Street, and Clapton Park, were brought together to form the Comprehensive Estates Initiative. The construction of each estate was similar: tower blocks, predominantly pre-fabricated and system-built, set within low-rise housing. The five estates contained amongst them 24 high-rise blocks of which only three, one apiece at Nightingale, Holly Street and Clapton Park, remain standing.

When the first residents moved in, they were enthusiastic about their new homes with modern conveniences, as Alice Burke records (p.223). For many, this was the first time they had a home with their own front door: a significant triumph that was, sadly, to be short-lived, for that front door would be needed more for security than for celebration.

For example, at Holly Street built between 1967 and 1971, there were four tower blocks along with half a mile of almost continuous five-storey blocks with a host of design problems. By the late '70s the council was working with tenants, developing radical proposals to localise the management and to overhaul the buildings. Despite a continuous programme of work, by 1986 yet more problems were becoming apparent, with the Director of Housing, Tony Shoults, arguing that the council should have gone directly for the radical option of redevelopment years earlier. Holly Street was simply too difficult and too expensive to maintain and to manage.

The grey 'low rise' blocks looked quite attractive with alluring names like Sycamore and Rowan Courts, but they were poorly built and had an internal corridor several hundred metres long, snaking across the development: a burglar's dream. Residents lived behind flimsy doors which could easily be kicked in (later replaced by high security doors), and while the police were responding to a call out to one address, the trouble makers could be exiting some distance away. The upper parts of the tower blocks were used for transmitting pirate radio stations. There were increasing levels of illegal occupation. Shops would not deliver within the estate, nor would mini cabs take residents home. A job application might be binned simply because of the address. The council publicly supported tenants' aspirations that comprehensive redevelopment (rich irony) was the only solution.

Meanwhile, by the River Lea, residents of the seven towers on the Trowbridge Estate had also been campaigning about the poor condition of their homes. The structural problems were exacerbated by the estate's isolated position, cut off from the rest of Hackney by the new motorway. Its angry Tenants' Association was emblematic of the demoralisation afflicting its residents.

In November 1983 the local MP, Brian Sedgemore, argued in the House of Commons that conditions in the tower blocks were so bad that they should be demolished (see p.28). The Conservative minister Sir George Young acknowledged in his reply: "The basic facts are that problems of rain penetration became apparent almost as soon as the first of the blocks were completed, with distressing results in some of the flats. Subsequently, a catalogue of other problems has been identified, such as inadequate ties and fixings, spalling mosaic, rotting window frames, condensation and noise problems."

Even a less-than-sympathetic Conservative government accepted responsibility to deal with this appalling situation. Funding was initially made available for repairs and overcladding, then for partial demolition, and finally for full demolition, resulting in Northaird Point becoming the first tower block in Hackney to be demolished in 1985.

Getting the funds

Hackney Council had a difficult relationship with the Conservative government, with a low point in 1985 when Hackney refused to set a rate until ordered to do so by the High Court. But it worked behind the scenes to convince the government that, given the requisite funding, it could tackle the backlog of poor housing.

By the late 1980s the council, led by John McCafferty, was in negotiation with Mrs Thatcher's government over a major package that would become CEI. The terms reflected Conservative priorities and contained some controversial elements:
- government would allocate significant funding but in return the council would no longer manage the redeveloped estates which would be mainly owned and managed by housing associations
- major housebuilders would be able to tender to lead the regeneration projects

• private developers could build housing for sale as part of each scheme

The involvement of housing developers reflected the government's view that they, as businesses, knew about securing best value; and also knew what people wanted to buy.

Hackney needed to be seen to deliver. CEI was established as a distinct unit co-ordinating the different agencies involved to ensure regeneration would be delivered on time and budget, and reporting directly to the leader of the council.

Although some work had already started at Trowbridge and Clapton Park, the main project came together around 1990, with major works starting in 1993.

Involving the Residents

Building on the innovative community engagement that had underpinned the regeneration of the Leaview Estate in the 1980s, the council was committed from the outset to effective resident involvement. An effective relationship gradually developed, although it took some years to overcome a legacy of mistrust. The residents' caution was understandable. They had been moved into 'new' estates delivered without their involvement, and had suffered the consequences of poor design and struggling management. That was an experience that they did not wish to repeat!

At Holly Street, where I was a project architect over many years, residents' ambition was simply that they did not wish to be experimented on by architects again. They wanted the same simple street patterns and straightforward housing that others enjoyed.

On the five estates, residents elected their own Estate Development Committee to ensure that their priorities were represented. Each estate developed its representative structures. At Holly Street, a range of sub-committees reviewed the emerging proposals from different perspectives, including design, provision for the elderly, and provision for young people. Residents helped to write the brief and worked with the architects over the ensuing ten years, agreeing to retain one tower block for older people managed by a tenant management co-operative.

At Trowbridge the resident's steering group expressed visceral opposition to high rise housing and sought a development of modest scale, simple design and high-quality new homes. They played a key role in selecting the architects to deliver their vision, and later took over managing their homes through their tenant management co-operative.

The CEI programme caused great disruption for tenants with development going on around them over a ten-year-plus programme. Not all residents were enthusiastic. Some felt settled and wished to be left alone. Some tenants, asked if they would move from a council tenancy to become housing association tenants in their new homes, wanted to remain as they were, although there were few properties available. Some tenants complained of being moved to poor-quality temporary accommodation while works progressed. There were a small number of leaseholders following Right to Buy, and they were bought out. For any squatters or illegal tenants, of which there were many, there was no offer of rehousing.

Despite these drawbacks, by 2005 CEI had successfully demonstrated that Hackney could deliver major regeneration projects. The council's housing department that was struggling in the 1980s has successfully developed and delivered not only one of London's largest mixed tenure estate regeneration programmes but also new build strategies. It continues with this ambitious housing programme today.

2006: A Tale of Hackney's Swimming Pools – Margaret Willes

London Fields Lido by night. After a long campaign, bathers got their wish to be able to swim after sundown. (Courtesy of Greenwich Leisure Limited)

Charles Dickens memorably opens his novel, *A Tale of Two Cities* about the French Revolution: "It was the best of times, it was the worst of times, it was the age of wisdom, it was the age of foolishness." This could apply, albeit less dramatically, to the opening years of the twenty-first century and the story of three of Hackney's swimming baths.

The pools in the newly built Clissold leisure centre were closed, after just 21 months in November 2003, amid local acrimony. Ken Worpole, speaking on behalf of the Clissold Users Group, explained that the heads at Hackney Council had been dizzied by the wonderful architecture that had cost a huge £34 million. "It is the wrong building at the wrong time in the wrong place", he declared to Jonathan Glancey for a report that appeared in the *Guardian* in March 2004. Complaints of blocked drains, dirty water from showers and slippery tiles were combined with reports of defects in the architecture, such as inadequate ventilation and glass walls around the pools retaining fetid water, along with problems with the associated sports halls. After extensive refurbishment, the leisure centre reopened in December 2007.

Amongst the points made during the Clissold Baths debacle was that Orthodox Jews and Muslim women were unable to use the 'changing village'. Swimming pools are not just about architecture or facilities, they are also social centres, and it is vital that the potential clientele is considered. In their new incarnation the Clissold pools are judged very good, suiting the new demographic of Stoke Newington, albeit at eye-watering expense. So, when in 2006 across the borough at London Fields, the unexpected happened, and the Lido was being prepared for reopening, one of the vitally important points to consider was just who were to be the users of the pool.

The London Fields Lido was first opened in 1932, paid for jointly by the London County Council (LCC) and Hackney Borough Council. The *Hackney Gazette*, covering its opening, described it as "the last word in up-to-date bathing pools … designed to trap all the sunshine the summer may see fit to yield". At this time many families in Hackney could hardly afford to take a holiday, so when a second open air lido was opened in Victoria Park in 1936, the chairman of the LCC Parks Committee proudly declared "We shall bring the seaside to East London. Why, this is as good as Margate."

Closed during the Second World War, London Fields Lido reopened after extensive restoration in 1951. It became a favourite summer venue, as could be seen in the home movies of my neighbours in nearby Appleby Road, where days out at the pool were intercut with annual pilgrimages to Kent to pick hops. But in the years that followed, expectations changed, holidays were spent not only in Margate, but also Marbella, and less hardy generations could not cope with the unheated water and basic facilities. The lido in London Fields closed in 1988, shortly followed by that in Victoria Park. While the site in Victoria Park was filled in, London Fields was not. Affection for London Fields endured with local residents mounting campaigns to clear the site of encroaching shrubs and weeds, painting the most-damaged woodwork, and installing a banner reminding the world that the lido was still with us. On one occasion the word went out that bulldozers were on their way to flatten the site, and campaigners prepared to man the barricades.

In 2004, however, Hackney Council was persuaded that London Fields Lido should and could be restored. According to Jules Pipe, then mayor, a trigger was what had happened at Clissold Pool. But undoubtedly the dauntless campaign mounted by the

London Fields Users Group, who lobbied over many years for the pool's return and who refused to be discouraged, played a major role.

S&P Architects, specialists in sports architecture, created a scheme for a 50 by 17 metre deck-level pool framed by colourful individual cubicles as well as changing rooms, and a shop serving both users of the pool and visitors. The water was now to be heated by gas-condensing boilers, so that bathers could enjoy the pool throughout the year. Seeing steam rise from the pool on a crisp winter morning before taking the plunge is an exhilarating experience.

London Fields Lido reopened in 2006, and has proved a triumphant success, catering for the influx of young people into the area, many of them finding an energetic early morning swim an ideal start to their long and stressful working days. This can present an interesting scenario, never dreamt of in the 1930s when the principal aim was to provide the residents of Hackney with light and air. One morning recently, from the relative safety of the slowest lane, I observed an elderly man paying his first visit to the new version of the pool. The attendants came to his rescue when he was outwitted by the locker key system. He then lowered himself into the fast lane and began to swim breaststroke, blissfully unaware of the freestylers bearing down upon him, their arms like sharks' fins scything through the water. Again he was rescued by the attendants, and I hope that it was not his last foray.

During the Olympics, the unusual length of the pool made it the ideal place for the US paralympic swimming team to do their training. In 2014, after a long campaign, floodlighting was installed allowing the pool to be open from 6.30 in the morning to 9.00 in the evening, every day, even weekends. Josephine Bacon of the London Fields Users Group reports that this decision has been very popular, with people telling her that it has changed their lives.

This happy story has, however, to be set against that of Haggerston Baths. While the outdoor lidos at London Fields and Victoria Park formed part of the idea of health and happiness of the 1920s and '30s, Haggerston, along with Clapton Baths, was created as a result of the late Victorian civic concern for the promotion of cleanliness along with fitness. Legislation was promulgated in 1878 allowing local authorities to borrow money to build indoor swimming pools. The baths in Clapton were opened in 1897, providing slipper baths and separate pools for men and women, amid Renaissance architectural splendour. Seven years later Haggerston Baths were opened, with a pool and slipper baths, along with a washhouse, housed in a building again in grand Renaissance style. Originally, the pool was open only in the summer months and emptied in winter because of filtration problems: instead, there was a sprung floor for dances.

A flavour of the poverty that prevailed in Hackney at this time is shown by the declaration of B.J.Wakeling, the Vice-Chair of the Baths and Washhouses Committee, at the opening in June 1904 that "great care should be taken, that no inducements are offered to cause the public washhouse to become popular with any members of the community other than the poorest". The playwright Arnold Wesker, who grew up in Clapton, describes visits to the washhouse in his memoirs. After buying his ticket, he would wait on a wooden bench to be called, and attendants would hammer on the door of anyone who overstayed his allotted time.

Both Clapton and Haggerston Baths endured rough rides during the twentieth century, but Clapton survived and has been adapted for the needs of the modern era as the King's Hall Leisure Centre. Haggerston Baths on the other hand were allowed to deteriorate from the 1980s, and on my last visit there I was horrified to meet up with cockroaches in the changing rooms. The baths closed on 11 February 2000 on safety grounds, and have remained closed ever since, despite valiant efforts by the Save Haggerston Pool campaign.

The civic pride reflected by the Grade II-listed building, topped by a cupola and a galleon, the Golden Hind, has paradoxically militated against its viability as far as Hackney Council is concerned. Maintaining swimming pools is an expensive business, and as I write this piece, London Fields Lido has closed while repairs are undertaken. The solution proposed by the council for Haggerston was to put the redevelopment of the building out to tender. The local residents made clear that their priority was to continue having a pool, and three of the bids received included such a retention. However, as the current Mayor, Philip Glanville, explained in early 2017 "the council has spent the best part of a year negotiating with a developer whose proposal included a pool. Unfortunately we could not get the reassurances we needed that the scheme proposed would actually be delivered."

It seems ironical that at a time when the population of Shoreditch is rising with new developments, bringing increasing numbers of health-conscious young people, the death knell has been sounded for Haggerston Pool.

Doomed, the magnificent bath at Haggerston. (Photo Lisa Shell)

2007: Beat the Bookies: the Old Town Hall becomes a betting shop – Ian Rathbone

Hackney's first town hall, now a Joe Coral betting shop, with Paddy Power just across the road. (Photo Simon Mooney)

In 2007, a group of residents started a petition against a proposed new betting shop opening in Chatsworth Road across the road from Rushmore School. The premises had previously been a DIY shop.

As a local ward councillor, I became involved in their campaign, and we went through the process of trying to stop planning permission and the granting of a licence by magistrates. We were shocked to find that the combined annual turnover of the two existing bookies amounted to around £9m, probably the combined turnover of all the other shops and businesses in the street.

The petition was handed in and I arranged a deputation to the full council where residents spoke about their concerns to a meeting of councillors from all parties.

About the same time, we heard that the Old Town Hall building in Mare Street was to become another bookies. The Old Town Hall had been the seat of local government in Hackney for most of the nineteenth century. It had subsequently been the Midland Bank, then HSBC. It is a handsome Grade II building right next to Hackney's oldest building, St Augustine's Tower. Now it was set to become another branch of Coral.

It seemed such a lowering of our heritage to see this landmark building converted to a betting shop. Such is the absurdity of planning legislation that the company did not need permission because betting shops were in the same planning category as banks and financial institutions and so there was no change of use. In fact pretty well any shop, café or takeaway could be converted to a betting shop without the requirement of planning permission.

What is more, the bookies were moving into Hackney in increasing numbers. Our investigations showed that there were eight in a short strip on Mare Street alone, five in Stamford Hill and three in Chatsworth Road Overall there were 64 betting shops in Hackney plus a bingo hall and four adult gaming centres, not to mention the private unlicensed gaming clubs behind anonymous shopfronts.

A big driver behind this growing plague was the arrival of fixed odds betting terminals (FOBTs) which provide simulated games like roulette, with stakes up to £100 per play and high prizes – a magnet for problem gamblers. Tax changes had made these machines highly profitable for bookies and the Gambling Act of 2005 had inadvertently added to the problem by limiting the number of FOBTs to four per outlet. Bookies were opening in clusters on busy shopping streets to get round this limitation.

Mare Street was just the kind of street that the bookies were drawn to. It has some established stores but intermixed with pound shops, pawnbrokers and traditional cafés: a street used by people from all sectors of the community and a street interesting to the bookies.

Beat the bookies: Hackney Council leads the campaign to control the scourge of betting shops. (London Borough of Hackney)

189

Father Rob Wickham, then Rector of St John at Hackney, was clear that he did not want another such establishment close to the boundary of his churchyard. We explored whether it was actually inside the boundary, but it wasn't. Coral opened and remains there to this day.

A turning point came when one resident, a reporter for the national *Observer* newspaper, wrote a double-page spread on the growing threat of betting shops, and the fact that they tend to orientate towards poorer areas where they play on fantasies about getting rich quick. Suddenly, it became a national issue.

Many people stood wringing their hands, saying it all was of concern but that nothing could be done. That changed in 2009 when the then Mayor of Hackney, Jules Pipe, made a passionate (for him) speech at a meeting of the full council about the evils of betting, in particular its cost to society in terms of family break up and job loss.

That year in July, all parties on the council backed a motion I proposed supporting the decision to use the Sustainable Communities Act to tackle the unacceptable spread of betting shops in Hackney. The Act had become law in 2007 and set up a new process whereby councils can request central government to introduce policies to "assist councils in promoting the sustainability of local communities". The scope of the Act was untested and we were asking central government to give us the power to turn the tide on this proliferation of betting shops.

We asked that the council's Community Safety and Social Inclusion Scrutiny Commission be tasked to investigate the problem and collect evidence to be used as a London-wide move to restrict the growth of gambling off- and online. I am grateful that the then Commission Chair, Cllr Deniz Oguzkanli, and my colleagues saw fit to instigate this special investigation.

The Commission held hearings and invited expert witnesses and residents to give evidence. The bookmakers took this seriously – not surprisingly as we were advocating bringing this free-for-all to an end. Responses were received from William Hill, Gala Coral, Betfred and the national head of PR for Ladbrokes.

The betting shop operators raised many issues. They took issue with our argument that Hackney was grossly over-stocked with betting shops and argued against using a national comparator on the number of shops per local authority area. They suggested that a fairer comparator would be the 10 inner London boroughs, most of them with social problems similar to Hackney They stated that problem gambling rates in the UK remain stable at just 0.6 per cent of the adult population, and argued that there was no evidence that the Gambling Act had made a substantial difference to the number of shops in the borough. They suggested that their shops attract people to local high streets and provide footfall, ensuring the vitality and viability of shopping centres.

We argued on the other hand that betting shops, which drain punters and their families of cash, undermine the vitality of shopping centres like Mare Street. We also pointed out the unquantifiable costs to the health and social services of the failure of families and individuals because of gambling addiction, and the human cost to individuals and communities.

The bookmakers did concede that there could be a problem with over-concentration in some areas and a representative from one betting shop chain went so far as to promise to donate up to £50k for a worthy cause in Hackney. Unfortunately, despite a lot of chasing by the council, and particularly by Cllr Oguzkanli, the donation was never forthcoming.

The Commission's report advocated that Hackney Council press the government to give it powers under the Sustainable Communities Act to use the planning system to regulate the opening of new betting shops, and I am pleased to say that this recommendation was adopted by the council. The council made submissions to the government in 2009 asking for powers to change guidance for the licensing and planning regimes so that it could take into account the concentration of betting shops in particular areas when deciding whether to grant permission for the opening of any new gambling premises. It pointed out that Hackney had three times the national average for a local authority area, mostly clustered in the poorer areas of the borough.

We were not helped by the fact that there was a dearth of social research to demonstrate and to quantify the human cost to individuals and families and communities, or the financial cost to social and health services caused by the gambling habit.

Unfortunately, the government met this submission with a dead bat. It said that the council "would need to demonstrate that there was a material planning difference between betting shops and other A2 land uses in terms of the impact on the environment", that "this would increase regulation", and that it "may not be cost effective to make a national change". A classic Sir Humphrey response.

With the tenacity for which Hackney is famed, Jules Pipe took the issue to London Councils and the then Mayor of London Ken Livingstone. When Paddy Power bought up the Railway Tavern at the bottom of the Narroway (and just across the road from the Old Town Hall), the two of them were pictured standing outside with a protest banner! A further submission for powers under the 2007 Act was made in 2014 in the name of 32 London boroughs and supported by 35 more councils outside London.

After eight years of sustained campaigning the government finally amended the law to give bookies their own planning use class. So now any company wanting to set up a new betting shop must apply for planning permission and the council will be able to take into account objections from local residents and also its own planning policies.

So something was achieved by the action of some residents wanting to see change in their local streets in Hackney in 2007. But sadly, not much. Since then there has been a small overall reduction in betting shops in Hackney. People are now at least more aware of the extent of the problem. And a new campaign to limit FOBTs is underway.

In spring 2014, hardly anyone noticed that the third bookies, the Chatsworth Road shop we had all campaigned against, closed.

Further Information

2007 Report of Hackney Community Safety and Social Inclusion Scrutiny Commission
http://www.hackney.gov.uk/Assets/Documents/concentration-of-betting-shops-09-10.pdf

2014 Submission under the Sustainable Communities Act
http://www.hackney.gov.uk/Assets/Documents/SCA-submission.pdf

2008: The Murder of Shaquille Smith: gang violence in Hackney
– Emma Bartholomew

In the wrong place at the wrong time: Shaquille Smith's photograph was released following his murder in St Thomas's Square. (Metropolitan Police press office)

Gang violence of the type which led to the senseless murder of Shaquille Smith still plagues Hackney. It is a depressing everyday reality for kids who are involved with gangs; not just gang leaders, but also kids who exist at or near the periphery of gangs – drawn into a world of violence controlled and initiated by others.

Shaquille was only 14 years old when he was fatally stabbed in the stomach in St Thomas's Square off Mare Street on 30 August 2008, just yards from his home. Shaquille's misfortune was to have been in the wrong place at the wrong time, when thugs from the London Fields gang were hell-bent on finding a target for a revenge attack on their rivals. His only mistake was to have been chatting with the brother of a gang member.

To this day it is common for non-gang members to be attacked just because they are friends with someone who is.

As I write, the sight of a shockingly huge pool of blood in Dalston's Tesco Express is still etched into my memory. The blood is surrounded by a pile of clothes left behind by a teenager who had stumbled in and collapsed after being stabbed on the pavement outside.

Whilst dramatic incidents like this sporadically make national headlines, stabbings go on every day. Much of the fallout from gang violence in Hackney and Islington is dealt with at the specialist trauma centre at the A&E unit in the Royal London Hospital in Whitechapel, where they may deal with three or four cases every single day. The regeneration which has touched some parts of the borough can be deceptive, and the influx of wealth is interspersed with pockets of deprivation where youths in gangs still rampage and hurt each other with knives – and sometimes guns if they can get their hands on them – in tit-for-tat revenge attacks.

Shaquille was the twenty-fifth teenager in 2008 to meet a violent death in London, and gangland violence appeared to be spiralling out of control. But in 2010 Hackney took the initiative by introducing the first Integrated Gangs Unit in the country, led by former borough commander Steve Bending. Police now collaborate with other agencies, including council youth workers and probation officers: sharing information, building a picture about where tensions lie, and targeting gang members they believe may be vulnerable, to offer them a way out. Figures seem to show that it's working, with gun crime down 63 per cent since the initiative's introduction, and offences where a knife was used to injure a victim aged under 24 came down from 218 to 65 per year in four years.

But essentially the essence of the turf war behind gangland disputes has not changed. While Yardies in Lower Clapton's 'Murder Mile' in the 1990s were competing to sell hard drugs like crack, it's thought that this latest spat, which saw the injured kid in Tesco, is over who's going to sell laughing gas to late-night revellers coming out of clubs and bars in Dalston.

Police don't generally like to name gangs, saying it's taken as a 'badge of honour'. But it is possible that, as I write, the most recent flare up has been between the Hoxton Boys and Islington's Red Pitch gang, vying over control of Dalston's 'late night economy'. In the space of two weeks there were seven stabbings, a shooting and two more close calls around the Hackney and Islington border due to tensions boiling over between rival gangs.

There's plenty of cash to be made out of the legal high nitrous oxide, sold on the street at £5 a hit, compared to the 40 pence it costs to buy online. Previously, sellers plagued the streets of Shoreditch, each one attracting queues of late-night revellers. Police were desperate to crack down on this trade because of the conflict it created between sellers, but lacked specific powers to stop it. The council helped by handing out fines for unlicensed trading and this enabled the Shoreditch late-night police team to stamp out street-corner dealing; then in 2016 a new law prohibiting nitrous oxide's sale came into force.

But the problem has drifted up the road to Dalston. At the time of writing (the end of 2016), police hope that a new late-night team will eradicate the trade. But it has become a well-organised business: kids on bikes are on standby, bringing in more laughing gas supplies to make sure that street sellers are never caught with an amount that would spark an arrest. Others act as look-outs, warning sellers when police are on their way. Compared to the time when the Yardies brought terror to 'Murder Mile' in Upper Clapton, the structures of gangs have become more complex, with hierarchical tiers of authority – much like the situation depicted in the US TV series *The Wire*, in which Hackney boy Idris Elba stars as the kingpin.

Nowadays, instead of 'big boys' like the Yardies acting out, the pawns lower down the chain will mark out the territory while the gang leaders make sure they never get caught red-handed. Youngsters carry out the street dealing which is most vulnerable to disruption by the police.

Police are always trying to keep tabs on the situation but, as Ian Simpkins, Partnerships Inspector for Hackney told me, it's a constantly changing picture. "It's so fluid," he said. "There's a gang tensions map which shows a mass of rivalries and alliances. It's like Greek politics. It's insane, London Fields might be allied to Gilpin Square but anti the three gangs in between. But that might change, and then Gilpin Square might be anti London Fields. High ranking individuals in one gang might fall out with others over non-payment for drugs that have been seized, or another money issue."

Technology has ramped up the ante, with professionally-produced rap videos posted on YouTube by rival gangs. In a case mirroring that of Shaquille Smith, Marcel Addai was set upon in September 2015 near his Hoxton home, when seven men from the Fellows Court gang rode into the area in three cars, intent on attacking someone from the Hoxton Boys. Marcel was stabbed 14 times after being chased through the streets. What stood out in the nine-week trial – during which all seven defendants blamed the others for his death – was the role social media now plays in fuelling disputes between gang rivals. Police drew on thousands of messages, posts and photos from Snapchat, Instagram and Facebook as evidence, with defendants making 'gang signs', or holding huge wads of cash allegedly earned from selling drugs.

Most chilling of all, the case shone a light on a bizarre world which sees gangs use professionally produced rap videos posted on YouTube to taunt each other – threats the judge said were "at the heart" of the attack. One of the videos shown as evidence during the trial sees Rikell Rogers lighting up what looks like a joint, saying: "Don't act like you don't see me, I've been lurking, been on the gully." But when Rogers was sent down as one of four men responsible for Marcel's brutal murder, my sons told me that their school friends were lamenting the imprisonment of Rogers, whom they lauded as a talented rapper.

Sitting through many gang murder cases at the Old Bailey, what I'm struck by is the lack of remorse shown by the killers. In 2015, four children and families were left in shock as a gangland feud spilled over into a Saturday's afternoon shopping, when Moses Fadairo was gunned down by Christopher Erunse in Chatsworth Road. Erunse, who had been pursued and stabbed first by a knife-wielding Moses, then took a pop at his brother Emmanuel in Mighty Meats butchers. At his trial, Erunse said he wished Moses wasn't dead, because otherwise he wouldn't be sitting there in the dock.

Despite the brazen nature of many gang attacks, the police are often impeded in gaining convictions by the fear and code of honour which stops witnesses from giving testimony. Shaquille's killers, however, did not escape justice. Six members of the London Fields gang were convicted of his murder, the oldest aged 20. They were given life sentences with minimum terms of 15 to 18 years. Cllr Ian Rathbone, Speaker of Hackney at the time, organised a peace march which ended at St Thomas's Square where a church service was held on the murder spot.

What makes these killings even more depressing is the sense of promising lives cut short. DCI Carl Mehta, who led the case against Shaquille's killers, described him as a "caring and considerate boy and an excellent sportsman who had a great future ahead of him". After the two shocking deaths of Marcel Addai and Moses Fadairo in 2015, mums of past victims and youth club The Crib held a peace march proclaiming "enough is enough". Whether that message will ever resonate with the gang members themselves remains to be seen.

2009: Woodberry Down Reborn – Ray Rogers

Comprehensive development, 21ˢᵗ-century style: the new Woodberry Park Estate. (Photos Monica Blake)

Woodberry Down is one of the largest regeneration projects of its type in the UK. The new Woodberry Down is being hailed as the future of urban living. "Surrounded by an exhilarating natural waterside environment and just 15 minutes from the City, Woodberry Down is the perfect place to appreciate an unrivalled living experience in London," say the developers, Berkeley Homes.

But the old Woodberry Down estate was the future once. The story goes back to 1936 when the London County Council identified the site of 64 acres, then mostly occupied by Victorian villas with large gardens backing on to the Stoke Newington reservoirs. The land was acquired, in the face of strong local opposition, to provide new homes for people to be re-housed, mainly from slum clearance areas in the East End. Construction was delayed by the war but began in 1946 and was substantially completed by 1951. The design finally adopted was by J.H. Forshaw, co-author of Abercrombie's visionary County of London Plan. The scheme was based on the German Zeilenbau principle of aligned tall blocks of five to eight storeys set in parallel. Strange as it seems today, the eight-storey blocks were the highest the LCC had ever built and the first with lifts. Considerable controversy attended the building of these new 'skyscrapers'. The first of these, Needwood House, was opened in February 1949. With 1,800 homes in total, the estate was built to a far greater density than the previous housing on the site but remained spacious with generous open spaces between the separate blocks.

My family moved into Needwood House in 1950 and my parents lived there for the next 20 years. My recollection of the estate is that it was, certainly in the 1950s, a good place to live. I went to the new Woodberry Down primary school and our doctor and dentist were both housed in the brand new health centre, the first of its type built for the infant National Health Service. In these years the estate was dubbed by one newspaper as the 'Estate of the Future', visited by dignitaries and housing professionals eager to see this grand scheme of community development. I recall the occasion we entertained a group of Russian visitors brought to see the estate, who were no doubt suitably impressed with the advanced workers' housing provided by the Labour-run LCC!

The estate was indeed a socially progressive development in its day. In addition to the first NHS health centre, Woodberry Down secondary school was one of the first comprehensive schools in Britain which achieved impressive results through to the 1970s when it was led by a celebrated headteacher, Michael Marland. Woodberry Down was described as "a type of Rosetta Stone" for the LCC's post-war standards in housing and welfare policy. The integration of housing, education and welfare facilities was an important milestone for the LCC and for Labour's social policy on a national scale.

In its early days the Woodberry Down estate had a thriving tenants' association with over a thousand members but, when the first generation of pioneers gave way to a more diverse community, the shared identity began to disappear. Sadly, the condition of the estate also deteriorated in the following decades, possibly not helped by changes in London's local government and changing times in which there was far less money available for estate renewal and maintenance.

The shortage of building materials after the Second World War meant that cost savings had been made in constructing some of the housing blocks and the secondary school. Some of the blocks suffered from structural defects and the school from ground subsidence, contributing to its closure by the mid-1980s.

In 2002, a structural evaluation reported that 31 out of 57 blocks were "beyond economic repair" with wide-ranging problems including subsidence, damp, faulty drainage, poor insulation, asbestos and lack of disabled access or lifts. The conclusion was that it would be more cost effective to demolish and rebuild rather than repair the existing buildings. Although this was a contentious issue at the time, the decision to redevelop the estate offered a rare opportunity for a new scheme providing housing on a grand scale; the largest comprehensive development in Hackney since the construction of council housing had ground to a halt some 20 years earlier.

From the start the scheme was ambitious with initially some 4,600 homes replacing the 1,800 existing dwellings, meaning a large increase in population density. The bulk of the additional homes would be private housing for sale in order to pay for the replacement of the rented housing. All existing social housing tenants wishing to stay were to be offered housing in the redeveloped scheme. The only group who lost out in this arrangement were leaseholders who had exercised their Right to Buy, as the market value of their homes fell far short of the cost of buying back into the new development. They have understandably been vociferous opponents of the redevelopment.

The layout of the new Woodberry Down was designed to create a new 'urban quarter' in place of the regimented layout of the former estate, creating new streets and garden squares, including a number of towers. The range of new facilities will eventually include three new public parks, a community centre and library, a new academy school and an extended primary school, a children's centre and retail and commercial opportunities. Leisure facilities nearby include the sailing club on the West Reservoir and the Woodberry Wetlands centre on the East Reservoir, opened by Sir David Attenborough in 2016. The intention is to create a community with a genuine sense of place.

Woodberry Down's original 1948 blocks. One of the blocks, Nicholl House, was used in the filming of *Schindler's List*. (Photo Chris Dorley-Brown)

The first masterplan for the new Woodberry Down was approved in 2007 leading to the grant of planning permission for the first phase. Construction began in 2009 with redevelopment planned to take place over the next 20 years. The first phase (called the 'kick start' site) saw the relocation of the first batch of re-housed tenants into new social rented housing overlooking the West Reservoir alongside private sector housing built for sale, including a 27-storey tower.

Future tenants who are re-housed are unlikely to be as fortunate. There has been relentless pressure from the developers to increase the density of the development and Hackney Council has also had to consider its ambitious housing targets discussed in Lisa Shell's article. The latest iteration of the masterplan provides for a total of 5,557 homes to be built by Berkeley Homes in conjunction with Genesis Housing Association over a further seven phases that will eventually replace the whole of the old Woodberry Down.

By a strange turn of the wheel of fortune, I was in charge of Hackney's urban design team during the planning of the new scheme. The council was determined that this huge new development would be exemplary in every respect and the first completed phase of social and market housing, with a mix of housing tenures and an idyllic setting facing the reservoir, has set a high standard of design and landscaping. Collaboration with the residents has far exceeded the normal level of 'consultation' usually on offer, with a community trust based in the new Redmond Community Centre jointly funded by the council and the developers.

Having said all that, the new Woodberry Down will house a very different community from that which moved in to their new council flats in the early 1950s. Typical responses were recorded in Woodberry Down Memories: The History of an LCC Estate in 1989. "The flats seemed wonderful when we first moved in," ran one. "I thought mine was marvellous compared to the conditions I was living in before... we had a couple of basement rooms." In contrast a contributor to a discussion about the Woodberry Down regeneration on the Municipal Dreams website in 2013 said, "I moved into the new flats in Woodberry Down over a year ago. I was one of the first to start renting in the area, from a Singaporean investor. All my neighbours rent from foreign absentee landlords."

Clearly, although the council had little choice financially – public funding for large-scale council housing development is simply not available – there are issues arising from the private sector led nature of the new development. Although the actual social rented housing stock has not diminished, and the proposed proportion of 'affordable' homes is relatively high, the preponderance of foreign investors, and the short term lets of the buy-to-rent market make for a poorer social mix. It has been said that the development already supports enough gyms for Sparta – a reflection of the type of community being created.

The original Woodberry Down Estate was a response to the housing shortage of the post-war years. The new Woodberry Down responds to the housing issues of today. To quote from Municipal Dreams, "So, welcome to the brave new world of social housing. Once our dreams were collective and, if the former Woodberry Down Estate never quite lived up to the hype, it represented, at least, an earnest and shared ambition to build high-quality housing and a real community for ordinary people. Will the new estate do that?" It is to be hoped so, but only time will tell.

2010: Going Round in Circles: the opening of the East London Line – Roger Blake

Dalston Junction Station in 1987, a year after closure. It was to be another 23 years before trains ran again.
(Photo Berris Connolly)

The Hackney Society was founded in the year before the last steam trains ran in scheduled passenger service and London Underground's Victoria Line opened. What a difference a half-century makes! It was also founded at a time when London's population had slumped by about a million from its 1939 peak of 8.6 million, with a further decline of one million by the early-1980s. But since then the population has risen by two million, to surpass that 1939 peak in early 2015, and with the prospect of yet more growth.

It is that population growth which underlies the capital's and the borough's rediscovery of rail as a quick and convenient means of transport – and a catalyst for growth and prosperity. Up to the 1980s we were still seeing lines and stations closed, and services reduced at those which remained. London Fields station closed after a fire in 1981, followed by Lea Bridge station in 1985. London Fields station was to reopen in 1986, thanks to GLC funding, although its services were then cut to weekday peaks-only from 1992. It was often eerily deserted, a rather threatening place to wait for a train, until a revival began in 1998.

And, meanwhile, Dalston Junction station and the link with the Broad Street terminus closed in 1986. The site of the former Broad Street station was sold off to become the Broadgate development, a beacon of the City of London's burgeoning importance as a financial centre. The viaduct carrying the railway into the City was cut off at the head, the remnant rapidly reclaimed by nature.

The one line which bucked the trend was the Hackney section of the North London Line which reopened in 1979 after an interval of 35 years. For three short years Dalston had the luxury of two stations, after Kingsland reopened in 1983 and before Junction closed in 1986. Since 2010 and the reopening of Junction, that former luxury has become necessity. The growth of Hackney in general, and Dalston in particular, has generated a combined station usage officially estimated at 11 million passengers in 2015/16, in the same league as Cambridge and Bristol Temple Meads, and ranked thirty-sixth out of 2,553 British stations.

Hackney had long lamented its image as a Tube-less borough, although Manor House station is actually (just) within the borough's boundary. The Hackney Public Transport Action Committee (HAPTAC) led by the late Roger Lansdown pushed the 'Hackney on the Tube' message. While the Chelsea-Hackney Line was seen as the ultimate goal (and now a realigned Crossrail 2), the northern extension of the East London Line had been seen as the 'low-hanging fruit' many felt they might live to see. The decapitated Broad Street viaduct came, after all, within a few hundred yards of Shoreditch station at Brick Lane, the little-used terminus of the East London Line.

Managers of the East London Line were among those with the vision to see the potential of an Underground line as a cross-river orbital link around a wider catchment of east London. Hackney saw it as the way to end the borough's negative reputation as 'difficult to get to'. Since 1964 the fire-ravaged ruins of the Bishopsgate Goods Depot had offered the prospect of a through route. The track-bed on the derelict viaduct had long been protected in a succession of Hackney Council development plans "for future possible railway use". That designation at one point helped stave off an idea from a cash-strapped council to sell off its asset, bought from BR for £1!

Hackney Council was a founder member of the East London Line Group (ELLG), an independent alliance of public and private-sector stakeholders formed in the early-1990s with Transport Minister Roger Freeman's words from his 1991 visit to the Bishopsgate Goods Depot site ringing in their ears: "If you want this railway you'll have to lobby for it." After the 'boom' of the late 1980s the language in the 'bust' of the early 1990s referred to an 'arc of deprivation' around inner north, east and south London. If that tag defined the problem, 'regeneration railway' later articulated a vision for a vital part of the solution. In mid-2002 the ELLG launched a brochure identifying £10 billion-worth of regeneration projects, mostly homes and jobs, to be supported by the railway in its catchment – a figure scrupulously assembled by Group officers then frequently quoted by others, and not once challenged.

What turned out to be a 20-year journey for the Group's members began formally in 1990 when London Underground published a consultation document anticipating the extended East London Line opening in 1994. A preview of an aged refurbished Metropolitan Line train exhibited by London Underground was accompanied by the confident expectation that "this is what you'll be getting on the extended East London Line". It tended to reinforce the official view of a Dalston-East Dulwich shuttle – merely an extension of the existing self-contained East London route. The ELLG's vision was very much more expansive, advocating through services to a wider spread of destinations, including at one time Finsbury Park and Wimbledon.

Hackney's ambition to be 'on the Tube' translated to 'on the Tube map' with the 2010 opening of the East London Line's northern extension into a completely rebuilt Dalston Junction Station. Hackney's ambition for 'Tube services' became 'Tube-style services', with 16 trains an hour running each way between Dalston Junction and Surrey Quays and served by spacious, high-capacity, air-conditioned, through-corridor, and trend-setting Overground trains. Restoration of the 'Western Curve' under the streets of Dalston in 2011 linked the new line to Highbury in the north. And following this, a largely new section of track was built to join the East London Line to existing suburban lines in the south, extending the service to Clapham Junction and creating London's first fully orbital railway. Growth in usage has been dramatic. The new station at Shoreditch High Street is now fifty-ninth in the national league – just behind Newcastle-upon-Tyne – and still rising!

Two of Hackney's new intermediate stations – Haggerston (opposite the original which was bombed and closed in 1940), and Hoxton (a major provider of visitors to the Geffrye Museum, such that the museum's expansion plans include a new entrance directly opposite) – filled the gap in what had been the borough's largest single built-up area beyond walking distance from a railway station. Names for other new stations were an issue. Your author's intervention steered 'Dalston' (actually one stop outside Carlisle) to Dalston Junction (the latter word having become synonymous over time with the crossroads). 'Bishopsgate' (nowhere near the street of that name in the City) became Shoreditch High Street, both to associate it with Hackney rather than Tower Hamlets and to succeed two previous Shoreditch stations, one behind Brick Lane, the other by Shoreditch Town Hall on the bridge over Old Street.

The East London Line project team also made the mistake of asking what sort of new bridge Hackney would like over the Regent's Canal. The council's officer representative needed no time; "a bow-string, like the one over Shoreditch High Street". Their engineers cursed me – it was quite a long span, over Dunston Road too! Another benefit arose from the demolition of its predecessor and the construction of the new bridge, and likewise with the construction of Hoxton station. Temporary road closures were necessary and your author speculated whether there was any need to re-open those roads, as people had become used to the alternatives and traffic volumes were anyway very light. The result is now plain to see – instead of roads, we have two new and permanent areas of public space.

The borough's love affair with London Overground extended in May 2015 when six other local stations on the Liverpool Street Line were taken over by Transport for London as part of the London Overground. Hackney now has 15 stations on the Tube map! This borough-wide coverage is symbolised by the recreated passenger link between the orbital route at Hackney Central and the radial route at Hackney Downs (the original link was opened in December 1885). The Hackney Interchange was opened officially on 12 August 2015. Your author's role as the council's project manager has been rewarded with a plaque on the wall at the Hackney Downs end of the elevated walkway. The business case for the link was vindicated when it achieved its four-year projected usage after just nine months.

What next? A new TfL concession for the Overground will bring even higher peak-hour frequencies on the North London Line, the prospect of some 24-hour weekend services, and new trains on Liverpool Street services in 2018.

Hackney's first directly-elected Mayor, Jules Pipe CBE, identified three top success factors in the transformation he oversaw of the look and feel of Hackney, and its public perception and reputation – clean streets, good schools, and London Overground.

A Dalston-bound train pulling into Hoxton Station. The skyline had changed beyond recognition since the trains last ran. (Photo Wayne Asher)

2011: Riots break out in Hackney – Meg Hillier

A burning car in Ellingfort Road, Hackney, at the height of the riots. (Photo Chris Dorley-Brown)

Disturbances broke out in Hackney Central just after three in the afternoon of Monday, 8 August 2011. Two hours later, it was clear that a full-scale riot was underway. But, very remarkably, by late morning the next day much of the clean-up of the damage had been completed. Hackney Council had started work in the small hours so that by the time #riotcleanup arrived – a cheering group of residents with brooms – there was little left to do.

Frantically I arranged to get back from my family holiday, which had only just begun, and, cheered by reports of the community spirit being shown in Hackney, I made a whirlwind visit to constituents. Pembury, despite much press coverage, had not been the centre of the riot. In fact, it was unscathed, with the main action on Clarence Road. Trelawney Estate had also been unaffected, even though looters had attacked Tesco on Morning Lane and the Burberry outlet store.

From the tenant hall on the Pembury Estate, I spoke briefly on the phone to the then Home Secretary, Theresa May. It was too early to have a full assessment of why the riots had happened, locally and across the country. Her main message was that justice for perpetrators would be swift, with courts sitting through the night: this was one of the few things government was able to control.

In the week that followed, I walked the streets with local councillor Ian Rathbone until 10 o'clock each night. Father Rob Wickham, then Rector of St John at Hackney and now Bishop of Edmonton, had worked with Ian and a group of residents following a vigil outside the church. This resulted in a street party in Clarence Road a week later with 500 residents and police enjoying tea, coffee and cakes, courtesy of our local Marks & Spencer, and making the front page of *The Times*.

International journalists were everywhere. In one interview a French radio journalist broke off mid-question to hold her microphone out as an ambulance went by, sirens blaring. Without irony she turned back to me and said, "I need some atmosphere". Apart from the impact on individuals and businesses, the biggest sadness was the attitude of people like the French journalist, determined to portray Hackney as a hotbed of crime and disaffection. It was depressing to have commentators peddle negative and outdated stereotypes. And the bigger issues would remain after the visitors had left.

With parliament recalled, I asked for a meeting with the Home Office Minister, James Brokenshire, and other MPs. We all wanted to know what support there would be for broken businesses and raised our concerns about the inability of the police to cope with a spate of violent riots across London.

At Hackney Council's CCTV headquarters I saw frightening footage of the riots from street level and from the perspective of the police line. The police had made the decision to kettle protestors to try to contain the riot. This meant that residents in Clarence Road and the north of Clapton Square were on the front line. Later it emerged that the police were very under-resourced at a critical time, leaving them unable to cope across London.

The borough fire commander had monitored live footage to advise his crews. If a fire was going to burn out it was left because of the risk of bringing engines into the middle of a riot. And, whilst there were car fires, no building was burnt down.

Later I reflected with another local vicar, Rose Hudson-Wilkin, and the borough police commander about the very different actions of that night. The optician at Boot's on Mare Street had pleaded directly with looters not to enter his property, and they let it be. Some people raided smashed-up shops, while others walked straight past. In one piece of footage a man cycled past a police car smashing its window with his cycle D-lock with a casualness that belied the violence of his act.

There were good news stories. After Siva's shop in Clarence Road was ransacked and looted beyond recognition, a fundraising campaign led by Ian Rathbone with local residents raised £30,000 in three weeks. Many, including Hackney Council, gave their time or goods freely to help get it back up and running. But it was many months before any compensation (promised "within weeks" by central government) trickled down, and it was not sufficient.

A nervousness lingered. One owner of a looted shop said to me, "I just shut up shop. In the end I have children and they are more important." The reputational damage was such that some of the specialist and marginal businesses have struggled to survive or closed, not helped by the slowness of the Mayor of London's riot fund to pay out. But in the end, the opening of the Westfield shopping centre at Stratford has done more than the riots to hit Hackney Central.

Reports began to come from council officers and commuters that they had overheard passengers on trains urging people to head to Hackney to get a piece of the action. This may be part of the reason why the average age of those arrested in Hackney was considerably older than elsewhere in the country. So, when disaffected youth and the social divide were brought up as factors, I resisted all calls for a curfew and refused to make snap judgements about causes.

Knitting the community back together. A street party on Clarence Road. (Courtesy of the London Borough of Hackney)

It was hard to be sure what had started the riots: we have a well-documented gang problem. The council and police have worked to identify gangs and this detailed knowledge means that Hackney often tops the 'league table'. But the riot was something different. Nationally, only 13 per cent of those arrested had links with gangs and those involved were disproportionately male (90 per cent), black and on benefits. Investigations later revealed that there had been a strong 'copycat' element, sourced mostly through social and other media.

In Hackney we pride ourselves on our diversity. The riots may not have been caused by the social divide, but conversations afterwards underlined that we must not be complacent about those left behind or marginalised as the world changes. Rose Hudson-Wilkin had rung parents of local teenagers to urge them to check the whereabouts of their offspring, and significantly not a single Hackney school pupil was involved. Our schools are now providing opportunities that young people don't want to throw away.

But for Hackney the riots came as a body blow on many levels. For community leaders, residents, emergency service and councillors, the images and comments about crime-ridden Hackney rankled. It was not the reality. Hackney's central location, and the fact that many journalists live locally, had helped put us on the map.

The long-term impacts of the riots are difficult to measure. At a conference held in Clapton, run and arranged by the community, it was highlighted that many of those vulnerable to gang violence and influence are below the radar of most of the authorities. Even though they had not been the main agitators during the riots, a strong view was voiced by local residents that these young people, vulnerable to grooming from gang elders, needed watching out for.

Likewise, these thoughtful residents knew who was at risk of marginalisation. But it can be difficult to connect people living below the radar to the support they need. Bureaucratic agencies are not the answer. Even now I worry about outside agencies who offer to 'solve' a problem in Hackney. Much better if those who know best – our youth leaders, tenant representatives and other community leaders – get more support for small-scale work.

The best role models are local – like James, the boxing coach at the Pedro Youth Club, and Nicolette, who ran the Morningside Estate youth centre in Portakabins for years. Both provided somewhere safe, warm and dry to hang out. I also highlighted to ministers organisations like the Crib in De Beauvoir and underlined how it wasn't so much about grand central government gestures as sustained local support. A little money goes a long way but here-today-gone-tomorrow initiatives don't work.

I still rail against the fact that too many of our teenagers are fearful of walking the streets. They must have the right to roam without fear.

The riots remain a scar on Hackney's history. The main perpetrators were dealt with by the home secretary's swift justice but I have since met some who have had difficulty getting work because of their criminal convictions. Locally, apart from improvements to shopfronts provided by the Mayor of London's riot fund, there's no physical reminder. Moreover, the social divide between the 'haves' and 'have-nots' in Hackney has widened to a gulf. With huge cuts to local services the small-scale projects in local areas that help connect people are struggling to survive.

2012: The Olympics and their Legacy – Ralph Ward

The Olympic Media and Broadcasting Centre under construction. Hackney fought vigorously to have it located within the borough as a future digital business hub. (Courtesy of the London Borough of Hackney)

2012 was the year the Olympic Games came to Hackney, if only just. The site for the Olympic Park was carved out of the old, ramshackle post-industrial Lea Valley that lay mostly beyond the borough's eastern edge. Hackney's share of the Park was limited to a few isolated hectares of remotest Hackney Wick, occupied by bus depots, tyre yards, a flea market, and perhaps appropriately, the remnants of the old Hackney Stadium. But this was enough to allow Hackney the status of an official 'host borough', and a seat alongside ministers and the Mayor of London on the Olympic Park Regeneration Steering Group (and more recently on the London Legacy Development Corporation). It was also enough to encourage Hackney Council to go in vigorous search of a share of the Olympic 'regeneration legacy'. And it was enough to provoke those for whom the land still held some meaning and value to kick up a noisy and perfectly reasonable fuss about how its authentic character had been obliterated by the Park's reimagining of a mythical Lea River Valley.

"The most enduring legacy of the Olympics," said the London 2012 bid document, "will be the regeneration of an entire community for the direct benefit of everyone who lives there." This marketing masterstroke proved irresistible to the International Olympic Committee. But what 'community' the bid was talking about, what these benefits might be and how a park, together with a collection of rather expensive sporting venues, could achieve this radical social outcome, remained unexplored. To Olympians this was just tiresome detail. But to many communities in Hackney it remains a puzzle. Who has benefitted and how is still not entirely clear.

But such is regeneration which focuses on places and not people. There is no obvious reason why Olympic regeneration should be any different, despite the rhetoric. Hackney's first venture into regeneration was 'Operation Clean-Up' in 1978. Buildings were cleaned, trees planted, railings around parks reinstalled. It is tempting and not difficult to the see the Olympics as its apotheosis – a super-duper Operation Clean-Up, albeit in one tiny and remote part of the borough.

Since 1978 Hackney has been immersed in regeneration. Estates have been Actioned. Cities have been Challenged. And the place *has* changed. Broadway Market – not a sinking ship but a submarine, as the graffiti put it in 1978 – was by 2010 as smart, 'vibrant' and cool as anywhere in London. Yet in 2010 Hackney was statistically still in the top (bottom?) three most deprived local authority areas in the country, according to the government's own 2010 Index of Multiple Deprivation (IMD). So the Olympic ambitions were always barely plausible. How far regeneration really benefits existing local communities rather than pricing them out of town, how far the bright new environments are inexorably claimed by a bright new clientele, are always hotly debated issues.

Local people were therefore circumspect about the promised impact of the Olympic Games. A survey of attitudes to the Games, commissioned by the Department of Culture, Media and Sport in the run up to 2012, revealed lukewarm attitudes among Hackney and its fellow host borough residents which contrasted sharply with the uncritical enthusiasm recorded in the rest of London. Of course a new park was nice to have but the Games also had downsides. Disruption and nuisance; the loss of some much loved features, notably the magical Manor Gardens allotments alongside the River Lea; over 5,500 established local jobs displaced from the Park including many good-quality unionised jobs in established businesses. There was a promise of several thousand new homes, but who was going to live in them? And why did the vast environmental expenditure poured into the Park stop so abruptly at its boundary? Even today the edge of the Park along the Lea Navigation is scrappy and unresolved, in sharp contrast to the Park itself. Hackney Wick still looks like a bomb has hit it (albeit a paint bomb).

As the Olympic Park took shape, Whitehall began to get exercised about the risk of 'cliff edges' appearing between the wealth of the Park and the apparent poverty of its surroundings. Not exercised a lot, but enough to wring the princely sum of £5m out of the Department of Communities and Local Government to fund improvements to the Hackney Olympic fringe beyond the Park boundary. Hackney put that towards the renovation of the bedraggled sports facilities on Hackney Marshes (but not sufficient to replace the bullet-ridden North Marsh changing rooms I recall using in all their Brut-drenched glory when turning out for Hackney NALGO in the 1980s).

One fascinating feature of the Hackney Olympic fringe, even today, is the startling contrast between opposing versions of urban life which appear to face off across the Lea Navigation. On the east bank is the managed and manicured Park, with its top-down planning and long-gestated corporate outcomes; on the west side, the *ad hoc*, organic happenstance nature of Hackney Wick. It is impossible to find the tiniest bit of graffiti on the Olympic Park – it is obliterated almost before it is perpetrated. Conversely, on the Wick it is hard to find a building that is not festooned with gaudy painted images. But things here are starting to change. Real estate values in the Wick are moving beyond the reach of the artistic community, studio space is declining, and new housing development is inexorably moving in.

The Games are now history and one senses that Hackney people have moved on. Their scepticism has been borne out. But among urbanists debate continues about the impact that the Olympics did and didn't have on Hackney. It certainly had a very big impact on that part of the borough that lies beneath the Park – its buildings and contours flattened! But beyond that, outcomes are difficult to identify and measure. And there is no logical reason why the Games should have had a wider impact in the first place. The concept of a wider regeneration legacy is an invented one, to support London's Olympic bid. In reality, the 2012 legacy ambitions and the money were focussed almost exclusively on the Olympic site itself.

But enough of the gloom. It is difficult to spend several billion pounds without some positive outcomes. (Though not impossible, as some other Olympic cities might reflect.) The Overground has been vastly improved, transforming accessibility from Hackney to the City, Stratford and the West End – and *vice versa*. Thanks to the Shoreditch/ Dalston component of this – the long-sought link once known as the 'East London Line Extension' – Hackney finally has its connections to the Underground network. Rejected by the Treasury for years because they saw no 'business case' in the link, the trains are now full. Whoever had the imagination to include this project in the essential 'Olympic transport package' deserves the Freedom of Hackney.

And then there is the mammoth Olympic Media and Broadcasting Centre, which Hackney fought vigorously to have located in its territory in the hope that it might be turned into a digital business hub. Somehow that dream is coming true. Renamed *Here East*, its description of itself as 'London's home for making – for innovators who are disrupting old ways of thinking and working to make the future better' has an attractive ring about it. With the imminent arrival into the building of UCL's robotic research and design department, the building offers an almost Ackroydian echo of the innovative character of the Wick in its industrial heyday (part of the building stands on the site of one of the Wick's 'world industrial firsts', the Carless factory where petrol was first refined). Possibilities of a symbiosis between *Here East* and the creative capacity of the Wick, and Hackney more generally, seem plausible, reinforced by the imminent arrival of the London College of Fashion, and satellites of the V&A, Sadler's Wells and University College, in the Olympic Park. There is interesting potential urban chemistry here.

Fundamentally, we are witnessing a radical change in Hackney's relative position, and potential role in London. The arrival of a huge new centre of gravity in East London at Stratford, means that the borough now looks east, as well as west, and can do both with confidence, with implications for its metropolitan role in ways that at the moment can only be guessed at.

But who is going to benefit from all this? Fed up with being poor, the host boroughs defined an Olympic goal, which they called 'convergence': within 20 years the social conditions for people living in East London would have risen to the London average. Hackney's statistics are certainly converging. The third most deprived borough in the country as recently as 2010, had risen out of the bottom 15, only five years later (IMD 2015). Its statistics continue to improve. Is the magic of the Olympics actually working? Have the Olympic sceptics been put to flight? Possibly. The Olympics may have contributed. How long this process will continue and where it might end is hard to predict. Equally hard to predict is how many people living in Hackney when the Olympic bid was won in 2005 will still be living there when 'convergence' has finally been achieved.

Here East – with the imminent arrival into the building of UCL's robotic research and design department, the building offers an echo of the innovative character of the Wick in its industrial heyday.

Hackney Wick still looks like a bomb has hit it, albeit a paint bomb. (Photos Glory Hall)

2013: Beards, Boozers and Breweries – James Watson

The Cock Tavern, Mare Street, voted London's most beard-friendly pub. Tim O'Rourke, head brewer at Howling Hops brewery, is behind the bar. (Photos Neil Martinson)

The East End of London once boasted a pub on every street corner. Between 1983 and 2013, 116 Hackney pubs closed; an attrition rate of almost 50 per cent. Half the borough's pubs had gone in just 30 years. This is consistent with a worrying national trend. At the height of the credit crunch in 2009, 59 English pubs closed every week. But well-managed pubs are regarded by many as vital community facilities, bringing neighbours together and enhancing social cohesion. Seminal works by Rick Muir (*Pubs & Places*, 2012) and Professor Robin Dunbar (*Friends on Tap*, 2016), have highlighted how pubs contribute to economic growth, sustainable communities, and mental wellbeing.

The Great British pub and the British-invented drink, cask beer (or real ale), are inextricably linked. People associate the ornate, iconic hand pump (beer engine) with the bar counter of the British pub. It is counter-intuitive to think that whilst the total number of pubs in Britain has fallen by a third since the end of the Second World War, the number of breweries is at an all time high at over 1,400. Hackney Brewery in Haggerston was established in 2011 and by 2013 the borough boasted a further five microbreweries plus three more at Hackney Wick and a brew-pub in Victoria Park.

Despite Britain having more coffee shops than pubs by 2016, the craft beer renaissance shows no signs of slowing, with an apparently insatiable demand for quality locally-brewed beer. The American influenced 'bottle shop' has arrived in Hackney with popular outlets on Lower Clapton Road and Well Street.

There is a 'beer scene' in most parts of London. Hackney was at the forefront of this revolution back in 2011. Today, the majority of the borough's pubs serve a good range of quality beer from London's 85 (and counting!) microbreweries. Many London brewers are at capacity and the romantic notion of a second-hand brew plant in a rented railway arch has had to give way to larger industrial premises. Beavertown, which commenced brewing in the back of the kitchen of Duke's Brew & Que on Downham Road in 2011, is now one of the leading global craft beer brands, operating from an industrial estate in Tottenham. The Five Points Brewing Company, founded in an arch under Hackney Downs Station in 2012 with just two staff, added a distribution warehouse and office in 2015 and now employs over 20 people, exporting beer to Spain and Italy.

Beneath the bustle of Mare Street, in the cellar of the Cock Tavern, voted 'Beard Friendly Pub of the Year 2014', a tiny brewery has produced over 100 different beer recipes in its four-year history. 2015 saw the opening of the country's first 'tank bar' (beers are served from tanks rather than kegs to ensure freshness and flavour) when Howling Hops acquired premises in Queen's Yard, Hackney Wick. Brewing still takes place in the Cock Tavern cellar, under the brand Maregade, producing artisan cask ale, mainly for dispense in the pub above, to the satisfaction of thirsty bearded beer connoisseurs.

The Cock was not always patronised by young men with skinny jeans and turn-ups, chunky brogues and designer lumberjack shirts, retrospective headwear and finely coiffed beards and moustaches. Nor did it attract their female counterparts. Up until its change of hands in summer 2012, it featured a reassuringly worn red carpet, fruit machines and regular karaoke. Beer was supplied by ubiquitous global corporate giants: Fosters, Carlsberg, John Smith's Smooth and of course Guinness. The clientele was a mixture of revellers and regulars. During the day, tar-stained hi-visibility jackets were a common sight. The transformation from hosting gritty tarmac-layers to hipster trend-setters is stark.

Yet it is a common trend, played out across a number of Hackney pubs and exemplified by the closure of the Windsor Castle in January 2013 following a drugs raid. This establishment was relaunched the following Easter as a contemporary gastropub with a wide appeal, particularly to families and females, two groups which did not feature in its previous incarnation. It is reassuring to think that a pub, situated at the bottom of 'Murder Mile' and for many years viewed as part of the problem, is now stylish, clean, welcoming and very popular with the community in Clapton: part of the solution in the move towards the area's commercial and social prosperity.

When the previous operator was forced out, due to the confiscation of his licence, a major concern was the threat of development. Developers are fond of the phrase 'much needed' when describing proposals for new housing, conveniently overlooking the all-important social dimension of sustainable development, which recognises that cohesive communities need shared spaces in which to interact. Half of London's closed pubs have ended up in residential use.

Whilst the planning system can act to safeguard key land uses by resisting the loss of community pubs, it is unable to determine or influence what *style* of pub will subsist. Many have lamented the demise of the traditional boozer. But it is a natural evolution that consumer tastes will change and, in the midst of a beer and brewing renaissance, discerning aficionados will reject the global brands in favour of locally produced quality beer, invariably more expensive and purveyed by a different breed of operator to the archetypal landlord. It is comforting to imagine that there might be space in Hackney for both types of pub, and perhaps even for a diverse range of punters in the same pub, but business needs often dictate a shift in offer towards the more affluent.

In 2012, at the height of the Olympic Games, the 147-year-old Chesham Arms in the heart of the Clapton Square conservation area was secretly sold to a property developer. Clapton Square is an oasis of calm, neatly sandwiched between the Narrow Way, Lower Clapton Road, and Morning Lane. A grass roots campaign, led by former regular Jonathan Sockett, swiftly gathered momentum and attracted much media attention, even featuring in a *Times* editorial. The fight for the Chesham Arms made Hackney Council look at pubs through new eyes. Councillor Guy Nicholson, Cabinet Member for Regeneration & Neighbourhoods said, "You've taken officers on a journey". And what an exhilarating journey it has been!

The controversial plans to demolish the Wenlock Arms in Hoxton in 2012 were defeated by the council through the innovative step of extending a conservation area to encompass the pub. This worked, but was hardly repeatable across the other 120-odd pubs in Hackney. The lessons learned at the Wenlock Arms led to the drafting of a pub protection policy within Hackney's local development framework. This would give the council a firmer footing in resisting the loss of valued community pubs in subsequent cases.

The policy was strengthened by the Chesham Arms campaign, the pub being Hackney's first Asset of Community Value (ACV). The council was galvanised into action by the unrelenting campaigning of the Save the Chesham team. Meg Hillier MP mentioned the pub in the House of Commons chamber. It seemed as though everyone in Hackney was aware of the campaign, yet still the developer maintained he would convert the pub into flats, even letting the top floor without planning permission. Having helped dismiss appeals against the ACV status and the enforcement notice for unauthorised change of use (from pub to residential), the campaign team worked closely with the council to secure the maximum possible planning protection. When it became clear to the owner that the Chesham Arms would have to remain a pub, he finally sought offers and a lease was signed with local publican Andy Bird, who relaunched the Chesham Arms to much celebration in June 2015.

The Chesham Arms has since been joined on Hackney's ACV register by the Prince Edward, the Duke of Wellington, the London Tavern, the Albion and a few others. These pubs are all characterised by being rather 'ordinary', yet very special at the same time and all four were very traditional and down to earth. There are many Hackney dwellers and visitors who do not feel comfortable in the new wave of ultra cool pubs. True diversity is achieved by sufficient provision for all tastes and preferences.

The relaunched Chesham Arms has successfully struck that very delicate balance by welcoming all members of the community and creating an ambience where the affluent incomer and the indigenous inner Londoner are mutually comfortable in the wider shared space. The oft-touted phrase, "Oh it used to be gritty but now it's been gentrified," need not be an inevitability when a pub changes hands. The answer must surely lie in well-managed establishments that have the broadest possible appeal. Besides, without choice and variety, the great British tradition of the pub crawl would not be possible! Hackney has some wonderful pubs within its enchanting neighbourhoods. Celebrate them and cherish them.

The Chesham Arms: local campaigners thwarted plans to close the pub by having it designated an Asset of Community Value. (Photo James Watson)

2014: The Demolition of Corsham Street: the price of redevelopment – Lisa Shell

Intimate, secluded and cherished: Corsham Street was lovingly photographed in all its seasons by its community of artistic residents, until the bulldozers moved in. (Photo Maria Ignacia Court)

In 2014 a whole block fronting one side of Corsham Street, tucked behind the Silicon Roundabout, was demolished to make way for an eleven-storey development of 541 student homes.

The industrial buildings that were lost dated from the early twentieth century. They ranged between two and four storeys with large multi-paned windows framed in yellow London stock brick. They were typical of the solid, high-ceilinged, well-lit and flexible buildings laid out within intimate street patterns that had evolved to accommodate furniture manufacturing for 100 years. And since the demise of that industry these attractive buildings had quickly become home to geeks and hipsters, from where they have kickstarted the Shoreditch tiger economy and nurtured it over the last 25 years.

Whilst these buildings were precisely the sort that defined Shoreditch's character they were also unexceptional. The nearby post-war housing estates meant that the Conservation Area boundary stopped a couple of streets short and so, in the absence of local or statutory listing, the buildings had no formal protection. It fell therefore to Hackney planners to assess the harm that might be caused to the character of the area in taking out such a street. The case officer advised the Planning Committee that "the demolition of the existing buildings on the site would not result in the loss of a heritage asset," despite this position conflicting with advice from English Heritage and Hackney's own conservation officer, Valerie Scott. Her damning assessment of the proposals had been withheld from the committee so that once it found its way into the public realm the council was obliged to dismiss it as "a personal opinion of a member of staff [which] did not reflect the views of the planning service".

Valerie Scott's report not only strongly objected to the loss of the buildings but also asserted that the development would have a detrimental impact on nearby historic buildings, including 18-35 Corsham Street, just across the road, by the renowned architect Sir Ernest George. She pointed out that Corsham Street was an assemblage of historic buildings of distinctive local character and concluded that "if the development were to go ahead, this unique identity would be lost".

Scott abruptly left Hackney's employ. Uneasy about the loss of the buildings, the Planning Committee deferred their decision until a second hearing. The Committee was presented at this second hearing with a heritage impact assessment dismissing the conservation concerns. This had been commissioned and paid for by the developers themselves with no expert impartial critique of that assessment. And so "the three monolithic blocks of anodyne design" as described by Scott, were constructed to "obliterate the historic interest of Corsham Street".

The sad episode at Corsham Street is well documented by those who fought alongside heritage experts to save it. Voluntary organisations such as Conservation Area Advisory Groups (CAACs), and the Hackney Society Planning Group, which I chair, work tirelessly to preserve Hackney's character and heritage values, reviewing up to 100 planning applications a week. But in seeking to temper the worst impacts of 'regeneration' as seen at Corsham Street, we have to understand and acknowledge the imperatives of development that are driving the council to disregard the value of the borough's historic fabric. We need to recognise that Hackney is under unprecedented pressure.

***

Housing shortage

The increase in population in the borough over the last ten years has been phenomenal. Hackney's 2015 population of 269,000 represents an increase of almost 33 per cent since 2001. Projections demand that the borough must build 30,000 more homes by 2033, adding a third again to its current stock. And, to support this new population, Hackney must provide infrastructure and services, including schools, medical facilities, and workspaces. Affordable housing is a bedrock of local employment as Kirsty Styles will warn us in the final chapter. If Hackney's boom falters then it risks slipping back into the poverty trap from which it has only recently emerged. Hackney has to build.

Austerity and private finance

Another incentive towards large-scale redevelopment is more patently financial. Since 2010 central government has reduced its funding contribution to Hackney by 35 per cent, forcing the council to rely increasingly on private finance to support its budget. In the current climate Hackney Council's principal wealth rests in property. Planning gains awarded to the council when approvals are granted, such as the Community Infrastructure Levy, help Hackney to pay for services whilst containing the Council Tax. The council relies on a reputation as a 'can do' borough, riding the tide of development pressures, and engaging 'constructively' with developers. In the process, concern for the long-term benefits of preserving heritage value slips clean off the radar.

Preserving the setting of heritage assets? Late 17th-century Lansdowne House and the modern pavilion permitted by Hackney planners. (Photo Laurie Elks)

Expertise

In any event, the council lacks the funding and expertise to compete with powerful developers who hire teams of specialists to push through proposals on their own terms. And beware the local authority that stands up to developers who wouldn't hesitate to claim for loss of profit, should they have to resort to the Planning Inspectorate to win planning approval at appeal.

So it is a new set of economic circumstances that threatens Hackney's heritage. In the last decade Hackney has witnessed a surge of major development projects that have transformed neighbourhoods, altered demographics, disrupted local businesses, and caused irreparable harm to historic environments. We are witnessing developments of a scale unprecedented since the 1970s. I have selected just three examples.

Dalston Square

In 2005 the council obtained permission to demolish their own historic buildings at the west of Dalston Lane, including the Victorian theatre which housed the The Four Aces Club and a terrace of Georgian houses, to make way for two rows of tower blocks facing on to a new pedestrian precinct called Dalston Square. The requirement for density obliterated any concern for the preservation of heritage, or recognition of the character or quality of the existing environment. These buildings had no statutory protection and there was no appetite or imagination to consider their potential future benefit to the town centre.

Dalston Lane Terrace

By way of consolation Hackney promised a 'conservation-led' regeneration of another Georgian terrace standing to the east of the Dalston Theatre, at the junction with Queensbridge Road. This time, the buildings fell within the compact Dalston Lane (West) Conservation Area, making up about half of its built footprint. In 2012 Hackney approved a scheme for 42 new flats within a contemporary steel-framed building, maintaining the façade of the old terrace. Hackney engaged as their development partner the building company Murphy who subsequently reported that there were no technical means by which any of the original fabric could be retained. Hackney was compelled to accept the total demolition of the terrace. Hackney's cabinet member for regeneration, Guy Nicholson, with unintended irony, offered reassurances that the new buildings would achieve a "good heritage likeness". And shortly after reassuring scores of objectors in a packed committee meeting at the Town Hall, that total reconstruction is a recognised form of conservation 'repair', another of Hackney's string of conservation officers, Peter Ashby, departed the borough.

The New Lansdowne Club

So what of the risks to Hackney's statutorily protected heritage assets? The late seventeenth-century house at 195 Mare Street is one of a handful of the borough's Grade II* listed buildings, and represents the kind of grand rural mansion that wealthy merchants once occupied, away from the stink of the city. Since being sold in 2004 the building has been repeatedly squatted and has fallen into disrepair. The Hackney

Society has kept constant watch, pushing the council to fulfil its statutory responsibilities and submitting opinions on development proposals.

So how did Hackney come to approve the redevelopment of the neighbouring plot at 197 Mare Street, which includes a white rendered 'pavilion' that visually enters and wrecks the setting of this important house? English Heritage (now called Historic England) advised that the applicant's first proposals were 'overbearing' and would 'diminish' the status of the house. The developer was required to submit revised proposals which were approved under delegated powers by a case officer who neglected even to consult Historic England on these quite different proposals, although they were no less obtrusive than the first scheme. To officers the new scheme 'ticked planning policy boxes' in providing eight new flats, and replacing an underused building with a 'more viable' development. But since its construction, Historic England have confirmed that if they had been consulted, as they should have been, they would have advised against the approving the proposals. So neither statutory listing nor Conservation Area status offered effective protection to this most important building.

We are now braced to witness mega-developments including a 35-storey tower of unprecedented footprint within the heart of the South Shoreditch Conservation Area at 201-207 Shoreditch High Street; and the total demolition of the canal-side Holborn Studios to make way for a seven-storey development of 64 new flats over fragmented commercial space. Several new 'major applications' are being received by the council each month.

The Hackney Society was formed in 1967 to defend its genteel nineteenth-century residential streets and squares from eradication, at the time threatened by government-funded social housing projects. Today the Society seeks to work with Hackney Council to protect the borough from a new corporate heritage enemy that is greedy, calculating and disparate.

Demolished: the buildings were typical of the solid, high-ceilinged, well-lit and flexible structures that had evolved to accommodate furniture manufacturing for 100 years. (Photo Maria Ignacia Court)

2015: A Hackney Grandmother's fight for Community Values
– Russell Parton

Alice Burke, community campaigner, in front of Nightingale Estate's sole remaining tower block.
(Photo Russell Parton)

Alice Burke is well known on the Nightingale Estate in Clapton, and not merely because she has lived there for more than 40 years. The 79-year-old retired auxiliary nurse and great-grandmother won a Pride of Britain Award in 2015 for fighting back against the gangs and criminals who blighted the estate, and for her role in its redevelopment.

The Nightingale Estate was built between 1967 and 1972 by the Greater London Council. Standing just north of Hackney Downs, it consisted originally of six towers standing 22 storeys tall and a sprawl of lower-rise terrace blocks. It was a product of the new Modernist urban vision first expressed by Professor Patrick Abercrombie in his *Greater London Plan* – the roads leading north from Hackney Downs all swept away in a vast scheme of comprehensive development.

Many of Nightingale's original tenants were rehoused from overcrowded accommodation with poor sanitation and amenities. By most accounts, they were delighted with their new homes. The flats were comparatively spacious, with their own bathrooms, and the towers provided spectacular views over Hackney Downs and beyond.

Alice and her husband moved into a ground-floor maisonette after a gas leak and explosion forced them to leave their flat in Stamford Hill. "We had this invitation to come and view it," Alice recalls. "I took my husband and as soon as I walked in I started crying. It was warm, it was lovely and it was brand new. It had three bedrooms and a bathroom I could use for my children, which was brilliant. I think it was 17 January 1975 when we moved in and it was snowing."

Early on, the estate lived up to Alice's first impressions. She made friends and joined the estate's Tenants' Association. There were local shops, social activities for adults and a youth club.

But things started to go awry. Inherent faults in the design and construction of the estate were exacerbated after the ownership and management of the GLC's housing stock was transferred to a reluctant Hackney Council in 1982 – at a time when the council's managerial competence was reaching a low ebb. Alice recalls that essential maintenance and repairs were left undone. As the buildings deteriorated the low cost methods of construction began to look like a false economy. "We'd go in the rent office and say that we needed a repair done, and they'd be so rude to you. Once they wouldn't empty the big bins and there were rats and mice in the bins and maggots crawling out of the bin chamber."

1960s blueprint: images of the old Nightingale Estate. (Photos Chris Dorley-Brown)

At the same time, crime and anti-social behaviour were on the rise. The estate's sprawling design, with its many alleys and walkways, made it, in one resident's words, "designed for skulduggery".

"It went from being a nice community to somewhere where you didn't want to live," says Alice. "We had a lot of burglaries, a lot of crime and unemployment. They were breaking into old people's houses, robbing them of their pensions and holding knives to their throats. There was a lady on my block who was over 90 and bed-bound. They broke into her house at nine o'clock at night and frightened the life out of her."

One evening Alice was mugged whilst walking home through the estate from bingo. "I heard someone running and then felt a bang in my back as he kicked me. I went flying and as I fell he went after my bag. He pulled me along the road until the bloody handle broke!"

The incident was a tipping point. Alice decided that something needed to be done, and that she was going to do it. "When I came here it was a nice place to bring my children up that was safe and clean, and I was buggered if I was not going to have that," she says.

Alice persuaded the police to increase patrols and make sweeps of the estate in search of drugs, guns and knives. "They'd come around and have tea with pensioners and anyone could tell them anything. It made the tenants feel safe."

In the late 1980s, the government launched Action for Cities which would see grants handed to ailing inner London estates to "make inner city decay a thing of the past". Nightingale was one of the estates urged to apply. Flats were in desperate need of refurbishment and the towers were particularly unpopular, with residents complaining of vandalism, smashed glass and broken down lifts.

To receive the money, the estate needed a new Tenants' Association. There hadn't been one for several years: a sign that residents felt powerless to make a difference. Alice and a friend volunteered to start up a new association. Alice became its Chair, and immediately set about raising morale and standards on the estate. She insisted that council staff wear badges and speak to residents with respect. "Within a month all the staff had badges and the whole atmosphere had changed in the office. And we went from one thing to another."

The Tenants' Association helped form an Estates Development Committee. Under the council's Comprehensive Estates Initiative, the committee drew up plans for the future. It consulted with residents and decided to demolish five of the hated towers and replace them with houses and lower rise flats. The remaining tower – Seaton Point – was to be refurbished to house the minority of residents who preferred the high rises. The committee applied for the government funding and received £65 million towards the scheme. It interviewed housing associations and contractors, and in 1990 the council went into partnership with Southern Housing Trust for the phased redevelopment of the estate.

Alice served on the design committee for the new houses, even going to Holland to investigate new 'tunnel forming' construction methods. She helped convince the architects that the new houses should include an attic room that could be converted into an extra bedroom, office or utility room, and persuaded the council that tenants should not be charged extra for it.

But while wheels were in motion to improve living conditions on the estate, crime was on the rise, with gang violence, muggings, burglaries and prostitution increasingly prevalent during the 1990s. Alice tackled this head on, confronting those she suspected of dealing drugs, and encouraging her neighbours to do likewise. "We had people giving drugs out on corners 100 yards from my front door. I'd go out and say 'sling your hook before I call the old bill'. And they'd move too. Those people have no courage, they're bullies. And I won't be beaten by a bully."

Alice suffered intimidation and even received a death threat. "My kids and my husband were worried, but I said if you let them get under your skin they've won – and I won't let them win."

More trouble arose when there was a delay between demolishing the first tower in 1998 and the next two – Embley Point and Southerland Point – which lay empty save for a handful of tenants. "In went the squatters, the drug dealers, the prostitutes, the gun runners… they all went in and squatted these empty flats," Alice recalls. "There were prostitutes and minders at the bottom where there were drug flats, these big blokes dripping with gold saying to tenants 'you stay in your flat and don't come out no more', bullying these tenants. Some of them were old – it wasn't funny."

Following a rave that lasted an entire weekend, Alice threatened to take matters into her own hands. "I said to the council, I'll get those tenants out, and you can please yourself what you do with the others. But I'm going to chuck a few petrol bombs in there tonight and blow the buggers up myself."

"The police were on to me that morning. The local copper said, 'You can't do that Alice.'" But the threat worked, as police raided the towers that same week. "One of the coppers showed me inside one of the drug dens," Alice says. "The front door was wired up from the mains, it had concrete on the inside with wires sticking in. If the police had touched the front door they'd have been electrocuted."

Embley and Southerland Point were demolished in December 2000, and the final pair – Rachel and Rathbone Point – followed in November 2003, with Alice and the DJ Trevor Nelson starting the countdown. "We watched this cloud of smoke go down the road. It was a great feeling to see this concrete hell turn into a load of rubble."

With refurbishment works completed in 2006, the Nightingale Estate is a very different place today. In a 2015 residents' survey, 94 per cent of respondents said they were satisfied with Nightingale Estate as a place to live, and 88 per cent said they felt safe walking through the estate at night. Alice says that the new homes made the estate a totally different community. "It was as if everyone woke up out of a sleep. People would walk through the estate, smiling, saying hello. They still do it."

It is still a mystery to Alice exactly who nominated her for the Pride of Britain Award. "It does feel good but I didn't do it for the fame, I did it for my kids and because it needed to be done," she says. "I think you've got to stand up and be counted in this life. It's no good leaving it until tomorrow because tomorrow never comes."

Further Information

A film about Nightingale Estate, made by residents, can be found at http://www.oureverydaylives.tv/blog/nightingale-estate

2016: The Silicon Roundabout, the Growth and Uncertain Future of Shoreditch Tech – Kirsty Styles

Looking up at Silicon Roundabout. (Photo Neil Martinson)

In the years since the Government launched its 'Tech City' initiative in 2010 – a 'start-up ecosystem' of new technology companies bubbling along in Old Street, 'Tech City' has gone from a half-joke nickname to a globally renowned innovation cluster.

On many international measures, London is now among the very best locations for technological innovation worldwide. It is estimated that 200,000 currently work in London's hi-tech sector, around one in five from Europe. Accommodating the highly skilled individuals that London will need is one of the challenges of Brexit.

The hub has a notional base in trendy Shoreditch, home to Silicon Roundabout. It is thought that there are thousands of tech companies clustered around Old Street, from one-person bands to big-name brands employing hundreds of people. But hi-tech has spilled out across London and Shoreditch's status as technology hub is being increasingly challenged. Shoreditch has nurtured all sorts of innovative companies. At one end of the spectrum is the early kids' mobile gaming leader Mind Candy, maker of Moshi Monsters. At the other is TransferWise, a money-transfer company started by two Estonians in Shoreditch in 2011 and now a 'financial unicorn' valued at over $1 billion. Increasingly it is the financial technology – fintech – businesses which are coming to the fore. Consultancy firm Deloitte has estimated that 44,000 people now work in fintech, pollinating Europe's finance capital with their ideas and talent.

Global technology brands have moved in with the likes of Google sponsoring a community space to support start-ups. Indeed, our home-grown heroes have now started getting mopped up by Silicon Valley companies, achieving that lucrative 'exit' acquisition. That includes artificial intelligence company DeepMind, behind the computer that famously beat a world-leader at the strategy game Go, which was sold to Google for hundreds of millions in 2014.

This part of Hackney has perhaps changed more in the present decade than in living memory – and this is just the beginning. Development plans include six towers proposed for the controversial Bishopsgate Goodsyard development and a £750 million transformation of Great Eastern Street (named The Stage as it takes in the site of Shakespeare's Curtain Theatre). Hackney ain't seen nothing yet.

The evolution of Hackney as a tech hub has been brought about by waves of creativity. It started with talented alternative, innovative types attracted by the grittiness of Shoreditch and its cheap rents, but has become increasingly subsumed into the worldwide industry of global business, venture capital, lucrative exit strategies. The challenge now is convincing creative people that the spiralling residential and office costs are still worth it, while the area is no longer able to promise the grit that inspired its earliest innovative inhabitants.

V.0: 'Version.0' of this innovation wave, as it is still known, was epitomised by Last. fm, started in a bedroom in Whitechapel in 2002. It provides a music curation service enabling subscribers to access millions of tracks through the net. It began with music-loving website developers sleeping on sofas, progressed to gaining backing from the huge venture capital firm Index Ventures, and was sold to CBS for £140 million in 2007. Last.fm got a name-check in David Cameron's maiden Tech City speech but, just as the edgy music scene in Shoreditch ate itself years before, the area has quickly become too expensive for the very companies that originally flocked to Hackney's roundabout.

V.1: Hot on the heels of these forerunners were the likes of Mimecast, Wonga and Huddle, 'version 1', when things started getting more serious. They aren't all household names, but their stories will go down in London start-up history.

Huddle, for example, is an online cloud collaboration tool enabling colleagues to work remotely and securely together across the globe. It started in 2006 co-habiting with six other venture capital backed companies in shabby offices called the White Factory in Old Street. They were later to be kicked out and the area is now the rather ominously named White Collar Factory. Huddle has hung on in Shoreditch (its co-headquarters are in San Francisco), with a worldwide client base and the resources to ride the Shoreditch boom; it was named 'Emerging Star of the Year' at the UK Tech Awards 2013.

But already, Hackney was sagging under the weight of its own success, struggling to support local innovators, while telling the whole world to come and invest.

V.2: Step in 'version 2' leader, the fintech upstart Crowdcube, founded in 2011 as the world's first crowdfunding platform: raising capital by peer-to-peer investment and enabling ordinary people to invest in technology start-ups. Crowdcube is part of the Shoreditch story in that its business model was spurred by the success stories coming out of Hackney, and it offers penniless start-ups an alternative for capital raising to the voracious clutches of the venture capital industry. Crowdcube facilitated its own first 'exit' when the car hire company E-Car Club, started with the help of £100,000 crowdfunding, sold out to Europcar in 2015.

But the founders chose vibrant Soho for its London offices and Exeter for its headquarters. Meanwhile its client base, fledgling tech companies, are increasingly establishing themselves in cheaper bases outside London.

V.3: Ernst & Young estimates that more than 1,000 international tech investments were made in London from 2005 to 2014, and people from all over the world are now making their home in this hip neighbourhood. Those working at 'version 3' companies, such as travel app Tripr, are forfeiting jobs in the City and can now safely go home to tell their mum they're working at a start-up without her thinking that's code for something sinister.

But Tripr, formed to build an online community for backpackers, ended up working out of a garage in South Kensington. That's because even 'co-working spaces', which seem to make up the majority of new offices in Hackney, are now too expensive when you're starting out.

Skills crisis

"Tech is eating its way into the lower skilled jobs on offer," says Deloitte's Angus Knowles-Cutler. His *Agiletown* report states that from 2001 to 2014, half of all secretarial jobs have gone in the city, along with more than a third of travel agents.

"But for the jobs that are disappearing, this is more than made up for – so we end up with net 300,000 more jobs, 200,000 of which are high-skilled. In the league table of global cities London leads in 22 sectors, including theatre, higher education and professional services. In the EU, it is the leading high-skilled city."

Knowles-Cutler believes that we need a permanent "chief talent officer to pull all of the strands together", an intelligent visa system; above all that we must "make sure that schools, colleges, universities are producing people into the workforce who've got the skills for the London of tomorrow".

Politicians are getting this message. In The Entrepreneurs Network's Parliamentary Snapshot of 2015, improving the skills of the domestic workforce was the top cross-party priority. And London's Mayor, Sadiq Khan, has taken the helm with the pledge of £5 million for "new opportunities for young Londoners aged between 15 and 25 years old in digital and tech".

The fruits of that public investment remain to be seen, but some of Tech City's biggest failures so far have been in local education.

In Hoxton, an offshoot of Hackney College, the specially-designed Hackney UTC (University Technology College), closed in 2015 following criticism by Ofsted and miserable failure in attracting pupils. College principal, Ian Ashman, complained that "the tech sector has been slower than we'd hoped to embrace the Tech City Apprenticeship programme".

And the STEM (science, technology, engineering and maths) Academy, close to Silicon Roundabout, has been blasted by Oftsed and taken over by an academy chain. A new technology college, Ada College, opened its doors in Tottenham Hale in September 2016. Hopefully it will take its spirit from the 'fail fast, learn fast' mantra that fills the pages of business books advising today's start-up hopefuls.

As Mr Ashman told *Tech City News*, the failure of the UTC "gives some credence to the criticism that the local population is not benefiting as much from Tech City growth as they might". He added that "we look forward to more companies joining us to bring more new local entrants, from more diverse backgrounds, into the Tech City talent pool". But the portents are not particularly promising.

Housing crisis

"One of the biggest risks we see to London's future success is the cost of housing", warns Deloitte's Knowles-Cutler. "There are lots of young, highly-educated people coming into London but it's a real struggle as the cost of housing goes up and up and up. But who owns the problem? We need a strategy that looks at the availability of housing, making the planning system more efficient, and public and private partnerships. For Tech City firms it's hugely important to the growth of the London economy.

Deloitte itself has started subsidising deposits and rents for its new young staff via a partnership with the Olympic Park's Here East project. But such an expensive solution is not an option for technology start-ups.

So far, the many initiatives taken nationally and by London councils have failed to close the gap between London's housing provision and its housing needs. London's new mayor recognises this as his greatest challenge for the years ahead.

Tech city vs our city

In the latest report from Hackney Council and Tech City UK, the government body tasked with overseeing developments in our borough and beyond, the tech sector delivered £9.17 billion to the area in 2015.

Hackney Council claims that local employment has increased from 55 per cent in 2006 to 69 per cent in 2015. But it's fair to say that tensions have grown between local people who remember Hackney before it was a playground for the world's high-tech elite and those who have just arrived.

In its latest report, Hackney Council claimed it will "challenge" property developers who appear only to build luxury apartments. But that either hasn't been backed up by action, or the decision, like the Goodsyard development, has been taken out of the council's hands. Indeed, the council's Invest in Hackney programme, launched in 2013, was a concerted effort to court landowners and developers to the area.

Those workers on low wages over in San Francisco, the place where people working in Silicon Valley go to sleep, have protested against things like free buses for Google employees. And they are quickly getting priced out of their homes. In the Hackney of 2017, the challenge is to avoid similarly becoming a tale of two cities.

Old and new side by side on City Road. (Photo Neil Martinson)

Afterword

In the opening piece of this book, John Finn documents the clarion call in 1967 to join the new Hackney Society: "I love Hackney. But what will it be like in 10 years' time?".

The late 1960s was a key time in the development of London. The planning system, created twenty years earlier, was starting to bite, and the unintended consequences for the built environment were becoming apparent. At the same time, the post-war housing crisis, for very good reasons, had been allowed to dictate development priorities; but it was now time to address some of the wider impacts. With the pace of change damaging the very environment that the planning system was supposed to control, the government paved the way for the first conservation areas, imposing a duty on London's boroughs to pay attention to their wider historic environment.

Within Hackney, residents formed action groups to slow down the developers' enthusiastic bulldozers. Concern was being expressed about the quality of the emerging architecture and construction, and over the threats to open space. Communities were beginning to campaign for the conservation of the decaying historic villas and mansions.. The air was full of talk of planning inquiries and compulsory purchase powers.

Many of these pressures are ones that we recognise across the capital, today, albeit in different ways. The demands on space are now much greater. The typical 'middle income' Victorian terraced houses were built with multiple, large families in mind, and with servants' quarters. Not only do we now expect this stock to accommodate fewer residents, but at the same time we encourage more people to live and work in our borough.

Undoubtedly, fifty years from now, we will be able to build quicker, higher, more reliably and more cheaply than we can at present. But we will be facing new problems, will have learned new lessons and will encounter new policy restrictions to keep everything under control.

The watchword in today's planning system is sustainability. It's a frequently over-simplified concept. Lying at its heart is an eye on the future, questioning whether anything we propose now might limit our ability to do something better, or even at all in that future. We have learned that resources are finite, and that short-termism creates problems (and waste) further down the line.

Even with current building and design standards that focus on long-term sustainability, it is not reasonable to expect all new builds to survive the seventy years or more for which they are supposedly intended. The best examples will survive because the market will find a new generation of occupants for whom they suit a need, and hopefully also because the civic movement of the time will be as active as it has been for the last fifty years, and will be campaigning to keep those best examples.

For all the focus on sustainability, we continue to struggle to weigh long-term goals against immediate pressures. And right now, so much development is in the hands of private developers that it effectively pits hard-nosed commercial interests against long-term visions in Hackney. These visions are too often seen as costly, idealised pipe dreams. The capital's boroughs have never been able to fight the might of the very money men upon whom they rely to provide them with the social infrastructure that they cannot afford, or are not allowed to build themselves. It's a modern phenomenon, but not one I'd wager will change any time soon.

In reality, true sustainability is a pipe dream. The housing crisis and emerging technology of the 1950s and '60s led us headlong into building high, without really understanding what the consequences might be. We know better now – up to a point. We continue to be hostages to sea changes in attitudes to space and our environment. We razed some of those 1950s and '60s tower blocks to the ground not only because of poor build quality, but because the physical environment turned out to be all wrong. Not just the little things like having to pass by five neighbours' living room windows to reach home, or cold and malodorous concrete stairwells: the whole inward-facing ensemble turned out to be somewhat inhuman.

Yet, just as the Victorians chose not to demolish the stand-out Georgian terraces that are still with us, the fittest estates have survived. Many of these were considered innovative at the time of construction and avoided some of the pitfalls, or have found a new market through sufficient renovation and refurbishment to make them more desirable. It will always be the fittest that survive our ever-changing social requirements.

Hackney's social housing stock is vast. The process of regeneration (a term loaded with nuance) is constant. Those estates high on the list for redevelopment aren't just the poorly designed ones, but those where the land use is not as dense as it now could be. The strategy is ever-changing. Demolition is starting to be seen by resident activists as an attempt to break up communities, and raises all sorts of thorny issues around the mixed tenure dream of private and public ownership existing alongside one another. A mix of redevelopment and refurbishment of the extant social housing stock is increasingly a favoured option, but it's hard to say which way the political wind will blow in fifty years from now. But I have no doubt the pressure to build more homes will continue.

Hackney in 2017 is stereotyped as the borough of bearded hipsters and yummy mummies, and of tech and night-time economies. They are labels that won't last long. If you are reading this in fifteen, ten or maybe even five years on, I dare say there are new words that people evoke when Hackney is mentioned. As social groups age and reach a critical mass, they gradually morph into another descriptor, or disperse to somewhere that better suits their needs. Today's Dalston hipsters are tomorrow's young families. In 2067, the new, trendy 25- to 30-year-olds will have a new moniker, and will likely be in a different neighbourhood: a never-ending cycle in action.

However, there is one significant pressure from the 1967 era that at first glance does not seem so cyclic, and has greatly diminished: cars. The 1960s and '70s saw immense pressure to enhance our road network. There were some truly awful, destructive schemes (even by contemporary thinking) across the capital. The scars of the epic war between private car ownership and pedestrians are evident throughout the world, and they come from a short period in history when the cars won. I challenge anyone to assert with any seriousness that the public realm in Hackney Wick or Homerton High Street benefits from the East Cross Route and the roads leading to it.

By comparison, Hackney in 2017 is positively anti-car, but even with the will, eradicating these scars is tricky. Car use continues to be somewhat contentious, especially where drivers are pitched against cyclists on back roads, but the scale of the shift in attitude is palpable. Hackney currently boasts some of the highest cycle usage and lowest levels of car ownership of any London borough – and by a margin. But reduction in car use must be predicated on a comprehensive public transport network and that places its own demands on land, demands which aren't always successfully resolved. I have no doubt that the conflict between personal vehicle use and mass transport will continue to be contentious well into the future. But I cannot speculate whether those battles will be for land on the surface, cavities 30 metres below ground, or space in the air 100 metres above it!

Sometimes I get a surprised response when I assert that the Hackney Society is not a historical society. The civic movement has never been about history – at least not in isolation. And it certainly was never about preservation at all costs. The Hackney Society, and the civic movement of which it forms a part, is about making history. Progress is not just inevitable, it is encouraged, but not at the expense of the eradication of our built heritage. We campaign to conserve, repair and reuse the best examples, and we let the weaker ones go. But in each case, we press for the very highest standards in design and construction that embody sustainability, to ensure that we don't repeat the mistakes of the past, and that development offers significant benefit to the wider public.

The planning system allows more latitude in this balancing exercise than we might like, and many modern developments are destined to become those that are first up for demolition when the next generation tires of the genre and has an appetite for the next big thing. But that does not mean that our current pleas have fallen on deaf ears. In fact, we can ill afford to stay silent. By speaking up for the finest of our heritage assets and by challenging developers to be part of our future heritage, we ensure that no-one forgets that the historic built environment is to be cherished. After all, who wouldn't want to be the developer whose vision is being admired and fought over fifty or a hundred years from now?

Nick Perry, *Chair, Hackney Society*

About the Authors

Wayne Asher is the author of *Rings Around London*, the first full-length study of the Ringway Plans, and of *A Very Political Railway*, which explores the near death and revival of the North London Line. He lives in Stoke Newington

Emma Bartholomew has covered crime and court stories in Hackney since 2008 in her role as a reporter at the *Hackney Gazette*. Her coverage of Old Bailey trials has included the murder of teenager Marcel Addai and the manslaughter of Moses Fadairo. She lives in Haggerston with her twin sons and daughter.

Brian Belton is an academic and writer in the field of professional youth and community work and informal education. Coming from an East London background, Brian entered youth work in Docklands in the early 1970s, later working in the field around the world. He is the author of many biographies and sporting histories, including *When West Ham Went to the Dogs*, and numerous books and learned papers.

Monica Blake is a library and information consultant who has lived in Hackney since 1980. She was a member of the Save the Reservoirs Campaign from 1987 until it disbanded in 2006. She edited the Campaign's newsletter from 1991. Since 1988 she has been a member of the Hackney Society, and now serves as a trustee where her responsibilities include editing Spaces.

Roger Blake worked for over 30 years with the London Borough of Hackney, from 1985-97 in the planning department, from where he led the council's input to the early stages of the proposed East London Line extensions, then until 2015 as principal transportation planner overseeing the council's contribution to completion of the ELL extensions project. Roger is now a director of the independent national campaign, Railfuture.

Duncan Campbell is a journalist who worked for the *Guardian* as crime correspondent and as news editor of *Time Out* and *City Limits*. He is the author of eight books, including *We'll All Be Murdered in Our Beds, the Shocking History of Crime Reporting in Britain*, *The Underworld* and a novel, *If It Bleeds*.

Jim Cannon lived in De Beauvoir for 41 years and was an active member of several local organisations and charities. He was a Labour councillor for De Beauvoir Ward from 1978 to 1986 when he was chair of various council committees, and in his last year was deputy leader of the council. He was a councillor for De Beauvoir again from 2002 to 2006.

Carolyn Clark is a community historian. She moved to Shoreditch in the early 1970s and is the co-author of *The Shoreditch Tales*. She was the first secretary of the Shoreditch Festival in 1979, edited *Shoreditch Views* Community Newspaper in the 1980s and wrote the regular Now and Then column in *In Shoreditch* in the 2000s. Her recent projects include the heritage of the Regent's Canal in Shoreditch and the heritage of Lower Clapton.

Maureen Diffley is an architect, originally from the west of Ireland. She has lived in Stoke Newington since the early 1980s with her husband and brought up their two children there. Maureen was a founder member of Stoke Newington Midsummer Festival in 1994. She is a passionate walker and is interested in building conservation, especially of vernacular domestic building.

Chris Dorley-Brown is a documentary photographer, filmmaker and archivist. He has published and exhibited widely and his work is held in public collections of the Wellcome Trust, Museum of London, BBC Archives, Hackney Archives and Tower Hamlets Archives. 2015 saw the publication of two widely acclaimed photo books, *The Longest Way Round* and *Drivers in the 1980s*.

Annie Edge started her working life in journalism. In 1990 she joined the London School of Economics as an academic researcher and continues to specialise in London-wide issues and education. More recently she has also acted as an educational adviser to groups of schools. She has lived in Hackney since 1978.

Laurie Elks has lived in Hackney since 1972. He is a trustee of the Hackney Society and Hackney Historic Buildings Trust and custodian of St Augustine's Tower, the borough's oldest building. He has campaigned for the protection of the Lea Valley since the 1970s. He was previously a lawyer working on the investigation of miscarriages of justice.

Mehmet Ergen came to London from his native Turkey in 1987. He was a co-founder of Southwark Playhouse and, as associate producer of Battersea Arts Centre, created the Grimeborn Festival of New Opera, which is now an annual feature of the Arcola's programme. In 2000 he co-founded the Arcola Theatre with executive producer Leyla Nazli, and remains its artistic Director. He continues to direct extensively in Turkey and is the founder and artistic director of Arcola's sister theatre in Istanbul, Talimhane Tiyatrosu.

John Finn has lived in Hackney for nearly 50 years and has strong family connections with the borough. After a working life as a typesetter, typographer and graphic designer, John qualified as a local London tour guide, and joined the University of Westminster's faculty of architecture and built environment, becoming director of their Clerkenwell and Islington guiding course in 2011.

Beth Green is currently working for the Diocese of London, supporting the ministry of the Church in the City. She graduated with an MA in history from SOAS, with a specialism in West African Pentecostal churches in London. She lives in Hackney, and is passionate about bringing history to life through the stories of everyday events and ordinary people.

Sean Gubbins is a keen student of Hackney's history. Since 2002 he has been devising and leading history walks in different parts of today's borough – see walkhackney.co.uk.

Patrick Hamill is an architect and has focused on major urban renewal projects in the UK whilst contributing to voluntary activities in Hackney. He has lived in the borough since 1977, becoming secretary of the Hackney Society and then its chairman. Patrick was a founder member of the Hackney Historic Buildings Trust and the Shoreditch Town Hall Trust.

Anna Harding trained as an exhibitions curator after studying history and history of art at UCL. Since 2005 she has been chief executive at SPACE, a non-profit artist support organisation founded in 1968 with its HQ in Hackney. Prior to this she founded the MA creative curating course in the visual arts department at Goldsmiths, University of London and was programme director for 8 years.

Julian Harrap is a conservation architect who lived and worked from a house in Mapledene Road during the early 1970s. As an active member of the Mapledene Residents Association and other local civic amenity organisations, he supported the case against Hackney Council's proposals to demolish the greater part of Mapledene and their subsequent proposals to infill the backlands. He now lives in an old house in Hoxton.

Meg Hillier is the Member of Parliament for Hackney South and Shoreditch and chair of the Public Accounts Committee. The cross-party committee scrutinises the value for money of public spending and holds the government to account for the delivery of public services. Meg was elected to Parliament in 2005 and previously represented Hackney as its first London Assembly member. She has lived or worked in Hackney for 25 years.

Rachel Kolsky is a prize-winning London Blue Badge guide. Focussing on the 'human stories behind the buildings', she specialises in quirky unknown areas of London, social history and Jewish London for which she has developed several tours in Hackney. She has published two books, *Jewish London* and *Whitechapel in 50 Buildings*.

Julia Lafferty was a founder member of the campaign to save Sutton House in the 1980s. She is a trustee of the Hackney Society, serves on the Clapton Conservation Area Advisory Committee and has written articles for Hackney Society publications and for *Hackney History*. She acts as secretary to the Friends of Clapton Cinematograph Theatre and as an advisor on heritage issues to Clapton Arts Trust.

Russell Miller is an arboriculturalist, ecologist and community activist. He is chair of the Ancient Tree Forum. He has been instrumental in creating local community-based environmental groups, including Tree Musketeers, Hackney Biodiversity Partnership, Sustainable Hackney and Abney Park User Group. He has lived in Dalston since 1990.

Russell Parton is a journalist and Hackney resident. He writes predominantly about the arts, with a particular interest in theatre and music. He founded the arts journal, *East End Review* and was deputy editor of the *Hackney Citizen* from 2015 to 2017

Michael Passmore is a historian specialising in social housing and town planning. In 2015 he was awarded a PhD by King's College London on the politics of council housing. He is a visiting lecturer in the Built Environment Department at University of Greenwich. Earlier Michael had a career as a chartered surveyor, working for a while for Hackney Council.

Nick Perry is the chair of the Hackney Society. From a keen but passive interest in architecture and the built environment, Nick began to engage more actively when a new Conservation Area was created in 2010 in the area where he lives. Since then, he has been involved in a number of campaigns to improve developments – and in particular their social benefits – which keeps him busy when he isn't at his day job, in IT for a legal publisher.

Daniel Rachel wrote his first song when he was 16 and was the lead singer in Rachels Basement. He was first eligible to vote in the 1992 general election and now lives in North London with his partner and three children. Daniel is the author of *Isle of Noises: Conversations with Great British Songwriters*, a *Guardian* and *NME* Book of the Year, and is a regular guest contributor on BBC Radio 5.

Ian Rathbone has worked all his life as a journalist, writer and designer and has received a number of national awards for campaigns, including one which significantly reduced street robbery in Hackney, and for his role following the disturbances of 2011. He has been a councillor for Lea Bridge Ward since 2002. Ian was born in Hackney and traces his family in the borough back to at least 1862.

Ann Robey is a historian specialising in economic, social and architectural history. She has worked for 30 years as a heritage professional for organisations such as the Survey of London, Historic England and the Georgian Group and is now a consultant. She has written ten Conservation Area appraisals for Hackney and is a former trustee of the Hackney Society.

Ray Rogers is an architect and town planner. From 2003 to 2009 he was head of the urban design and conservation team at Hackney Council, and before that a historic buildings inspector at English Heritage. He is co-author of *Behind the Veneer: The South Shoreditch Furniture Trade and its Buildings*. His interest in the Shoreditch furniture trade was prompted by the knowledge that his grandfather was a Shoreditch cabinet-maker.

Alan Rossiter is an artist, designer and public art consultant who has worked in Hackney since 1972 and lived in the borough from 1977. Alan was organiser of the Hackney Marsh Fun Festival and Fireshow, first artistic director of Chats Palace and associate director of Free Form Arts Trust.

Lisa Shell founded Lisa Shell Architects in 1998. After fighting the 2014 campaign to save Dalston Lane Terrace, she took up the chair of the Hackney Society planning group, which encourages high quality and sensitive design and seeks to reduce the potential harm to Hackney's built environment. She also sits on the Dalston Conservation Area Advisory Committee.

Christopher Sills moved to Hackney in December 1957 and joined the Young Conservatives in January 1958. A year later he became their honorary secretary and has remained active in the local Conservative party ever since. He first stood for the council in May 1962 and has fought numerous local elections and by-elections ever since. In total, he has served 21 years on Hackney Council in many different circumstances. He is currently deputy chairman (political) of Hackney Conservatives.

Richard Simmons is a town planner and urban regeneration specialist with long experience of working in East London. A planner for Hackney Council from 1978 to1985, he was chief executive of Dalston City Challenge between 1993 and 1997. He teaches city planning and urban design at the Bartlett School of Planning, University College London, and at the University of Greenwich.

David Sloan first came to Hackney as a medical student in 1968 and lived and worked in the borough for most of the next 40 years. As a GP based in Lower Clapton Health Centre, he took a particular interest in pregnancy and maternity services. In 2000 he was appointed director of public health for Hackney and the City of London

Kirsty Styles has worked as a journalist, editor, podcaster and campaigner in East London, and beyond, for the past five years. Kirsty presents the New Economics Foundation's weekly economics podcast, has been the B2B tech editor at the *New Statesman*, and previously editor at *Tech City News*. She has lectured widely on the future impact of technology.

Geoff Taylor has lived in Hackney since 1971, when he came to the borough to teach. He has been a member of Hackney Council since 2002 and is currently cabinet member for finance. His book *A Parish in Perspective* chronicles an aspect of Hackney history in an earlier period of rapid change.

Simon Thomsett has spent his working life in the professional performing arts world and many of those years running theatre, including 14 years at the Hackney Empire. He joined the Empire in 1995 as general manager, subsequently headed up the £20m refurbishment and redevelopment project leading to the theatre's celebrated re-launch in 2003, and later became chief executive.

Muttalip Unluer was born in a village near Ankara in 1955 and arrived in London in 1973. He started work in the rag trade as a machinist and opened his own textile factory in 1982. He has worked closely with the Turkish community for many years, especially with voluntary organisations. In 2002 he was elected as a councillor for Stoke Newington Ward and became the Speaker for Hackney for the year 2009.

Linh Vu arrived in Hackney as a refugee with her father in the early 1980s and continues to live in the borough. She graduated with a degree and diploma in architecture and, after working as an architect and helping to run the family's Vietnamese Canteen, went on to open her own restaurant in Hackney. Linh also works with Queen Mary University of London and the Refugee Council on projects and films concerning child migration.

Ralph Ward joined Hackney Council planning department in 1978 to work on its nascent Inner City Partnership Programme. He left Hackney in 1989, but continued to work on East London development planning for various public agencies before becoming DCLG's Olympic planning and regeneration advisor in 2003, probably as the only person in Whitehall who knew where Stratford was.

Suzanne Waters is a Hackney resident, who has many years' experience working in arts and heritage. She has taught at Birkbeck College, worked for English Heritage and now at the Royal Institute of British Architects where she has catalogued the drawings and archives of Sir Denys Lasdun. She is also a member of the Twentieth Century Society.

James Watson is a campaigner, activist and pub evangelist. In 2014, James co-founded the social media network, @ProtectPubs, which campaigns for reforms to the planning system, and his successful lobbying of ministers led to a fundamental revision of national planning law in April 2015. He also serves as the Greater London region pub protection advisor for the Campaign for Real Ale. He lives in Homerton, is a keen beer drinker, but does not have a beard.

Jessica Webb was first elected as a councillor for Hackney Wick Ward in October 2000. She has been re-elected a number of times, for which she is very grateful. She also works for the RMT trade union. She lives in Hackney Wick with her family.

Stuart Weir became a Labour councillor for the De Beauvoir Ward from 1972 to 1976. He left *The Times* to work for the Child Poverty Action Group in 1970, returning to journalism with the *New Society* and *New Statesman* magazines, founding Charter 88 in 1988 and moving to head the research organisation, Democratic Audit, at Essex University in the 1990s.

Winstan Whitter was a professional brand-sponsored skateboarder before becoming an award-winning filmmaker. His credits include *Rollin' Through the Decades*, *Legacy in the Dust: The Four Aces Story* and *You Can't Move History*. He has curated exhibitions across Europe; co-produced film festivals including the London Film Festival 2015; and contributed to books including *Dramas and Dissent: Twelve Glorious Years in a London Borough*.

Margaret Willes spent her career in book publishing, latterly as publisher at the National Trust. Since retiring, she has written several books, including *Gardens of the British Working Class*. She is a trustee of the Hackney Society, and has particular responsibility for the publications, acting as editor of *Hackney: An Uncommon History in Five Parts* published in 2012.

Anne Woollett was chair of Hackney Marsh Users Group from 1989 to 2007. She was involved in planting trees on Hackney Marshes and in what is now Wick Woodland, establishing the Tree Nursery, and fighting to minimise the loss of the wildlife habitat of the Marshes to development. Anne now lives in Norfolk where she is still involved in environmental activities.

Ken Worpole is a long-standing Hackney resident and member of the Hackney Society and is the author of many books on architecture, landscape and public policy. He has a special interest in the social history and literature of East London, as well as the history and landscape of Essex. His website is: www.worpole.net

Hackney Society Publications

Hackney Society Publications

From Tower to Tower Block, 1984

Buildings at Risk in Hackney, 1987

Hackney Houses, 1987

Loddiges of Hackney, David Solman, 1995

Famous Women of Hackney, 1998

Twentieth Century Buildings in Hackney, Elizabeth Robinson, 1999

Hackney: Modern, Restored, Forgotten, Ignored, Lisa Rigg, (2nd ed, 2013)

Hackney: An Uncommon History in Five Parts, Margaret Willes (ed), 2012

For more information, see www.hackneysociety.org